Beyond the E

GW01418628

Beyond the Borders

American Literature and Post-colonial Theory

Edited by
Deborah L. Madsen

Pluto Press

LONDON • STERLING, VIRGINIA

First published 2003 by Pluto Press
345 Archway Road, London N6 5AA
and 22883 Quicksilver Drive, Sterling, VA 20166-2012, USA

www.plutobooks.com

British Library Cataloguing in Publication Data
A catalogue record for this book is available from the British Library

ISBN 0 7453 2046 5 hardback
ISBN 0 7453 2045 7 paperback

Library of Congress Cataloging in Publication Data applied for

10   9   8   7   6   5   4   3   2   1

Designed and produced for Pluto Press by
Chase Publishing Services, Sidmouth, EX10 9QG, England
Typeset from disk by Stanford DTP Services, Towcester, England
Printed and bound in the European Union by
Antony Rowe Ltd, Chippenham and Eastbourne, England

Contents

Part 3 Post-colonialism in the Border Regions

Part 4 American Post-colonialism at Home and Abroad

Introduction: American Literature and Post-colonial Theory

Deborah L. Madsen

Post-colonial theory provides a powerful approach to ethnic literatures of the United States and of those political regions significantly influenced by U.S. political or cultural imperialism, such as Hawai'i, Puerto Rico, Southeast Asia, and areas of Central America such as Haiti and the Dominican Republic. The essays collected here use post-colonial theory as a powerful lens through which to read these diverse literatures and to question the constitution of national ethnic literatures. It is a diverse body of writing with which contributors engage; what draws these very different texts together is the way in which they owe much of their thematic shape to perceived tensions with the colonial power exerted by the U.S. In this introduction I attempt to explain these post-colonial commonalities, which bring together scholars of Vietnamese, Indonesian, Burmese-American, Filipino/a, Hawaiian, Asian American, African American, Puerto Rican, Haitian and Latin-Caribbean, Chicana, Native American and Canadian First Nations literatures. First, however, the uses of the term "post-colonial" in this book need clarification. The term has been employed in a range of diverse readings and interpretations for the past two decades. Consequently, the term has accumulated meanings and associations. In this book, each contributor argues from their own perspective about what they call the "post-colonial", calling upon those contexts that are most relevant to the body of literary work and the particular theoretical approaches they address. Some contributors choose to hyphenate the term (post-colonial); others choose to elide the two parts of the term (postcolonial): each critic chooses to represent the term in the form that is most appropriate to the argument they are developing. A number of recurring post-colonial themes do emerge: displacement or diaspora, exile, migration, nationhood, and hybridity. While individual essays employ the concept of the post-colonial in quite specific ways, then, the collection as a whole uses the

1

term broadly, to encompass all the complex processes of colonization and decolonization.

In the course of its varied history "post-colonialism" has acquired three primary meanings. First, post-colonialism refers historically to writings produced in a previously colonized nation after its independence from colonial control. In this sense, all literature produced in the United States after the War of Independence could be called post-colonial. However, the colonial status of the Native American "nations" of the United States in the same period is much more difficult to conceptualize. Native American literatures of the United States and Canada could perhaps be better described as post-colonial in a second meaning of the term, where it is used to encompass the whole complex of historical and cultural processes, starting with the pre-colonial period and leading up through independence from colonial control to a state of decolonization. Post-colonialism in this second sense describes then four (often overlapping) phases: the pre-colonial, colonial, independence, and de-colonized periods of a nation's development. Contributors use this second meaning of post-colonialism to describe aspects of the Vietnamese, Indonesian, Burmese, Filipino/a, Hawaiian, Asian American, African American, Puerto Rican, Haitian and Latin-Caribbean, Chicana, Native American and Canadian experiences of colonialism. These experiences are very different and vary according to history and geography: many European powers held colonies in these places with a consequent diversity of cultural effects. For example, the island of Hispaniola, which is now divided into Haiti on the one side and the Dominican Republic on the other, has seen the impact of Spanish and French colonization, about which Latin-Caribbean Americans write from their perspective as migrants to the United States. Situations such as this open up a third meaning of "post-colonialism" that is used by contributors in this book. In this third sense, it is the critic, rather than the text or its author, who adopts a post-colonial perspective. This is most clearly the case in the essays written by John Peacock and Myriam Chancy, both of whom are concerned to analyze the ways in which their own post-colonial status, as members of colonized cultural groups (Native American and Haitian respectively), is inscribed in their practice as readers and writers, teachers and scholars of American literature.

This collection of essays works from the premise that the ethnic variety of the contemporary United States calls for a redefinition of inherited notions of "American identity". Post-colonial theory is the tool that enables the cultural study of a reformulated identity. The questioning of American cultural identity takes two forms: on the one hand, essays explore how the multiethnic nature of the United States impinges upon writing by members who self-identify with American ethnic minorities (Native American, Chicano/a, Latino/a, Black, Asian American, Hawaiian), while other essays explore how the literatures of what might be broadly conceived as "border" regions (the Caribbean, Central America, Canada) or literatures of regions in which America has had a colonial impact (particularly countries of Southeast Asia) are influenced by definitions of "America" that carry a heavy colonial inflection.

In the opening essay Chadwick Allen reviews strategies for reading contemporary indigenous literatures within the context of post-colonialism in order to conceptualize the United States as a site of ongoing colonialism vis-à-vis American Indian peoples. The larger comparative frame he employs represents a movement from the colonial/post-colonial world safely "out there" toward the colonial/post-colonial world unexpectedly "at home" in the U.S. He begins with representations of "classic" colonial and post-colonial situations in Africa, then moves to representations of settler colonization in Aotearoa/New Zealand, and finally home to the complicated colonial/post-colonial situation of the U.S. A second comparative frame is created by juxtaposing texts produced by colonizers with texts produced by colonized or formerly colonized indigenous peoples. Third and fourth comparative frames arise as comparisons are made among different colonizers and among various indigenous peoples. An additional comparative frame is engaged by comparing post-colonial theory's abstractions of "the" colonial or post-colonial situation with specific representations by individual writers.

From Allen's discussion of the relationships among post-colonial African, indigenous Aotearoa/New Zealand and Native American literatures, we move to the post-colonial tensions that inform relations between Native America and the U.S. Issues of "nation" and nationhood, which are prominent in contemporary post-colonial literary studies, are taken up by Lee Schweninger and Cara Cilano, who address Native American literatures as "post-colonial", in that a focus on "nation" emphasizes the consequences that resulted from Native American contact with the dominant U.S. In the context of post-colonial literary studies, there has been a preoccupation with nationhood in relation to globalization and its effects. This has given rise to debates over whether the "nation" is still a viable model of political and economic organization, and a foundation for unified cultural identities. Within Native American literary studies the concept of "nation" can be seen to signify a desire for autonomy, self-determination, and equality not unlike those sought by "Third World" countries. However, the location of Native America within the geography and history of the United States renders problematic the articulation of a "national" identity in the work of many Native American authors.

In his essay, "Origin Story," John Peacock brings the pursuit of national identity to the personal level as he tells the story of how he was transformed from a "white Native Americanist" to a "white Native American(ist)." The story of his discovery of his lost maternal origins is embedded in a discussion of what may be spoken of outside, as opposed to inside, particular cultural groups. His starting point is the experience of teaching Leslie Marmon's Silko's novel *Ceremony* in the context of the Native American (Laguna) oral traditions that Silko explicitly acknowledges as influences. He notes that Laguna writer and critic Paula Gunn Allen, in her essay "Special Problems in Teaching Leslie Marmon Silko's *Ceremony*," argues on the one hand that native ethics forbids the telling of sacred stories outside the clan, but on the other hand many native texts do not make sense unless these stories are explained and understood. John Peacock searches among various sources for a solution to this dilemma and discovers in the process his own undisclosed story and that of his family, which reveals to him a new and valuable post-colonial perspective.

My own contribution to the discussion focuses on the concept of counter-discourse, developed by Helen Tiffin in relation to classic post-colonial texts such as J. M. Coetzee's novel *Foe* which retells the Robinson Crusoe story from the perspective of the colonized. I want to apply this concept to the post-colonial conditions represented in contemporary Chicana writing. The U.S. colonization of the Hispanic Southwest in the course of the nineteenth century, through the Mexican–American War and subsequent Treaty of Hidalgo, left a legacy of loss and dispossession that was experienced by many as a second colonization, following the initial impact of the Spanish 300 years earlier. In addition, Chicana writers such as Gloria Anzaldúa claim for Chicanas a second colonization by the Mexican patriarchy, operating through the ideology of *machismo*. Writers such as Helena María Viramontes and Ana Castillo use counter-discursive strategies to "write back" in resistance to the narratives of the masculine, Chicano canon. But this is not all. The experience of colonization is represented in gendered terms through images such as the figure of La Malinche, the woman given by her people to Hernán Cortés, who became the mother of the hybrid Mexican race. La Malinche is, however, an ambiguous figure, interpreted by critics like Octavio Paz in *Labyrinth of Solitude*

(1959) as the origin of macho violence and Chicana passivity. I argue that writers such as Sandra Cisneros and Ana Castillo use the strategies described in post-colonial theory as "counter-discourse" to engage and deconstruct the oppressive cultural narratives that are a legacy of Mexican America's colonial past.

It is post-colonial travel theory that is engaged in the following essay. Alasdair Pettinger uses work on ethnography and travel writing by Mary Louise Pratt and James Clifford to consolidate this body of theoretical work, which to date has neglected the area of African American travel writings. In his discussion of texts like David Dorr's *A Colored Man Round the World* (1858); Booker T. Washington's *The Man Farthest Down* (1912); Langston Hughes's *The Big Sea* (1940) and *I Wonder As I Wander* (1956); and Colleen McElroy's *A Long Way from St Louie* (1997), Pettinger argues that travel abroad gave African American writers the opportunity to develop attitudes towards the United States on the one hand and the countries to which they travelled on the other that were informed by broadly colonial perspectives. So, while black authors took advantage of the opportunity to criticize the racial politics of the United States, they were also tempted to adopt what Pettinger calls "imperial" personae in relation to the people and countries they wrote about. He makes the case that these travel texts represent a post-colonial stance with respect to the United States but a colonial stance with respect to the rest of the world.

From Native American to Mexican American to African American literatures, we move to Asian American literature in the United States. Rajini Srikanth's discussion of the term "Asian American literature" addresses some of the ways in which the assumption that "American" signifies "United States" is problematic and a major limitation of the term. A similar limitation arises from the insistence that Asian American writers write about the experience of living in the United States as an Asian. The focus upon the United States within those texts that have attained canonical status produces a disproportionate emphasis upon issues of identity, voice, empowerment, racism, cultural hybridity, and belonging which does not adequately reflect the reality of contemporary Asian America. For example, since the 1980s foreign-born Asians have outnumbered native-born Asians in the United States. This means that for many Asian Americans, nations and "homes" other than the United States are as psychologically important as the United States. Indeed, many South Asians, Filipino/as, and Vietnamese watch as their ancestral homelands engage in the process of decolonization, establishing themselves as independent nations free of colonial control. In texts written by such authors, issues of diaspora and post-colonialism are urgent themes. Srikanth's essay focuses upon texts that offer a nuanced and complex vision of what Asian American literature might be, that lead to an interrogation of the term itself; texts that enable us to see the ways in which Asian Americans must confront anew issues of citizenship, nation, and belonging.

Post-colonial concepts of mimicry and imitation inform Mary Condé's essay, "Forging a Post-colonial Identity: Women of Chinese Ancestry Writing in English." Starting with the paradigmatic example of the Eaton sisters, Condé surveys the representation of disguise and the fabrication of cultural identity in the work of a range of texts produced by women of Chinese American (though the distinction between the U.S. and Canada is rendered ambiguous by some of these writers) ancestry. The Eaton sisters were born of an English father and missionary-educated Chinese mother; the family finally settled in Canada but Edith spent much of her professional life in the U.S. Edith self-identified with the Chinese American community, despite the pervasive anti-Chinese prejudice of the time, and wrote under the pseudonym of Sui Sin Far. Winnifred wrote under the pseudonym of Otono Watanna and identified with a then-popular Japanese exoticism, with which she had no blood connection and for which she has subsequently been criticized. Condé explores the cultural pressures exerted by Asian and American influences that have shaped the storytelling traditions that have developed within the work of Chinese American women writers in the United States in the course of the twentieth century.

Srikanth's discussion of Filipino/a literature within an Asian American context is developed by A. Noelle Williams, who presents Filipino/a literature as a challenge to definitions of American literature as constituted by texts written by and about residents of the U.S. In her representation, Filipino/a writing is a key component of a revisionist Asian American literature, described by Rajini Srikanth, that incorporates diasporic and colonized literatures. Williams draws attention to the invisibility of the Philippines in American history, society, and culture and argues that this is a consequence of the invisibility of American colonialism to most Americans. After the Spanish–American war, the United States appropriated the Philippines as American territory and assigned Filipinos to the category of U.S. nationals, a category which simultaneously obscured Filipinos' status as indigenous inhabitants of a foreign land taken by force, and prohibited them from claiming United States citizenship. In these terms Filipino narratives of migration can be seen as more than narratives of immigrant goals and experiences –

as tales of double exile and migration within the same political entity and through a similar cultural realm.

Paul Lyons discloses the status of Hawaiian literature within a colonial/post-colonial theoretical context. He observes that most Americans are unaware that Hawai'i is an American colony: this despite President Clinton's Apology to Native Hawaiians on Behalf of the United States for the Overthrow of the Kingdom of Hawaii in 1993 on the centennial of the Overthrow, which President Grover Cleveland acknowledged in 1893 to have been an illegal "Act of War." Cultural production in Hawai'i is thus intimately tied to American colonialism. Literature in Hawai'i is threefold; it is produced primarily by *haole* (whites), locals (primarily descendants of Asian plantation workers), and Hawaiians (those tracing their ancestry back before the 1778 arrival of Europeans). Local literature varies a great deal; it is in many contexts discussed as an Asian American literature, but it has often allied itself with issues of Hawaiian sovereignty as well. In addition, much of the recent *haole* literature, written by those born in Hawai'i or who have lived much of their lives in Hawai'i, deals with local and Hawaiian themes, raising questions of propriety, appropriation, custodial rights. On the face of it, "local" literature seems ambivalently "American" and Hawaiian literature not an American literature at all, despite its obvious entanglements with American culture and language. Lyons discusses how attempts at infusing "local" and "Hawaiian" content into "American" literature destabilizes the very concept of "Americanness."

In the essays that follow, tensions between distinct national identities are explored in relation to U.S. Puerto Rican, Haitian, Dominican, and Latin-Caribbean, Canadian, and Southeast Asian literatures. In her essay, Frances Aparicio mobilizes the linguistically hybrid term of Puerto Rican identity, "AmeRican," which signifies "American" while it simultaneously reaffirms the U.S. Puerto Rican subjectivity (read "I'm a Rican"), inscribed over the former imperial term in a kind of cultural and political palimpsest. The tensions between these two identities have been amplified by the rise of Puerto Rican diasporic literary production, which has destabilized traditional binaries of Self/Other represented in earlier insular texts. Diasporic authors such as Laviera, Esteves, Algarin, Pietri, Ortiz Cofer, Hernández Cruz, and others have foregrounded the contradictions experienced by the U.S. Puerto Rican subject, who "belongs" to both and to neither culture. The incorporation into the Anglo-American canon of insular authors such as Rosario Ferre and Esmeralda Santiago, and the publication in English of the dramatic works of Pedro Pietri have blurred linguistic and national borders. Aparicio argues that this transnational circulation of literary texts makes U.S. interests an integral component in reconceptualizing the U.S. Puerto Rican literary corpus as a part of "American" literature.

Myriam Chancy begins her essay with the example of Puerto Rican writer Ana Lydia Vega and her ability to represent the ways in which hegemonic relationships in and among the islands have disrupted revolutionary movements of decolonization between islands, which share a common history. In her short story "Cloud Cover Caribbean," three men, one Haitian, one Dominican, and one Cuban are fleeing their Caribbean nation states for a new beginning within the U.S. They are rescued by an American ship but are immediately categorized as "niggers," a categorization which is quickly confirmed by a Puerto Rican voice. Starting with this short narrative, Chancy explores how recent writers from the Caribbean negotiate the cultural terrain between the axes of "nationality" and "solidarity." Chancy argues that in proportion to its mainstream acceptance, Caribbean literature has neglected to address issues of pan-Caribbean history, which are informed by inherited colonial and racial codes. Recent works by Ana Lydia Vega, Edwidge Danticat, Cristina García, and Julia Alvarez suggest that women writers of the Caribbean are advancing new definitions of Caribbean identity, which may help to redefine pan-Caribbean relationships.

On the northern border of the United States, Canada's First Nations are also seeking to redefine colonial relationships by reclaiming stories of time and place, maps and metaphors, that interpret not only the past but also the present and future. Richard Lane focuses on two authors in particular, Tomson Highway and Eden Robinson, to examine the ways in which indigenous identities, places and stories have been re-coded, through a range of anthropological, cartographic, educational, literary and juridical discourses. He examines Robinson's novel *Monkey Beach* (2000), as an example of a post-colonial text that responds to such a re-coding of the location of place and identity: In this essay Lane explores the colonialist strategies of mapping and re-coding and counter-strategies by which First Nations writers have responded through contemporary fiction.

In the following essay, Laura Peters turns to the issue of national boundaries and allegiances, in relation to the post-colonial experience of indigenous Canadians. The concept of "borders" encapsulates the dilemma faced by the indigenous peoples of North America who have seen colonial borders and frontiers overtake their longer-standing affiliations. The U.S./Canadian border divides the Blackfeet tribe nominally into "Americans" and "Canadians"; their ethnic affiliation as a group has been placed under erasure. Peters addresses the racialized historical assumptions underlying the term *Canadian* as she explores the ways in which those who identify themselves as indigenous not only negotiate their ethnic identity in relation to the issues of nationhood and national belonging, but also how contemporary identities are negotiated in relation to inherited concepts of indigeneity. She focuses upon the work of Thomas King within the context of his larger project to articulate a contemporary indigenous identity which is neither Westernized nor held to a notion of stereotypical and pre-historical "authenticity."

In Southeast Asia, literatures are developing that owe much of their thematic shape to perceived tensions with the colonial power exerted by the U.S. For example, Renny Christopher argues that the literature produced by Vietnamese diaspora writers since 1975, and the literature being produced by writers in the Socialist Republic of Viet Nam, represent new literary forms that fuse the Vietnamese prose tradition with U.S. literary influences. The anthology *The Other Side of Heaven: Postwar Fiction by Vietnamese and American Writers* edited by Wayne Karlin, Le Minh Khue and Truong Vu brings together works by Euro-Americans, Vietnamese Americans who fought for the Republic of Viet Nam, and Vietnamese who fought for the National Liberation front and Democratic Republic of Viet Nam. This anthology represents the ways in which a new dialogue among Americans, Viet Kieu (exiles), and Vietnamese is helping to shape a new literature. Christopher highlights the subgenre of "return" narratives – narratives by Vietnamese diaspora writers that attempt to create a syncretic, transnational viewpoint through which to discuss issues of exile, home, and dislocation caused by war and cultural conflict, and the forging of new identities.

Julia Shackford-Bradley discusses three novels published in the late 1980s and 1990s by Southeast Asian women writers: Jessica Hagedorn's *Dogeaters* (1990), Wendy Law-Yone's *Irrawaddy Tango* (1993), and Ayu Utami's *Saman* (1998). She argues that these texts use intricate forms of intertextuality to represent the Foucaultian workings of power within post-colonial politics of the Philippines, Burma, and Indonesia. *Irrawaddy Tango* provides a focus for discussion of a new genre emerging in Southeast Asian fiction, in which women writers like Ninotschka Rosca (Philippines), Duong Thu Huong (Vietnam), and Ayu Utami (Indonesia), engage with the political urgencies of their homelands through innovative narrative strategies. At the same time, *Irrawaddy Tango* is read as an American novel, one which, the author implies, could never be written in "Daya"/Burma/Myanmar. Exiles and nationals alike are shown to suffer from a sickness of the tongue brought on by 30 years of dictatorship following the colonial experience. Shackford-Bradley argues that these novels occupy a particular place within the field of American post-colonial literature in which "home," or the nation, becomes the primary location of the story, while the American experience is what allows the protagonist to fulfil her potential. The insider/outsider dynamic represented by American post-colonial texts like these is explored further in Geraldine Stoneham's discussion of such issues as national identity, multiculturalism, and post-colonialism within the context of the experiences of immigration and assimilation.

In all of these essays contributors are led to ask whether in our discussions of American multiethnic literature we are naturalizing inherited concepts of American cultural identity as being equivalent with the United States. Not only the canon of "American Literature" but perhaps especially the authors, texts and traditions excluded from that dominant cultural category carry the burden of America's colonial history. The rationale for exclusion reinforces arbitrary national divisions based upon the partitioning of the Americas into North–Central–South divisions that serve the interests of the United States. The extension of this process into Asia and the Pacific furthers the dominant definition of America *as* the United States. The essays gathered in this collection address important questions about the complicity and potential for resistance offered by the practice of literary study, and specifically the study of American literature.

REFERENCES

Ahmad, Aijaz, 1992. *In Theory*, London: Verso.

Ashcroft, Bill, Gareth Griffiths and Helen Tiffin, 1989. *The Empire Writes Back: Theory and Practice in Post-Colonial Literatures*, London: Routledge.

Ashcroft, Bill, Gareth Griffiths and Helen Tiffin, 1998. *Key Concepts in Post-Colonial Studies*, London: Routledge.

Barker, Francis, Peter Hulme and Margaret Iversen, eds, 1994. *Colonial Discourse/Post-Colonial Theory*, Manchester: Manchester University Press.

Boehmer, Elleke, 1995. *Colonial and Postcolonial Literature*, Oxford: Oxford University Press.

Chambers, Iain and Lidia Curti, eds, 1996. *The Post-Colonial Question: Common Skies, Divided Horizons*, London: Routledge.

Child, Peter and Patrick Williams, 1997. *An Introduction to Post-Colonial Theory*, New York: Prentice Hall/ Harvester Wheatsheaf.

Fraser, Robert, 2000. *Lifting the Sentence: A Poetics of Post-Colonial Fiction*, Manchester: Manchester University Press.

Gurr, Andrew, ed., 1997. *The Politics of Post-Colonial Criticism*, Special Number of *The Yearbook of English Studies*, vol. 27.

Harasym, Sarah, ed., 1990. *The Post-Colonial Critic: Interviews, Strategies, Dialogues: Gayatri Chakravorty Spivak*, London & New York: Routledge.

Kiberd, Declan, 1996. *Inventing Ireland: The Literature of the Modern Nation*, New York: Vintage.

Lazarus, Neil, 1999. *Nationalism and Cultural Practice in the Post-Colonial World*, Cambridge: Cambridge University Press.

Loomba, Ania, 1998. *Colonialism/Post-Colonialism*, London: Routledge.

Madsen, Deborah, ed., 1999. *Post-Colonial Literatures: Expanding the Canon*, London: Pluto Press.

McLeod, John, 2000. *Beginning Post-Colonialism*, Manchester: Manchester University Press.

Mongia, Padmini, ed., 1996. *Contemporary Post-Colonial Theory: A Reader*, London: Arnold.

Moore-Gilbert, Bart, 1997. *Post-Colonial Theory: Contexts, Practices, Politics*, London: Verso.

Walder, Dennis, 1998. *Post-Colonial Literatures in English: History, Language, Theory*, Oxford: Blackwell.

Williams, Patrick and Laura Chrisman, eds, 1993. *Colonial Discourse and Post-Colonial Theory: A Reader*, Hemel Hempstead: Harvester Wheatsheaf.

Part 1

Ethnic Literature and Post-colonialism

1

Indigenous Literatures and Postcolonial Theories: Reading from Comparative Frames

Chadwick Allen

Difficult questions arise when we attempt to teach post-contact American Indian literature not simply as one voice among many in a multicultural United States – a thin strand in an increasingly dense fabric (to employ one popular metaphor) – but rather as an *indigenous* literature produced and consumed within a global context of historic and ongoing colonialisms.

First, as instructors and scholars, we have to decide to what degree we will ask our classes to engage the large bodies of postcolonial criticism and postcolonial theory (see Moore-Gilbert 1997 for useful discussions of the distinctions and overlaps between these). The latter's tendency toward all-inclusive generalization has come increasingly under attack (see McClintock 1992; San Juan 1998), and we have to decide up-front how we will introduce this often controversial work to students, especially undergraduates, who may have no prior experience with literary or cultural theory. Should we assign "early" postcolonial theorists, who are more likely to be accessible in the undergraduate classroom – say, the less violent Frantz Fanon of *Black Skin, White Masks* (1952), or Albert Memmi's even-toned *The Colonizer and the Colonized* (1957), or passages from Aimé Césaire's passionate and poetic *Discourse on Colonialism* (1955)? Or should we forego these foundational texts and assign more recent "cutting edge" theorists, who are likely to have been compelling forces in our own graduate educations and critical work – say, the often convoluted but always fascinating "high" theory of Gayatri Spivak, Homi Bhabha, and their many followers? Should we attempt to cover the history of the field of postcolonial literary studies as it has developed in the English-speaking academy over the past several decades

– including the rise of vocal detractors, like Aijaz Ahmad – or should we focus on what we think will be most relevant to the particular literature our students will read during the ten or fifteen weeks of the term? Should we privilege the "indigenous" theorist over the "metropolitan" and, if so, exactly who will we count as indigenous (only North American Indians? what about Hawaiians or other Polynesians? writers from the Caribbean or Latin America? Chicanos? Africans? African Americans?) and how will we justify our inclusion or exclusion of those theorists who are difficult to categorize? More mundanely, should we gloss theory as part of a lecture series, and therefore tightly control what kinds and what levels of theory students can draw upon in their readings of primary works, or should we ask students to wrestle with at least excerpts from key theoretical and critical texts?

Equally daunting, we have to decide how much historical, cultural, and/or linguistic context we will provide students for each of the primary American Indian texts we assign, and to what degree we will expect students to actively draw on these contexts in their responses to specific works in class discussions or presentations, in shorter and longer essay assignments, and on exams. As with postcolonial theory, choices here range between depth and coverage, relevance to specific works and a sense of fairness: If the 1890 massacre of over 200 Sioux men, women, and children at Wounded Knee, South Dakota, is a relevant context for a particular American Indian novel, short story, or poem, how graphically should we describe the horrific violence of that event – with which many if not most non-Indian undergraduates and graduate students will be unfamiliar – and how much do students need to know about changing Sioux customs at the time, tensions in local and national politics, settlers' fears and fantasies, individual personalities within the Sioux bands and within the cavalry, related battles and massacres, the legacy of Wounded Knee for both American Indians and other American citizens over the course of the twentieth century, and so forth? Similarly, if we wish to assign the evocative and often personally moving work of contemporary Navajo poet Luci Tapahonso, how much do students need to know about Navajo physical and social geography, the history and legacies of the 1864 Navajo Long Walk, Navajo oral traditions and ceremonial life, or the pronunciation, grammar, vocabulary, and typical syntax patterns of Navajo language (of which Tapahonso is a native speaker)? To complicate matters further, how much do students need to know about any indigenous author's biography or family history?

Beyond deciding what to include on the class reading list or in our lectures in terms of depth and coverage, those of us who teach at colleges and universities with predominantly White, middle-class student bodies must often work hard to convince our students that colonialism is a relevant context not only for early, often violent, encounters between indigenous North Americans and Europeans – where distinctions between colonizer and colonized seem relatively clear – but also for nineteenth- and twentieth-century American Indian literature and cultures, where such distinctions are often more complicated and lines can appear blurred. Part of the problem can be getting students to dissociate the word "colonial" from the historical period of the original 13 British colonies in what is now the northeastern United States. However, more of a challenge is asking literature students who are unfamiliar with both American Indian history and the political, social, economic, and psychological complexity of the American Indian situation today to grapple with the concept of an ongoing U.S. colonialism vis-à-vis indigenous individuals and communities. (Instructors have to decide whether or not they wish to raise the issue of U.S. colonialism offshore as well.) Students who have been taught by their families, by their elementary and secondary schools, by their churches, and by the dominant media to think of the United States as a safe haven from religious, ideological, and cultural persecutions that happen "out there" in other parts of the world can find the application of a colonial/postcolonial paradigm to the situation of American Indians intellectually frustrating, emotionally disturbing, or even personally offensive. Every term in which I have taught American Indian and other indigenous literatures in the context of colonialism, I have had undergraduate students become visibly upset during discussions of the roles Christian missionaries played in the encroachment and administration of colonial systems. Other undergraduates and graduate students have found it difficult to read about or to discuss the details of physical and psychological violence committed against American Indian men, women, and children, especially when that violence, like the kidnapping of indigenous children to be shipped off to boarding schools or the forced sterilization of indigenous women, has occurred in the contemporary era rather than in the distant past. Occasionally, students who have been taught that the mid-twentieth-century European Jewish Holocaust is incomparable with any other world event have expressed their unease with American Indian writers like Vine Deloria, Jr. (Sioux) and Sherman Alexie (Spokane/Cour d'Alene), who compare Jewish and American Indian experiences as similar experiences of survival in the face of attempted genocide. Thus, the issue of *how* students are likely to respond to the use of a colonial/postcolonial paradigm in the study of contemporary American Indian literature and cultures raises its own set of difficult questions about what to include on the syllabus and how to approach specific materials and issues in the classroom.

One approach I have found useful for inviting undergraduate and graduate students to consider American Indian literature as an indigenous literature within the context of ongoing colonialism is to organize the syllabus around a series of comparative frames. When this organizational structure works, my students – the undergraduates of which, especially, are mostly from Ohio and are mostly White and middle class – are able to effectively investigate texts that represent diverse peoples and cultures, and that reveal often violent histories, with which they have had little or no prior experience.

In my undergraduate courses on colonial and postcolonial representations, I establish the larger comparative frame as a three-part movement from the colonial/postcolonial world safely "out there" in toward the colonial/postcolonial world unexpectedly here "at home." Given the specific areas of my own interests and research, we begin with representations of "classic" colonial and postcolonial situations in Africa, then move to representations of settler colonization and its aftermath in Aotearoa/New Zealand, and finally home to the complicated colonial/postcolonial situation of the United States. I sometimes include Canadian First Nations texts in the final unit, which then becomes focused on North America rather than exclusively on the U.S. The advantage of this type of organization is that students who have never before dealt with the history or aftermath of colonialism as it affects indigenous peoples are not immediately confronted with personally disturbing issues of their own nation's or, potentially, their own European or American ancestors' responsibility and guilt. In plain language, White, middle-class students are less likely to feel attacked, and they are less likely then to shut down and refuse to engage in class discussion. Ideally, this three-part movement toward "home" encourages students to develop a critical vocabulary and a larger comparative context with which to more objectively confront and analyze their own nation's ongoing colonial history.

Within each unit the assigned readings create a second comparative frame by juxtaposing texts produced by European or American colonizers with texts produced by colonized or formerly colonized indigenous peoples. In the unit focused on Africa, for instance, we begin by reading several brief contextualizing essays on Africa's history and changing political geography. Students are usually surprised to discover the role Europe played in drawing the map of the African

continent we know today. We then investigate one or more representations of Africa written by "colonizers." At different times I have
assigned, either singly or in combination, Joseph Conrad's celebrated
European novel of physical and psychological exploration, *Heart of
Darkness* (1899), which students are likely to have studied before, but
with much less attention to history, politics, or race; Edgar Rice
Burroughs' American pulp adventure classic, *Tarzan of the Apes* (1914),
which students are surprised to find in the "serious" literature classroom,
but which readily raises a variety of issues about stereotyping and White
fantasies of the "other"; and Marcel Griaule's French anthropological
text, *Conversations with Ogotemmêli* (1965), which is available in English
translation and which invites students to think about the roles power
and personality play in the West's supposedly "objective" analysis of
non-Western cultures. Next, we juxtapose these with one or more "post-
colonial" novels of African response to European colonialism. I often
use Nigerian author Chinua Achebe's *Arrow of God* (1964). Many undergraduates, of course, will have already read Achebe's better-known
Things Fall Apart for another class. I have also paired Isak Dinesen's
popular and romantic European description of a White woman farmer
in colonial Kenya, *Out of Africa* (1937), with Kenyan author Ngugi wa
Thiong'o's early postcolonial novel *Weep Not, Child* (1964). This juxtaposition can be especially powerful, since Ngugi writes from the
perspective of the same Kikuyu people who worked Karen Blixen's
plantation, and since *Weep Not, Child* basically picks up the story of
the Kikuyu where Dinesen's work leaves off. Having been pleasantly
lulled by the lush imagery of Dinesen's story of personal fulfillment in
Africa, many students find Ngugi's far bleaker vision of Kenya's difficult
attempts to remove the yoke of colonial control – the very control that
made Blixen's personal independence possible – a disturbing but eye-
opening discovery. When I use this pairing, I also assign at least one
contextualizing essay about Kenyan political history.

Whenever materials are available, I try to bring in appropriate visual
aids, so that students can see the places and peoples about whom they
are reading, including clips from documentary and feature films on
video. Burroughs' *Tarzan of the Apes*, for instance, works particularly
well in this regard, since it can be used as an occasion for demonstrating how dominant images of Africa and Africans, as well as dominant
images of the White man in Africa, have developed – and not developed
– in Hollywood films from the 1930s through the 1990s. I also make a
point of bringing contemporary African music into the classroom, so
that students can experience African languages and musical styles.

In these undergraduate classes, I tend to spend a greater amount of time on the African unit than on the New Zealand or U.S. unit, partly because the history of European colonization and official decolonization in Africa sets up a useful model against which students can compare deep settler colonization in Aotearoa/New Zealand and the United States, and partly because I sense that, as I suggested above, my students are most comfortable with discussing colonialism and postcolonial theory in relation to these "distant" places and texts. By the time we have finished the unit on colonial and postcolonial representations of Africa, students are better equipped to name issues and to analyze literary strategies that will be relevant in the subsequent units.

In the second unit I begin with mini-lectures on New Zealand geography, complete with maps (my students are often not sure exactly where New Zealand is located), and on Maori history, culture, and contemporary demographics. I then assign excerpts from an early Pakeha (British) representation of Aotearoa/New Zealand, like *Our Maoris* (1884) by Lady Martin, the wife of a British missionary who lived in the Auckland area between 1842 and 1874. The "benevolent" paternalism of Martin's text (which students often decide, instead, to name a colonial *ma*ternalism) makes for a productive comparison to Dinesen's and Conrad's perspectives on Africans. Next, we juxtapose Martin's colonial text with several short, "postcolonial" works written by Maori authors since 1970: Apirana Taylor's brief but moving poem "sad Joke on a Marae" (1979), which draws on both classic and contemporary Maori imagery to describe colonial dispossession; Witi Ihimaera's short story "The Greenstone Patu" (1977), which alludes to the 1840 Treaty of Waitangi and which presents a Maori worldview that openly challenges typical Pakeha notions about the value and ownership of property; and Patricia Grace's lyrical second novel *Potiki* (1986), which offers both an aesthetically beautiful reading experience and highly charged messages about ongoing attempts at colonial expropriation and indigenous land rights. For most American students, these texts will be their first exposure to Maori culture and Maori language, and in addition to lectures on history and culture, I provide a translation sheet of the Maori words and phrases Grace deploys in her novel – except for the novel's ending, which is written entirely in Maori. I ask students to speculate about the ending's likely or possible meanings given the preceding passages written in English, to grapple with the experience of linguistic exclusion, and to consider the possible literary, personal, and political reasons Grace may have had for presenting her novel's ending exclusively in

Maori language before I lead them through a translation and discussion of the passage in class.

In this unit I might show clips from feature films like *Utu* or *The Piano* while discussing Pakeha representations of Aotearoa/New Zealand, and from the Maori written and directed feature films *Ngati* and *Once Were Warriors* while discussing contemporary Maori authors. (The former of these will be difficult to locate in the U.S., but the latter is widely available on video.) I also like to show the Maori-produced documentary *Bastion Point Day 507*, which documents an important Maori anti-colonial activist event – as well as the New Zealand government's violent response to that event – in the late 1970s. (Unfortunately, this film, which was first shown on New Zealand television in 1981, will also be difficult to locate in the U.S.) As in the African unit, I make a point of bringing contemporary music into class. Students are usually surprised to discover that Maori produce their own pop, rap, and hip-hop music, often bilingually and sometimes exclusively in Maori language, and that this music often carries anti-colonial messages. Because I am able to translate Maori lyrics into English for my students, I spend an entire class period on exploring the conventions and implications of this contemporary Maori music. Because the music produced by Maori pop, rap, and hip-hop artists can seem more culturally familiar than unfamiliar to American young people, at this point in the course my sense is that many students begin to think about the postcolonial issues we have been discussing in the first two units in more personal terms, especially the continuing psychological impact of European colonization on indigenous peoples.

Finally, in the third unit, we arrive "home" to the United States. Readers of this essay will be aware of the wealth of appropriate contextualizing materials and works produced by European and American "colonizers" with which to begin this unit. I am personally fond of assigning John Filson's 1784 Daniel Boon narrative, because it codifies many of the conventions that became standard in "frontier" and "western" literature written by members of dominant American culture, and because subsequent generations have reinvented Boon(e) and his narrative in a variety of forms and for a variety of purposes (see Slotkin 1973). The Boon text is also useful for opening a lecture or discussion about the history of U.S. – as opposed to European – colonial expansion in North America. As in the previous units, we then read "postcolonial" works by indigenous writers. Here again, readers of this essay will be aware of the wealth of appropriate materials written by U.S. American Indians and/or First Nations peoples of Canada. I have used different

American Indian works each time I have taught a course like this, and I have experimented with assigning only works written since the 1960s as well as with assigning a variety of American Indian works written in the nineteenth and twentieth centuries. My students have responded particularly well to Blackfeet and Gros Ventre author James Welch's historical novel *Fools Crow* (1986), which is set in Montana in the late 1860s and which ends with the event of the 1870 Marias River massacre; Welch is a descendant of one of the massacre's Blackfeet survivors. Part of this novel's appeal, I think, is that while it was written in the 1980s, its setting in the relatively "safe" nineteenth century, combined with Welch's even tone and well-developed non-Indian as well as Indian characters, allows students to explore issues of violent colonization in the western United States with some level of objectivity. My students have also responded well to the short stories of Mohawk First Nations author E. Pauline Johnson, which were published in the first decade of the twentieth century and which present surprisingly "feminist" as well as pro-Native women protagonists, and to contemporary poetry and short narratives written by Alexie and Tapahonso. While questions of guilt and the dominant culture's contemporary responsibilities toward indigenous individuals and communities inevitably surface during this unit – as do questions about American Indian high-stakes bingo and casino gambling enterprises – in my experience, if I encourage students to think comparatively, these discussions tend to be invigorating and productive (although rarely anything approaching conclusive) rather than alienating or debilitating. Students find particularly instructive comparisons to contemporary Maori desires and demands in Aotearoa/New Zealand, about which they tend to have become sympathetic during unit two.

I am less likely to show clips from feature films in the North American unit, because I assume that students have already seen a variety of film and television representations of American Indians. If undergraduates say they are unfamiliar with classic westerns, I will show something like *Stagecoach*'s fight scene with the Apache. Many students are likely to have seen Kevin Costner's *Dances With Wolves*, Disney's *Pocahontas*, or television's *Dr. Quinn, Medicine Woman*, making it possible to discuss these images without bringing in clips. The recent release of the American Indian-written and directed film *Smoke Signals*, however, offers a great opportunity to introduce students to Native-produced film images of American Indians, especially if there is time to screen this film in its entirety. Moreover, a number of good documentaries on American Indian peoples and history were produced during the 1990s.

I often show relevant segments from the documentary series *500 Nations*, for example; this series includes on-camera interviews with contemporary Native people, often the descendants of indigenous people involved in tragic historic events like the 1864 massacre of Southern Cheyenne at Sand Creek, Colorado. Perhaps even more so than in the previous units, I feel it is imperative for students who may never have personally met an indigenous North American to see and hear living Indian people. As in the other units, I make a point of exposing students to contemporary indigenous music: here, everything from powwow singing and drumming to folk harmonies, country and western to rock and roll, and reservation rap. By now students are prepared (and often eager) to hear this variety of musical production from American Indians, as well as to analyze the pro-Native and anti-colonial messages some of this music contains.

As the term progresses, third and fourth comparative frames arise as students become able to make comparisons among the works of different European and American colonizers and among the works of various indigenous peoples. Such comparisons can be actively encouraged by setting aside certain class periods as "comparative days," and/or by requiring comparisons in writing assignments and exam questions. This aspect of the course – active comparison – is essential for the comparative frames approach to have any significant impact on students. If comparisons across and among histories and cultures are left up to the students themselves, they are likely to see a course like this as simply a sequence of discrete, mostly unrelated, units of knowledge – colonialism in Africa, colonialism in Aotearoa/New Zealand, and colonialism in the U.S., for example – rather than as an effort to build a complex but integrated base of knowledge about a larger object of study designated by the terms "colonial" and "postcolonial" that includes the United States and its indigenous peoples.

It is here that the study of postcolonial theory really becomes important in the undergraduate classroom, for it can provide the tangible "glue" to hold together the seemingly discrete units of a course organized in this manner. In a sense, students engage an additional, fifth comparative frame throughout the course by comparing various theorists' abstractions about "the" colonial or postcolonial situation, about colonial discourse, or about postcolonial literary production with the specific representations they are reading by individual writers from a variety of cultures, geographies, historical periods, and subject positions within multiple hierarchical systems of power.

Before beginning the first unit, therefore, I introduce basic vocabulary. On the first or second day of class, I ask students to write out definitions for the following terms: "colonization," "colonial," "postcolonial," "discourse," "colonial discourse," "frontier," "settler," "native," "indigenous." Students often remark on the difficulty of this exercise, and it seems to stir their interest in the first reading assignments. For the next class meeting, I have students read selections from one or more foundational theoretical texts that offer definitions for at least some of these terms, perhaps Memmi, Fanon, and/or Césaire. In class, we go over the terms I asked them to define during our previous meeting and, on a handout, I provide provisional definitions for these terms based on the assigned readings, but also on other theoretically informed texts, like the introduction to Williams and Chrisman's *Colonial Discourse and Postcolonial Theory: A Reader* (1994) or Sara Mills's volume titled *Discourse* (1997). I stress the ambiguity and situatedness of terms like "settler," "native," and "indigenous," and I offer multiple, even contradictory definitions for terms like "postcolonial." I also give students Annette Kolodny's useful definition of "frontier" and introduce them to the additional term "contact zone," as defined by Mary Louise Pratt. At a minimum, students need this vocabulary, as well as the knowledge that scholars do not agree on its precise definitions, to begin to critically engage the primary readings. I make it a point to refer to this vocabulary throughout the course and to encourage students to continually refine their understandings of individual terms.

Depending on which specific primary texts we read in a given term, I assign other relevant theoretical and critical works, usually excerpts, although I prefer to gloss "high" theory when it is relevant, often as a means for initiating class discussion of a particular text, rather than to ask undergraduates to try to read its typically difficult prose. Early in the term, I give a brief mini-lecture on the history and contemporary concerns of the field of postcolonial literary studies – and raise concepts like colonial discourse analysis, postcolonial hybridity and mimicry, and so forth – but I expect most undergraduate students to focus mainly on the primary texts assigned in class. If we read Conrad in the African unit, I will assign Achebe's famous 1977 essay "An Image of Africa: Racism in Conrad's *Heart of Darkness*" as well as a response to Achebe by a critic who disagrees with his charge. If I assign novels by Achebe or Ngugi, I will assign brief examples of their critical work and/or their more theoretical work on the role of English in African literature. During the New Zealand and U.S. units, I raise the issue of so-called "indigenous theory" and give examples of the exciting work being produced by indigenous scholars, particularly those who identify as Maori or American Indian.

In contrast to my large undergraduate classes, in my smaller graduate seminars I assume students will have at least some prior experience with U.S. multicultural literature, including American Indian, and at least a limited exposure to world literatures. (In practice, of course, this is not true of every graduate student.) Instead of a three-part comparison, I offer graduate students a more focused comparative frame so that they can investigate and compare two indigenous minority literary traditions within the context of ongoing colonialism in more depth. Again, given the specific areas of my own research, I ask students to compare the twentieth-century literary work produced by members of a specific American Indian nation or region (for example, the Sioux, the Plains, or the Southwest) with the contemporary literary work produced by New Zealand Maori. I also ask graduate students to read a wide range of postcolonial criticism and theory. Particularly important to a course like this is having students juxtapose theoretical models developed in response to literatures produced in the "classic" postcolonial situations of Africa, India, and the Caribbean with emerging theories that respond specifically or comparatively to indigenous minority or "Fourth World" situations like those of American Indians and New Zealand Maori. In these graduate seminars, I devote considerable attention, usually toward the end of the course, to analyzing "indigenous theory" and to considering its potential implications for influencing or ignoring the larger body of so-called "orthodox" theory. Some parts of this body of theory and criticism are more rigorous than others, most of it will be completely unfamiliar to graduate students, and all of it is highly provocative. Of particular interest for a course that investigates how American Indian literature can be read as an indigenous literature in the context of an ongoing U.S. colonialism is the work of American Indian writers and scholars Simon Ortiz (Acoma), Jack Forbes (Renape/Lenape/Sapori), Gerald Vizenor (Chippewa), M. Annette Jaimes (Juaneño/Yaqui), Elizabeth Cook-Lynn (Crow Creek Sioux), Louis Owens (Choctaw/ Cherokee), and Jace Weaver (Cherokee).

While there are potential drawbacks to the comparative frames approach I describe above – I can think of no approach to teaching within the parameters of a 10- or 15-week term that does not have its drawbacks – one of its advantages is that it invites students to rethink their sense of the exceptional quality of "American" literature and to reconceptualize that literature's connections to other world literatures and to world events like colonization, settlement, resistance, and their aftermath.

REFERENCES

Achebe, Chinua, 1964. *Arrow of God*. New York: Doubleday, 1967.

Achebe, Chinua, 1977. "An Image of Africa: Racism in Conrad's *Heart of Darkness*." Rpt. in *Heart of Darkness: A Norton Critical Edition*, ed. Richard Kimbrough, 3rd edn, New York: Norton, 1988, pp. 251–62.

Alexie, Sherman, 1993a. *First Indian on the Moon*, New York: Hanging Loose Press.

Alexie, Sherman, 1993b. *The Lone Ranger and Tonto Fistfight in Heaven*, New York: Atlantic Monthly Press.

Burroughs, Edgar Rice, 1914. *Tarzan of the Apes*, New York: Penguin, 1990.

Césaire, Aimé, 1955. *Discourse on Colonialism*, trans. Joan Pinkham, New York: Monthly Review Press, 1972.

Conrad, Joseph, 1899. *Heart of Darkness: A Norton Critical Edition*, ed. Richard Kimbrough, 3rd edn, New York: Norton, 1988.

Cook-Lynn, Elizabeth, 1996. *Why I Can't Read Wallace Stegner and Other Essays: A Tribal Voice*, Madison: University of Wisconsin Press.

Deloria, Vine, Jr., 1969. *Custer Died For Your Sins: An Indian Manifesto*, New York: Macmillan.

Dinesen, Isak, 1937. *Out of Africa*, New York: Vintage, 1961.

Fanon, Frantz, 1952. *Black Skin, White Masks*, trans. Charles Lam Markmann, New York: Grove, 1967.

Filson, John, 1784. "The Adventures of Col. Daniel Boon; Containing a Narrative of the Wars of Kentucke" in *The Discovery, Settlement and Present State of Kentucke*, New York: Corinth Books, 1962, pp. 49–82.

Forbes, Jack, 1987. "Colonialism and Native American Literature: Analysis," *Wicazo Sa Review*, 3, pp. 17–23.

Grace, Patricia, 1986. *Potiki*, Auckland: Penguin.

Griaule, Marcel, 1965. *Conversations with Ogotemmêli: An Introduction to Dogon Religious Ideas*, London: Oxford University Press.

Ihimaera, Witi, 1977. "The Greenstone Patu," *The New Net Goes Fishing*, Auckland: Heinemann, pp. 107–18.

Jaimes, M. Annette with Theresa Halsey, 1992. "American Indian Women: At the Center of Indigenous Resistance in North America" in *The State of Native America: Genocide, Colonization, and Resistance*, ed. M. Annette Jaimes, Boston: South End, pp. 311–44.

Kolodny, Annette, 1992. "Letting Go Our Grand Obsessions: Notes Toward a New Literary History of the American Frontiers," *American Literature*, 64.1 (March), pp. 1–18.

Martin, Lady, 1884. *Our Maoris*, London: Society for Promoting Christian Knowledge.

McClintock, Anne, 1992. "The Angel of Progress: Pitfalls of the Term 'Postcolonialism,'" rpt. in *Colonial Discourse/Postcolonial Theory*, eds Francis Barker, Peter Hulme, and Margaret Iversen, Manchester: Manchester University Press, 1994, pp. 253–67.

Memmi, Albert, 1957. *The Colonizer and the Colonized*, trans. Howard Greenfeld, Boston: Beacon, 1967.

Mills, Sara, 1997. *Discourse*, London: Routledge.

Moore-Gilbert, Bart, 1997. *Postcolonial Theory: Contexts, Practices, Politics*, London: Verso.

Ngugi, 1964. *Weep Not, Child*, Portsmouth, NH: Heinemann, 1987.

Ortiz, Simon, 1981. "Towards a National Indian Literature: Cultural Authenticity in Nationalism," rpt. in *Critical Perspectives on Native American Fiction*, ed. Richard F. Fleck, Washington, DC: Three Continents Press, 1993, pp. 64–8.

Owens, Louis, 1992. *Other Destinies: Understanding the American Indian Novel*, Norman: University of Oklahoma Press.

Pratt, Mary Louise, 1992. *Imperial Eyes: Travel Writing and Transculturation*, London: Routledge.

San Juan, E., Jr., 1998. *Beyond Postcolonial Theory*, New York: St. Martin's Press.

Slotkin, Richard, 1973. *Regeneration Through Violence: The Mythology of the American Frontier, 1600–1860*, Middletown, CT: Wesleyan University Press.

Tapahonso, Luci, 1993. *Sáanii Dahataa/The Women are Singing: Poems and Stories*, Tucson: University of Arizona Press.

Taylor, Apirana, 1979. "Sad Joke on a Marae," in *Eyes of the Ruru*, Wellington: Voice, 15, p. 15.

Vizenor, Gerald, 1994. *Manifest Manners: Postindian Warriors of Survivance*, Hanover: Wesleyan University Press.

Vizenor, Gerald, 1998. *Fugitive Poses: Native American Indian Scenes of Absence and Presence*, Lincoln: University of Nebraska Press.

Weaver, Jace, 1998. "From I-Hermeneutics to We-Hermeneutics: Native Americans and the Postcolonial" in *Native American Religious Identity: Unforgotten Gods*, ed. Jace Weaver, Maryknoll, NY: Orbis Books.

Welch, James, 1986. *Fools Crow*, New York: Penguin.

Williams, Patrick, and Laura Chrisman, 1994. "Colonial Discourse and Postcolonial Theory: An Introduction" in *Colonial Discourse and Postcolonial Theory: A Reader*, eds Patrick Williams and Laura Chrisman, New York: Columbia University Press, pp. 1–20.

Part 2

Post-colonialism at Home

2

"Going Into a Whole Different Country": Postcolonial "Nation"-hood in Native American Literature

Lee Schweninger and Cara Cilano

A focus on issues of "nation" that are prominent and urgent in post-colonial literary studies today allows us to look at Native American literatures as "postcolonial" in their own right, in that a focus on "nation" in these literatures emphasizes the abiding realities that resulted from Native Americans' histories of contact with dominant U.S. groups. That is, we want to draw attention to the contentiousness and ambiguity surrounding the status of "nation" as it applies to both fields of literary study. In the context of postcolonial literary studies there has been a pre-occupation with ideas of geography, history, nation, and global interconnectedness, as is evidenced by the explosion of commentary on globalization and its effects. In the literature of some formerly colonized countries, too often labeled "Third World" or "developing," "nation" represents a long-sought-after, if difficult to attain, autonomy that, ideally at least, promised/-es some degree of self-determination and equal political and economic standing on the global stage. However, under the heading of globalization, many critics from diverse fields, including literary studies, debate whether the "nation," as a mode of political and economic organization, as well as an idea around which to build unifying identities, still exists. Such debates take shape from the imbalanced political, cultural, and economic relations between countries, not to mention the increasingly visible presence of transna-tional alliances that base their identities upon religion, for instance, and that characterize global interconnections in the late twentieth- and early twenty-first centuries.

Within Native American literary studies, the concept of "nation" can be seen to signify a desire for, or a claiming of, senses of autonomy, self-determination, and equality akin to those sought after or held by "Third World" countries. Yet, given Native Americans' histories with the United States, histories that resonate with those from countries more traditionally thought of as postcolonial, such as Zimbabwe and India, for instance, the secure and unproblematic articulation of a "national" identity in the literatures of many Native American authors remains elusive. As Elizabeth Cook-Lynn (Dakota) asserts, the "people of America's First Nations find themselves struggling with the myths of their own national status against a long history of denationalization" (1996: 86). From the perspectives both of postcolonial and Native American literary studies, "nation" proves to be a slippery concept whose meaning shifts according to which country, whose people, "nation" is meant to signify.

Any analysis of basic or neutral definitions of "nation" (that is, if definitions are ever neutral) illustrates where and why the term becomes hard to pin down. According to Rob Wilson and Wimal Dissanayake's definition, which clearly reflects Benedict Anderson's influences, "nation" is "an 'imagined community' of coherent modern identity through warfare, religion, blood, patriotic symbology, and language" (1996: 3). By contrast and in somewhat greater detail, Ward Churchill defines nation as "consist[ing] of any body of people, independent of its size, who are bound together by a common language and set of cultural beliefs, possessed of a defined or definable land base sufficient to provide an economy, and evidencing the capacity to govern themselves" (1998: 3). Both of these basic definitions hit upon the ties that bind: language; and cultural beliefs, which would include things such as religion. Though implying each other, the non-overlapping elements of these definitions – warfare, blood, and patriotic symbology, on the one hand, and land, an economy, and self-government, on the other – indicate where the concept gets slippery: while any group, "independent of its size," could define itself as a "nation" thanks to shared language and culture, only those "nations" with *power* could define themselves as such through the additional definitional components of warfare, blood, symbology (or metanarrative), land, an economy, and self-government. Warfare, the claiming of land, and the ability to self-govern, which includes the enforcement of laws, are all obvious exertions of power. Less explicitly, a reliance on blood involves power in that it is exclusionary, and it must have the force to remain inviolate or pure, even if only putatively so; blood sets normative boundaries, including those that mark race, class, ethnicity, sexuality, morality, etc. In a similar way, symbology or the metanarratives that give shape to the stories and myths of a "nation" are exclusionary at base in that they often depend upon binary oppositions to bolster their viability. For instance, during the Age of Empire, what it meant to be English depended a great deal on having Indians and Africans as foils. Further, the race and ethnic tensions that exist in England today testify to the still extant exclusionary definitions of Englishness. Likewise, in formulations of U.S. identity, the denigration of Native Americans as uncivilized or, conversely, the romanticization of them as noble savages, continues to play a foundational part. Finally, the possession of an economy that provides self-sufficiency at the very least assumes prior possession of a workforce, markets, and resources, both natural and financial. Not only does the possession of such things suggest social and political stability, but also points to some of the reasons why many "nations," such as England and the U.S., sought (and still seek) (neo-) colonial domination.

Within postcolonial literary studies the slipperiness of "nation" involves both the common elements of language and culture, as well as the power elements just discussed. In terms of defining "nation" along axes of shared language and culture, much literature from post-colonized places points toward the difficulty of finding that common ground, since the geographic boundaries drawn by the formerly colonizing powers bind groups "nationally" who would otherwise define themselves differently, even oppositionally. Take, for instance, Salman Rushdie's 1980 novel, *Midnight's Children*, which deals with the violence, confusion, and long-lasting ramifications of Partition. As for the power issues that coincide with defining "nation," many formerly colonized places that became "nations" in the twentieth century lacked fundamental infrastructural elements, such as a firmly established legislative system or functioning economic base, that severely inhibited and continues to inhibit these "nations'" abilities to occupy a place in world organizations in a self-determining fashion. For instance, in a 1988 interview with Bill Moyers, Nigerian novelist Chinua Achebe explained that the reason why so many "developing" African "nations" were having such troubles with corruption in their newly formed democracies was that the colonial project was a totalitarian system that offered its colonies no model of how to run an efficient and effective democratic government, not to mention how to enter into global capitalism in a sustainable and equitable manner (Achebe 1994).

To develop this focus on "nation" in Native American literary contexts, we want to focus primarily upon Native Americans' histories of contact with the dominant U.S., as these histories give rise to the power dynamics – geographic, historiographic, and legislative in nature – that Native American literatures point toward as complicating factors in claims to "nation." More specifically, this focus on histories of contact enables us to examine Native American literatures in terms of issues of sovereignty, which implicitly or explicitly revolve around the reservation as a material legacy of Native Americans' contact with the U.S. government. Such literatures problematize the articulation of a "national" identity or claiming of sovereignty on the part of Native American communities, as they draw upon other corollary legacies of contact, such as: the ability of treaties and other historical events to connect Native American communities and the U.S. government in equitable and just relationships; and troubled conceptions of citizenship, as Native Americans struggle with understanding how to identify themselves on individual and "national" levels.

"Nation"-hood, as defined by Wilson and Dissanayake, as well as by Churchill, for instance, in a Native North American context, as it is grounded and defined by the geographic place of the reservation, can exist only from the point of view of historical contact with whites. With this insistence on the prevalence and pervasiveness of contact, Native American "nations" invite specific kinds of historical or, more precisely, historiographic considerations. Before outlining the contours of these considerations, however, let us first underscore how a framework built around contact disallows, for instance, any nostalgic tendencies, and this lack of nostalgia tends to preclude a fictive return to pre-contact days, since it predicates the articulation of a "national" identity on the part of Native American communities.

Even though the vast majority of works comprising what constitutes the Native American literary canon is devoted to post-contact representations and depictions of Native American life in concert with the effects of contact, there are examples by writers who seem to imply that some form of return to a pre-contact era or culture is desirable and even possible. The ambiguous ending of Linda Hogan's (Chickasaw) *Mean Spirit* (1990) is suggestive of a family's ability to follow a mysterious, sometimes invisible, red road into a world that essentially pre-dates contact. Similarly, in her novel *Power* (1998), Hogan seems to suggest that Omisto can somehow return to her pre-contact Panther clan in the swamps of southern Florida. One might make a similar argument of Leslie Marmon Silko's (Laguna Pueblo) *Ceremony* (1977), except that Tayo's healing is in large measure dependent upon a medicine man who lives very much in the twentieth century and maintains that the stories have to change with the times in order to retain their vibrancy and efficacy. It has also been suggested that N. Scott Momaday's (Kiowa) novel *The Ancient Child* (1989) advocates some return to a pre-contact pristine Kiowa past, but such a reading overlooks the fact that Set would never have known to return to the historically sacred Devils Tower (Bear's Lodge) in the first place if it had not been for the pan-Indian and Western influences of his lover and spiritual guide Grey.

Unfortunately, in the novel *Mountain Windsong* (1992), Robert J. Conley (Keetoowah Cherokee) belies or betrays the book's thematic structure and movement when he suggests that the protagonists, the two lovers Whippoorwill and Oconeechee, can come together as a sort of pre-contact Cherokee Adam and Eve on the newly acquired "reservation" in North Carolina. Such a possibility is suggested early in the novel, when a somewhat mysterious character ("he had just materialized there and then" and is flanked "by two, large snarling, black wolves") stands outside the crowd and asserts that if the Cherokee follow the white men's ways, their culture is doomed (Conley 1992: 36). In order to stay where they belong they must heed his advice:

> Throw away your steel knives and iron pots and guns. Burn the white man's clothes you wear. Throw away the glass beads you use for decoration and learn again how to prepare the quills of the porcupine for use as decoration. Speak your own language, the one God gave the Cherokees. Kill your cats and pigs and horses. Be Cherokees. That is the only way to be saved. (Conley 1992: 36)

Other novels of homecoming, in contrast, are very dependent upon an acceptance of the effects of contact and colonization in one way or another. In the first place, one might argue, if one comes home to a reservation, that character is not necessarily returning to a post-contact environment. Nor do characters tend to return as essentialized Indians to a pristine past. When Archilde returns to the reservation at the beginning of D'Arcy McNickle's (Salish) *The Surrounded* (1936), for instance, he enters an arena torn by allegiances to both his Salish mother's world and his Spanish emigrant father's. "When you came home to your Indian mother you had to remember that it was a different world" (McNickle 1936: 3). Indeed, the novel's title suggests the thorough intertwining of multiple cultures. In Momaday's *House Made of Dawn* (1968), in another instance, Abel's return is entirely dependent upon his ability to incorporate the many things he learns as a result of his stay in Los Angeles. In undertaking the final dawn run, he practices a Jemez Pueblo tradition, but as he runs he recites a Navajo healing song he has learned from his Navajo friend Ben Benally in L.A. Also, it is through the Kiowa trickster Tosamah that the reader, if not Abel himself, learns that migration and incorporation of other cultures' artifacts and/or customs are a fundamental part of their own culture and thus their survival:

> Along the way the Kiowas were befriended by the Crows, who gave them the culture and religion of the plains. They acquired horses. . . . They acquired Tai-me, the sacred sun dance doll, from that moment the chief object and symbol of their worship, and so shared in the divinity of the sun. Not least, they acquired the sense of destiny. (Momaday 1968: 129)

As such examples suggest, the impossibility of a return to a pre-contact era rests upon the whole reality of the reservation as an obvious result of contact. We mean to say, the geographical place of the reservation truly matters because, first, the American Indians' existence there is historically determined; and, second, the concept of "nation" in a post-contact context depends on territory and literal boundaries; hence, "national" identity comes about because of the place where the nation is found. Such a notion of the importance of the land is asserted by Vine Deloria, Jr. (Yankton Sioux), and Clifford M. Lytle, who argue for "the primacy of land in the Indian psychological makeup. ... [A]s land is alienated, all other forms of social cohesion also begin to erode, land having been the context in which the other forms have been created" (1984: 12).

Moreover, much Native American literature frames the geographical location of the reservation as the place from which to assert sovereignty, an idea that, in Native American literary and political contexts, also relies upon histories of contact. Whereas the national metanarrative of the dominant U.S. tends to write the Native American out of the history of itself as a nation, Native American claims to sovereignty emphasize contact and the continuing connections between themselves and the federal government, a connectedness that Chadwick Allen views as a sort of supervised sovereignty (2000: 7). As Charles F. Wilkinson explains, "This separatism [between the Native American tribes and the U.S. federal government] is measured, rather than absolute, because it contemplates supervision and support by the United States" (1987: 14). The reservations themselves act as the sites of supervision and support, as they came about out of treaty agreements and are still the places – geographically and socially – at which the dominant U.S. government deals with Native American communities. Current relations between the U.S. government – at both the state and federal level – and Native Americans on reservations include trying to find ways of dealing with the horrifying conditions on reservations. Louis Owens characterizes these conditions:

> [T]he poorest and most desperate places in America are Native American reservations, populated by indigenous peoples who commonly live with as much as 85 percent unemployment, deplorable health care and even worse education, horrifying rates of alcohol and drug addiction, an epidemic of fetal alcohol syndrome, and the highest suicide rates and lowest life expectancy of any ethnic group in the nation – all the effects of institutionalized racism. (2001: 21)

Another area of current contact between Native American communities and the U.S. government involves "legally" identifying oneself as an Indian. Kathryn Shanley points out what a logistical and ridiculous nightmare some Native American individuals and communities undergo as they try to enroll as "Indians" with the federal government:

> [U]nder many tribal enrollment policies, if a tribal person's parents are from different nations, but the individual cannot document at least one-quarter blood quantum in one parent's nation, he or she cannot be counted as being Indian at all. [Moreover,] over one hundred tribes have yet to complete the lengthy and expensive process required to establish recognition as tribes. (Shanley 2001: 42)

Finally, it is important to acknowledge that not all peoples who identify themselves as Native Americans reside on the reservation. Consequently, "nation" in Native American contexts insists not only upon a history but also upon a continuance through the present and the future of contact between the first peoples and the treaty co-signers.

Such an insistence grounds itself in the solidity or reality of treaties as historical documents; that is, at base, claims of sovereignty invest treaties with enough force to structure and ensure the reality of Native American "nation"-hood for both Native Americans themselves and for outsiders to these nations. Yet, contentions regarding the forcefulness and enforceability of treaties abound. For instance, at the Conference on Indian Tribes and Treaties that took place at the University of Minnesota in April of 1955, Julius Nolte, Dean of Extension, articulated the general contradiction and confusion that exists in U.S. legal relations with tribal nations:

> there is a great deal of confusion as to the legal aspects of the relationship of Indian and whites. This confusion . . . is the diversity that exists in the kind of treaties and agreements that have been made by the

United States with different tribes. There have been interpretations, not only of the treaties themselves, but of statutes that have been passed pursuant to the treaties . . . which have been diverse and conflicting. (Quoted in Vizenor 1981: 49)

Thirty years later, in their study of Indian sovereignty, *The Nations Within* (1984), Deloria and Lytle acknowledge the need for trust and stability between the concerned parties, but they are very careful to distinguish between sovereignty or self-determination and self-government: "self-government is not and cannot be the same as self-determination so long as it exists at the whim of the controlling federal government" (1984:19). That is, maintain Deloria and Lytle, self-government is not nationhood and does not represent sovereignty because it is not "free and uninhibited" (13). In addition to distinguishing between self-government and self-determination, Deloria and Lytle articulate the problematic and complex nature of nationhood. Despite the federal government's slogan of "government-to-government relationship" in specific dealings between the United States and any particular Indian nation, they suggest, the "idea of two governments meeting in some kind of contemporary contractual arrangement on anything approaching an equal bargaining position itself seems ludicrous" (7). In the face of such skepticism, however, Deloria and Lytle remain hopeful. Self-government with all its shortcomings is still a position from which to aspire: "it is an exceedingly useful concept for Indians to use when dealing with the larger government because it provides a context within which negotiations can take place" (15). Yet it cannot be regarded as a final solution. Deloria and Lytle insist that Native American nations need to continue to strive for sovereignty. Such insistence shows up in literature in the fiction of Gerald Vizenor, for instance, when a character at a trial concerning repatriation rights asserts that 'sovereignty is a natural tribal right, not a benefaction or grant from proud flesh patricians, the heirs are sovereign and the court hears our stories" (1991:78).

As a starting point for the discussion of the genesis and development of the concept of "domestic dependent nations," that is, of self-government but not self-determination, Deloria and Lytle refer to the legislative and judicial decisions surrounding the Cherokee removal policies of the 1830s. When the Cherokee attempted to file an action against the state of Georgia, Justice Marshall maintained on the one hand that the "Cherokees were not a foreign nation," but in another decision, on the other hand, he acknowledged that the "Indian nations had always been considered as distinct, independent political communities, retaining their original natural rights, as the undisputed possessors of the soil, from time immemorial" (Deloria and Lyle: 17, quoting *Worcester v. Georgia*, 31 U.S. 6 Pet. 515, 559 [1832]). The result of these contradictory elaborations of what constitutes nationhood is a sort of power vacuum in which neither the federal government, the state government, nor least of all the tribal government has final authority. Even though the federal government established treaties guaranteeing the Cherokees sovereignty and the rights to their land, it failed to honor these treaties. During the 1830s after the U.S. Congress had signed into law the Cherokee Removal Act, the federal government broke both the 1785 Treaty of Hopewell and the 1791 Treaty of Holston – treaties which provided the Cherokees with a form of sovereignty and rights to their lands.

The "treaty politics" of the Cherokee removal – which embody the confused and contradictory conceptions of the "nation"-hood of various tribes held by the United States government – have inspired several recent Native American writers to investigate ideas of "nation"-hood through fiction. For novelists Conley and Diane Glancy (Cherokee) discussions of what sovereignty means play important roles. Conley's novel, *Mountain Windsong*, is in a sense a montage that juxtaposes several levels of narration as it tells a story of Cherokee removal. In addition to a story (of the experiences of two lovers separated by the removal) within a story (of a grandfather relating this history to the narrator), the novel includes pieces of a highly romanticized poetic account of the couple's experiences and the texts of several actual historical documents – including the actual text of the 1835 removal treaty and a protest letter Ralph Waldo Emerson sent to then-president Martin Van Buren. In quoting Emerson, Conley questions the very nature of what constitutes a nation. Emerson refers to what he calls the criminal act of removing the Cherokees from their homelands:

> We only state the fact that a crime is projected that confounds our understandings by its magnitude, a crime that really deprives us as well as the Cherokees of a country for how could we call the conspiracy that should crush these poor Indians our government, or the land that was cursed by their parting and dying imprecations our country, any more? (76)

The obvious disjunction between Emerson's stance and that of an individual Cherokee, John Ross for example, is that Emerson's loss of country is purely symbolic. The Cherokee's is both symbolic and painfully literal.

Within the fabric of her historical novel, *Pushing the Bear* (1996), one of Diane Glancy's characters recalls the removal decisions from the point of view of the Cherokees who were fighting Georgia's intrusions onto their land and into their treaty rights: "We claimed the Supreme Court had original jurisdiction. The Cherokee Nation is a foreign nation and the Court can intercede. But the Court ruled against us. Marshall said we were in a state of pupilage and were not a foreign country inside Georgia." As a result, suggests another character, Knobowtee, the "Chief Justice declared us a domestic, dependent nation ... . Our relation to the U.S. is a ward to his guardian" (21). In a sense, then, Glancy's novel fictively illustrates Chadwick Allen's conception of Native American "nation"-hood as supervised sovereignty. Within his essay Allen talks about Glancy's novel in terms of how it "Complicate[s] both the dominant culture's and American Indians' typical understandings of [the Cherokee Removal] and, further, ... raise[s] the troubling issue of Indian complicity: the specter of the American Indian 'victim' as sometimes-collaborator with colonial power" (2000: 14). Glancy's use of multiple narrators throughout the novel allows her to provide the political history that underlies the main plot, a plot that tells of a Cherokee family undergoing the forced removal from the North Carolina homeland to Indian Territory in present-day Oklahoma. Glancy's and Conley's insistence on the continued presence and importance of history corroborate the contention that Native American sovereignty exists in unique relation to the different tribes' relationships with the federal government.

In addition to contemporary accounts, one finds reference to the ambiguity of "nation"-hood and sovereignty in earlier works as well. In *Life Among the Piutes* (1883), Sarah Winnemucca Hopkins (Paiute) recalls that the government told different versions of what the land meant. One agent tells Winnemucca's people that the land is theirs, "that this land was ours for all to work and make us homes here" (1883: 144). Another agent tells them that "this government land, not land for us" (1883: 144). Thus, as early as 1883, Winnemucca is pointing out the contradictions and problematics of the concept of American Indian "nation"-hood.

Whereas a reliance on a history of contact allows some Native American authors to articulate a "national" identity, this same history of contact operates differently for other Native American authors who use it to render ambiguous any sense of a "national" identity. Thus, instead of emphasizing how a history of contact stabilizes certain conceptions of "national" identity, we now want to shift focus slightly to illustrate how some Native American literatures challenge Native American claims to sovereignty or "nation"-hood. Accordingly, the reservation, a geographical location often at a far remove from tribes' earlier lands, becomes a vexed site for the grounding of any secure articulation of a "national" identity because of the sense of dislocation it imparts to the peoples contained there. The demographic reality of non-reservation Indians also illustrates a pervasive sense of dislocation. As Louis Owens contends: "Above all, Native Americans have been deprived of land and of the dignity that derives from the profound and enduring relationship with homeland" (2001: 18). Without the geographical and ideological/cultural grounding that a sustained and sustaining sense of "homeland" supplies, select Native American voices, as Owens further argues, "might in fact accurately be described as what postcolonial theories have called 'migrant' or 'diasporic'" (2001: 11). Moreover, Owens extends the terms "migrant" and "diasporic" to include non-reservation Native Americans as well, asserting that "through many generations of displacement and orchestrated ethnocide [non-reservation Native Americans] are often far from their traditional homelands and cultural communities" (12). An anxiety of a sort arises, then, and this anxiety makes difficult any stable identification of a geographical place or, for that matter, of a more metaphorical sense of a "homeland" that could serve to conjoin Native Americans so that they could articulate a cohesive "national" identity.

In effect, then, for the shift we now want to make in our discussion of how some Native American literatures render the status of "nation" ambiguous, we want to connect a problematized view of "nation" to the contested site of the reservation, that explicit marker of a history of contact, so as to forward conceptions of identity that express a dis-ease with being part of a "nation." Sherman Alexie (Coeur d'Alene) treats this "disease" humorously in a scene from his screenplay *Smoke Signals* just before the characters Victor and Thomas leave the reservation:

VELMA: Yeah, do you guys got your passports?
THOMAS: Passports?
VELMA: Yeah, you're leaving the rez and going into a whole different country, cousin.
THOMAS: But it's the United States.
LUCY: Damn right it is. That's as foreign as it gets. I hope you two got your vaccinations. (1998: 40–41)

The tension underlying Alexie's humor resides in an ambiguous sense of "nation," particularly as this tension manifests itself in what it means to be a citizen of a given "nation." To understand how "national" identities correlate to certain ideas of citizenship, we suggest that much Native American literature figures citizenship in a "nation" – that is, the sorts of rights that accrue to an individual who is a citizen – as operating on a sliding scale that often works to the disadvantage of Native American characters precisely because they are identified by the court system as Native Americans. Donna Kay Maeda asserts:

> Underlying the narrative of liberal justice are the epistemological and moral foundations of the individual. In liberal justice rights are to be applied "neutrally" and "objectively" to individual persons without regard to race, gender, culture, or other differences. Such differences, when acknowledged, are generally understood to be qualities of individuals. [...] [However,] liberal neutrality, objectively, and universal individualism actually project and hide privileged group positionings. (Maeda 2000: 84–5)

In short, the problematic development of a sense of "nation" for Native Americans bears a corollary: the problematic development of Native Americans as rightful citizens.

Claims of Native American sovereignty complicate claims to rightful citizenship in both internal and external ways. From an internal perspective, for instance, the long history of conflict and disputation between Native American communities and the U.S. government have made it difficult for these communities to declare definitively their own status as "nations." As a result, the individuals who identify with these communities hold an ambiguous "rightful" standing, in the legal sense at the very least. According to Kathryn Shanley, the branches of the U.S. federal government cannot even come to an agreement over what their relationship to Native American tribes is: "The difference between judicial and legislative views [of the U.S. government's relationship to Native Americans] seems to be equivalent to the difference between fiduciary principles (the government's trust relationship to Indians based on treaties) and fiscal principles (the government's legislative allocation of those treaty responsibilities)" (Shanley 2001: 42). In addition, other factors, including non-reservation or tribal-affiliated Indians, render complex claims to "rightful" citizenship: of what "nation" are such individual citizens – the U.S.? A tribe?

From an external perspective, the supervisory role that the U.S. government purports to play in relation to Native American communities calls the nature of Indians' "national" citizenship and rights into question. Throughout their long history of contact, the U.S. government has often inappropriately interceded into the affairs of individual tribes. Fergus M. Bordewich, in his book, *Killing the White Man's Indian: Reinventing Native Americans at the End of the Twentieth Century* (1996) discusses specific incidents and acts of legislation that mark the historical interactions between the U.S. government and various Native American communities. From a position that wants to recognize the legitimacy of Native American claims to national sovereignty, Ward Churchill explains the inter-national significance of these sorts of intercessions: "For any country to set out unilaterally to impose its own internal system of legality upon another is to adopt a course of action which is not just utterly presumptuous but invalid under international custom and convention (and, undoubtedly, under the laws of the country intended for statutory subordination)" (1998: 5). Moreover, Shanley illustrates the questionable nature of Native American citizenship vis-à-vis the "rightful" American kind:

> Since most Americans lack an understanding of what treaties guarantee Indians and why, they reduce Indian experience to the lowest common denominator, according it only the Euro-American sense of "right" by experience. Non-Indian hunters are usually at odds with treaty hunting and fishing rights, because they feel equally entitled to all resources; tourist industries around the country use Indian lore and images to entice consumers and yet fight to prevent Indians from exercising their rights to be Indian. (Shanley 2001: 31)

From both inside and outside Native American communities, then, "Native American" as an identity marker inserts some sort of "difference" on both individual and collective levels – which undoubtedly springs from their long history of contact with whites – that makes Native American citizenship a difficult concept/entity to define.

Native American authors often present these questions of "what rights?" and "whose law?" by depicting encounters between mainstream laws and the behavior of particular Indian characters. Like questions of sovereignty, questions of legal status in both criminal and civil matters are often central in Native American literature. Prior to 1885 many tribes did enjoy sovereignty in that a given nation was free to try and punish tribal people according to their own custom, for instance. However, by passing what was called the Seven Major Crimes Act in 1885, Congress essentially annulled the former treaty right of sovereignty. The 1885 act deprived Indian tribes of criminal jurisdiction. As a "nation" within a nation, then, tribal people are confronted with the paradox of being acknowledged as one nation but subject to the laws and customs of another. In his novel *Skins* (1995), Adrian C. Louis (Lovelock Paiute) points out this paradox of "nation"-hood. Ernie Eagleman, the captain of the tribal police force on the Pine Ridge reservation, complains to the novel's protagonist, Rudy Yellow Shirt: "We're steers – we're a castrated department, a castrated tribe. Technically even though we got a court system, this tribe don't even have the authority to punish a murderer" (1995: 91).

Depictions of the lack of jurisdiction or of legal status often take place in courtrooms and thus serve as a means for the authors to demonstrate the ambiguities of "nation"-hood or sovereignty in that they expose the legal powerlessness of Native American tribes or individuals and at the same time call into question the concept of American justice. The authors often seem to ask what it means to be a citizen of any particular "nation," especially when the laws of that "nation" are not acknowledged or respected by the mainstream culture or legal system. Indeed, the inevitable jurisdiction that the U.S. government claims over tribal "sovereign nations" explicitly illustrates how these "nations" are postcolonial.

Perhaps one of the most renowned court scenes in Native American literature is the brief allusion to Abel's murder trial in Momaday's *House Made of Dawn*. Like so many other Native American characters, Abel has been taken from the reservation to be put on trial in a U.S. court for a crime that must be understood from both a tribal and a mainstream, white context. The novel makes manifest the unwillingness and inability of the dominant culture, which makes and carries out the laws, to accept or acknowledge the worldviews or ethical systems of the "colonized" culture. During the testimony, the priest, Father Olguin, articulates this inability when he offers his opinion of Abel's act: "I believe that this man was moved to do what he did by an act of the imagination so compelling as to be inconceivable to us" (Momaday 1968: 101–2). According to the prosecution, "he killed a man – took the life of another human being ... . He committed a brutal and premeditated act which we have no choice but to call by its right name" (101–2). Tosamah, Priest of the Sun, offers the reader a somewhat sarcastic reading of the event: "And do you know what he said? I mean, do you have any idea what that cat said? A snake, he said. He killed a goddam snake!" (149). Like Olgin's comment in the courtroom, Tosamah's sarcastic outburst draws attention to the dominant culture's absolute failure to acknowledge a radically different worldview.

The rationale for the murder of a state trooper, recounted in both Silko's "Tony's Story," in the collection *Storyteller* (1981), and Simon

Ortiz's (Acoma Pueblo) "The Killing of a State Cop," in the collection *Men on the Moon* (1999), is similar. Tribal sovereignty would not apply in this instance in that, although the murder took place on the Acoma Reservation in New Mexico, the victim was not Acoma and therefore the government would have interceded, regardless of sovereignty. Silko, however, especially suggests how the state trooper was perceived as a witch by the killer and so, within a very specific Pueblo context, the two Acoma men committed a crime other than the one the state of New Mexico charged them with. According to Silko's depiction, the narrator has not killed a policeman, has not killed a human being. Tony explains what he has done: "Don't worry, everything is O.K. now, Leon. It's killed. They sometimes take on strange forms" (1981: 128). Before the shooting, Silko suggests that this is indeed a story about rights. Leon tells the narrator that the two of them have the right to be on the highway, a right that the vindictive state trooper does not acknowledge. The narrator questions Leon's logic: "I couldn't understand why Leon kept talking about 'rights,' because it wasn't 'rights' that he [the trooper] was after, but Leon didn't seem to understand" (1981: 127). As the story makes clear, the two Acoma men – who may have had the legal right to be on the highway – did not have that right according to the state trooper who harasses them. That he pursues them onto the reservation suggests they have no sanctuary there either.

In Linda Hogan's *Power* (1998), Ama's crime of killing an endangered Florida panther is viewed and judged by two completely different standards, reflecting two different worldviews. In the context of sovereignty, however, it is clearly the non-Indian law and the Florida state court that take precedence. Even though Ama herself wants desperately to be convicted, the judge declares a mistrial for lack of evidence; there is no gun, no panther hide, no flesh. Only after this trial do the Taiga people themselves try Ama:

> They will hear her out and they will listen to me [says the narrator] and then decide her innocence or guilt and what will become of her. Here it doesn't matter what was decided in the marble building in town. It doesn't matter what's written on paper. The old people are the ones who know the laws of this place, this world, laws stronger and older than America. (1960)

Despite Hogan's powerful rhetoric here, the ironic truth underlying the narrator's statement is that Ama is free to face a tribal court only because she is not in a state prison. Any notion of tribal power or standing is further undermined in that the Taiga people's judgment is based on a lie. The people have hope "because Ama has not shattered [their] world with truth" (174). Such a reading suggests the deep irony of the chapter title, "The Place of Old Law." The old law, finally, has no place: the state courts have precedence and, as the reader knows, the tribal court lacks the facts on which to base a sound decision.

A prime literary example of how a Native American civil law goes unacknowledged by white America is in Pauline Johnson's short story, "A Red Girl's Reasoning," from the collection *The Moccasin Maker* (1913). After the white man, Charlie, marries an Indian woman, Christine, he discovers that her parents (an English trader and an Indian woman) were not married by a priest or a magistrate: "The marriage was performed by Indian rites," explains Christine (11). Aghast at this information, the husband accuses her of having disgraced herself and her parents, because she has, in his words, declared that her parents "were never married" (114). When Charlie asks her why her parents were not married by the "law," Christine questions the very concept: "Law? *My* people have *no* priest, and my nation cringes not to law" (116). Because he refuses to recognize the customs of her nation as legitimate, she denies those of his: "Why should I recognize the rites of your nation when you do not acknowledge the rites of mine?" (117). Johnson is acutely aware of the double standard between the English colonizer and the North American Indian colonized person, and she makes her point all the more poignant by demonstrating it in the very intimate and personal context of a marriage. At the risk of being arbitrary, one could argue that her metaphor for the colonizing process itself is a marriage, a marriage of two parties that distinctly are unequal from the very beginning. Like a literal marriage, suggests Johnson, a colony cannot survive if the rights and privileges of one party are denied or left unacknowledged.

Just as some Native American writers offer fictional accounts of the historical Cherokee removal as a means of depicting issues of "nation"-hood, Linda Hogan provides a fictional account of the exploitation of the oil-rich Oklahoma Osage during the 1920s in *Mean Spirit*. In order to comment on issues concerning rights of citizenship, Hogan depicts the imbalance and legal loopholes as she describes many of the ways the Indians were legally cheated out of their land, money, and oil rights. Unlike many other reservation tribes, the Osage had retained the mineral rights to their land even after the allotment act had deprived them of their reservation. As a result, when oil was discovered on Osage land, many Indian landowners became quite rich. With the wealth, came exploitation. As Terry P. Wilson demonstrates, Osage author and historian John Joseph Mathews (Osage) felt that "the Osage people ... became industry, and flocking to them from all ends of the earth came every type of person, rats as well as fairly decent citizens" (1985: 155).

Even the "fairly decent citizens," in Hogan's hands, are seen to be self-serving, greedy racists who ignore law and civility. In the Spring of 1923, for example, "nearly all of the full-blood Indians were deemed incompetent by the court's competency commission. Mixed-bloods, who were considered to be competent, were already disqualified from receiving full payments because of their white blood" (Hogan 1990: 241). Once deemed incompetent by the courts, the individuals were assigned non-Indian guardians who had immediate control of all assets. The character Moses Graycloud, a fully competent rancher, who is deemed legally incompetent, is assigned two guardians:

> he was assigned two legal guardians, and any further lease money that might have been earned by his grazing leases would have to go through the attorneys. By the time they deducted their legal fees, for service rendered to him, he owed them large sums of money. They impounded and sold a car; his cattle were taken from him, his bull bought, and even a telescope was sold to the attorneys. (241)

A court scene in this novel suggests that even though the law is willing to try a white man who has been accused of murdering several Osage people and profiting from the insurance policies he has sold them, there was to be no such thing as a fair trial. It was immediately clear to one character, for instance, that "the trial was going to be beset with numerous problems, missing witnesses being only the smallest of the difficulties." After the first day, "many of the Indian people gave up on justice and went home" (332, 333). With such examples, Hogan is merely reflecting the historical reality of the exploitation of the Osage that took place during the 1920s and 1930s.

What is remarkable about what these numerous court scenes have in common is that the sense of tribal law, the notion of any tribal sovereignty is without exception subjected to U.S. law, even when that law is bent and reshaped to favor the whites. At best, in this fiction, an Indian character can hope to get off on an insanity plea, whereas a white will benefit from missing witnesses and bribed jurors. In these novels the federal or state courts rarely recognize tribal sovereignty, and they inevitably depict the Native Americans as relatively powerless in the face of the United States government. As McNickle makes plain at the end of his novel *The Surrounded* (1936), "It made no difference whether they stayed at home or went to the mountains. When they were wanted, by priest or agent or devil, they would be sent for, and that was all" (286). In the context of having or not having power, Deloria argues that "[s]overeignty and power go hand in hand in group action. One cannot exist without the other" (1970: 123). As the literature makes clear, Native Americans are without the power sovereignty would afford them.

In *The Heirs of Columbus* (1991), Gerald Vizenor (Anishinabe) articulates this notion of interdependence between sovereignty and power, when a federal judge, Beatrice Lord, who decides in favor of the heirs (those crossblood tribal descendants of Columbus and Samana), allows a floating bingo casino near the headwaters of the Mississippi River:

> The federal court finds in favor of Stone Columbus ... the notion of tribal sovereignty is not confiscable, or earth bound; sovereignty is neither fence nor feathers. The essence of sovereignty is imaginative, an original tribal trope, communal and spiritual, an idea that is more than metes and bounds in treaties. (1991: 7)

Later the same federal judge, in the context of the repatriation of medicine pouches and human remains, determines that "we must hear more to determine the standing of human remains in federal court." She must hear more, she says, before deciding how, or even if, "the repatriation of tribal stories and the sacred animals" can be a crime (1991: 69).

With such passages, Vizenor calls into question normative stances concerning sovereignty. In this post-modern courtroom "peopled" with comic (and surreal) characters, such as a talking panther, a whistling mongrel, a vanishing graduate student shaman, and the Anishinaabe descendants (heirs) of Christopher Columbus, Vizenor insists on the complexities and intricacies of sovereignty and "nation"-hood. From the tribal perspective, the narrator insists, rather than "material evidence" in this particular hearing "the evidence would be stories in the blood and the most original shadow realities ever presented at federal court" (1991: 64). In another instance, Stone Columbus, as a crossblood descendant of the explorer, writes a letter to the president asserting the heirs' rights to the tithes promised to Columbus upon his "discovery":

> These rights and capitulations have never been abrogated by treaties, conquest, or purchase; therefore, since we are the legal heirs of the unpaid tithe on this continent, be so advised, that unless your government pays the inheritance due, we shall annex, as satisfaction of the tithe, the United States of America. (1991: 160)

Such sarcasm and insight demand that the reader, like the federal judge or the president, rethink any preconceived notions of what constitutes "nation"-hood and the sovereignty that comes with it.

As literary texts like Vizenor's demonstrate, there remains ambiguity surrounding the status of "nation." Native American writers have co-opted the language and genres of the colonial power or nation and have made claims for autonomy and self-determination. Yet, as Vizenor argues in *Fugitive Poses* and elsewhere, the very concepts of "Indian" and "nation" are colonial inventions: "The *Indian* is a simulation and loan word of domination" (1998: 14). In this context, the very concept of "nation" is of necessity also a colonial invention and as such must remain in ambiguous relation to a dominant colonial power, and Native American writers will continue to grapple with these ambiguities.

REFERENCES

Achebe, Chinua, 1994. *World of Ideas*, produced and directed by Gail Pellett. 28 min. Public Affairs TV. Videocassette.

Alexie, Sherman, 1998. *Smoke Signals*, New York: Miramax Books.

Allen, Chadwick, 2000. "Postcolonial Theory and the Discourse of Treaties," *American Quarterly* 52. Project Muse. William Randall Library, UNCW, Wilmington, NC. 17 April 2002 <http://muse.jhu.edu/journals/american_quarterly/v052/52.1allen.html>, 7.

Bordewich, Fergus M., 1996. *Killing the White Man's Indian: Reinventing Native Americans at the End of the Twentieth Century*, New York: Doubleday.

Churchill, Ward, 1998. "The Tragedy and the Travesty: The Subversion of Indigenous Sovereignty in North America," *American Indian Culture and Research Journal*, 22.2.

Conley, Robert J. 1992. *Mountain Windsong*, Norman: University of Oklahoma Press.

Cook-Lynn, Elizabeth, 1996. *Why I Can't Read Wallace Stegner and Other Essays: A Tribal Voice*, Madison: University of Wisconsin Press.

Deloria Jr., Vine, 1970. *We Talk, You Listen: New Tribes, New Turf*, New York: Delta.

Deloria Jr., Vine and Clifford M. Lytle, 1984. *The Nations Within: The Past and Future of American Indian Sovereignty*, New York: Pantheon.

Glancy, Diane, 1996. *Pushing the Bear: A Novel of the Trail of Tears*, New York: Harcourt.

Hogan, Linda, 1990. *Mean Spirit*, New York: Ivy Books.

Hogan, Linda, 1998. *Power*, New York: Norton.

Hopkins, Sarah Winnemucca, 1994. *Life Among the Piutes*, 1883; rpt, Reno: University of Nevada Press.

Johnson, E. Pauline, 1913. *The Moccasin Maker*, intro., annotation, and bibliography by A. LaVonne Brown Ruoff, Tucson: University of Arizona Press, 1987.

Louis, Adrian C., 1995. *Skins*, New York: Crown.

Maeda, Donna Kay, 2000. "Subject to Justice: The 'Cultural Defense' and Legal Constructions of Race, Culture, and Nation" in *Postcolonial America*, ed. C. Richard King, Urbana: University of Illinois Press.

Magdaleno, Jana Sequoya, 2000. "How (!) Is an Indian? A Contest of Stories, Round 2" in *Postcolonial Theory and the United States: Race, Ethnicity, and Literature*, ed. Amritjit Singh and Peter Schmidt, Jackson: University Press of Mississippi.

McNickle, D'Arcy, 1936. *The Surrounded*, Albuquerque: University of New Mexico Press, 1978.

Momaday, N. Scott, 1968. *House Made of Dawn*, New York: Harper and Row, Perennial.

Momaday, N. Scott, 1989. *The Ancient Child*, New York: Doubleday.

Ortiz, Simon, 1999. *Men on the Moon: Collected Short Stories*, Tucson: University of Arizona Press.

Owens, Louis, 2001. "As If an Indian Were Really an Indian: Native American Voices and Postcolonial Theory" in *Native American Representations: First Encounters, Distorted Images, and Literary Appropriations*, ed. Gretchen M. Bataille, Lincoln: University of Nebraska Press.

Rushdie, Salman, 1980. *Midnight's Children*, New York: Knopf, 1981.

Shanley, Kathryn, 2001. "The Indians America Loves to Love and Read" in *Native American Representations: First Encounters, Distorted Images, and Literary Appropriations*, ed. Gretchen M. Bataille, Lincoln: University of Nebraska Press.

Silko, Leslie Marmon, 1977. *Ceremony*, New York: Signet.

Silko, Leslie Marmon, 1981. *Storyteller*, New York: Little, Brown.

Vizenor, Gerald, 1981. *Earthdivers: Tribal Narratives on Mixed Descent*, Minneapolis: University of Minnesota Press.

Vizenor, Gerald, 1991. *The Heirs of Columbus*, Hanover, NH: University Press of New England.

Vizenor, Gerald, 1998. *Fugitive Poses*, Lincoln: University of Nebraska Press.

Wilkinson, Charles F. 1987. *American Indians, Time, and the Law: Native Societies in a Modern Constitutional Democracy*, New Haven, CT: Yale University Press.

Wilson, Rob and Wimal Dissanayake, eds, 1996. *Global/Local: Cultural Production and the Transnational Imaginary*, Durham, NC: Duke University Press.

Wilson, Terry P. 1985. *The Underground Reservation: Osage Oil*, Lincoln: University of Nebraska Press.

3

Origin Story: On Being a White Native American(ist)*

John Hunt Peacock, Jr.

I first read U.C.L.A. professor Paula Gunn Allen's essay "Special Problems in Teaching Leslie Marmon Silko's *Ceremony*" after a Laguna Pueblo student of mine told me his elders would disapprove of the class reading aloud the traditional origin story Silko put in writing in her novel. It is "not to be told outside the clan," Allen agreed, explaining that "the protectiveness of native people, particularly Pueblos, toward their traditions is legendary" (1990: 383) – sacred stories were secretly performed in underground kivas under ritually prescribed circumstances; Indians who told such stories to whites were once threatened with ostracism, loss of land or water rights, physical punishment, or even death – "but the reasons for that protectiveness are perhaps not so well known" (1990: 379). Traditionalists believed that telling origin stories at the right time renewed the growing season, but telling them at the wrong time or in the wrong way led to potentially *"tragic consequences"* (1990: 380, italics in original) for the community and the land itself: seasons might not occur or might occur at the wrong time; the stories' important powers might be misused, released without effect or with the wrong effect (Peacock 1996b: 54–5). The problem Allen said she had teaching *Ceremony* was that "[p]edagogically, I believe I should give specific information to students ... what prayers, rituals and spiritual activities occur at the Pueblo that have bearing on the novel. ... Ethically, as a professor, I see this kind of methodology as necessary, but ethically, as an Indian, I can't do it. ... I don't have any solutions or resolutions" (1990: 385).

Not all Indians agree that the particular oral stories Silko incorporates in *Ceremony* are sacred. They're "like T.V., just for entertainment," said Tony and Wilma Purley (quoted in Sequoya 1993: 469), two contemporary residents of Mesita, the village where many traditionalists

* Research and writing funded by the American Philosophical Society.

relocated after Silko's white great-grandfather Robert Marmon and his brother Walter precipitated what Silko acknowledges as "all kinds of factions and trouble [that] complicate[d] the already complex politics at Laguna [and] upset Laguna ceremonialism" (Silko 1981: 256). What began as a matter of establishing borders – the Marmon brothers came to Laguna in 1870 on a U.S. government contract to set out boundary markers – turned into a matter of mixing bloodlines when the brothers stayed on and reared large families with Indian wives. The daughter of the chief of the Jerena-Shikani medicine men married Walter, who was appointed government teacher in 1871. Robert served as the first Anglo-American governor of Laguna during the great split between traditionalists who removed their altars from Laguna and progressives who tore down its two *kivas*. No *kachina* dances took place for some time. They had resumed by the time Silko was growing up, but she was never included in clan activities to the same extent as full-bloods, and helped out but did not dance at ceremonies (Peacock 1996a: 4, 1). "[A]t the core of my writing," she writes, "is the attempt to identify what it is to be a half-breed or mixed-blood person, what it is to grow up neither white nor fully traditional Indian" (Silko1980: 188).

Maybe the best way to handle the special problems in teaching *Ceremony* was to teach students exactly what those problems were. Toward this end I was encouraged by Gerald Graff's *Beyond the Culture Wars: How Teaching the Conflicts Can Revitalize American Education* (1992). However, an eminent white Native Americanist, A. Lavonne Ruoff, at the Newberry Library's D'Arcy McNickle Center for the History of the American Indian, cautioned me against pressing the issue in print. Native scholars do not themselves agree that all sacred material should be off-limits. Osage scholar Robert Warrior at Stanford University points out that many sacred oral traditions are public knowledge, having been in print for three generations (thanks to ethnographers in the 1940s and 1950s, native writers in the 1960s and 1970s, and literary scholars in the 1980s and 1990s.) As for scholarly access to this material, Warrior expresses "personal frustration about who gets to be Indian versus first-rate analysis" (1997: n.p.); while Cherokee scholar Dan Littlefield of the American Native Press Archives quips "Joseph Conrad was a Pole who wrote in English about Belgians in Africa" (1997: n.p.).

Looking for a way to proceed, I studied the case of a Navajo elder who, believing his people would survive only as long as their stories remained wet with breath, but unable to find a young person in the tribe interested in learning them, passed them on to Utah State University linguist J. Barre Toelken, whom the elder adopted. After the elder's death, however, his wife asked Toelken to return the tape recordings of the two men's 30-year collaboration; she feared her husband's spirit would wander unless those powerful stories were put to rest with him. It could be seen as a cultural sacrilege not to give them back, but, as some of Toelken's colleagues argued, an academic sacrilege to do so. The elder's wife intended to destroy the recordings. Toelken returned them but implored her to keep them in the event a young person ever became interested in learning them in the future. Instead of taking the "objective" stance of a researcher not obliged to share in the worldview of those he studied, Toelken decided that by playing by their rules, he learned more about their culture as well as his own. "Not that this matters necessarily to Indians," he added (1997: n.p.).

The question of whether aboriginal resources should be shared with non-natives is addressed (at least with regard to natural resources) by Silko herself in a public policy statement she co-authored with two political scientists. "Replacing Confusion with Equity: Alternatives for Water Policy in the Colorado River Basin" argues that Pueblo farmers should not have to share aboriginal water rights with whites upstream as long as the latter have alternative water sources for their own survival and the survival of their crops and livestock. But when those whites do *not* have enough, Silko *et al.* argue, Indians have an obligation to share, and whites not to use more than for their survival needs. Thus, uranium miners have no right to deplete the aquifers by 13,279 gallons per minute all over the Grants Mineral Belt in northwest New Mexico (Garcia 1983: 47). It is estimated the aquifers will need 5,000 to 50,000 years to effectively replenish themselves – not long compared to the quarter-million-year half-life of their radioactive contamination by those same uranium miners (LaDuke and Churchill 1985: 119–20).

As for sharing sacred stories about the land's origin and care, Silko writes elsewhere that after Hiroshima "[h]uman beings were one clan again" (1977: 246). "Whether you were a Hopi who believed in traditional ways or ... a Madison Avenue Lutheran, all human beings faced the same possible destruction ... the day after the first [atomic] bomb was detonated" (Silko quoted in Fitzgerald 1980: 34–5). Silko shares sacred stories about care of the land with whites, even as she criticizes what she regards as nonessential appropriations of those stories by poets Gary Snyder and Robert Bly (1979: 3–5).

Was it essential then that I teach the origin story in *Ceremony*? I finally asked native scholars on a conference panel. What was essential, they suggested, was for me to teach the stories my own people didn't want to discuss about their past and present Indian relations. A way to teach without becoming sanctimonious – "much of contemporary Indian criticism is cant," in Dan Littlefield's words (1997: n. p.) – would be to start with my own family, they said – the story of my own Indian relations. When I said that I didn't think my family had had any Indian relations, the native scholars reminded me that any white family that had been in this country for long (as mine had) probably had Indian relations. They suggested I might be surprised by what I found (Piatote 1997: n.p.).

What would happen, I wondered to myself, if I actually followed this advice? The first thing I found out was that in 1954, when I was five, my paternal grandfather, a Washington, D.C. lawyer and former Commerce Department official, unsuccessfully defended before the U.S. Supreme Court the timber rights of the Tee-Hit-Ton Indians of Alaska. He appealed that the decision showed "complete misconception [and] studied avoidance ... of the recognized principles of international law" (Peacock 1989: 1) in denying compensation to the Tee-Hit-Ton for timber rights that had been taken over by a national park and then sold for clear cutting to a timber consortium. The legal defeat became a notorious precedent in Indian law. As for my grandfather's own compensation as the Tee Hit Ton's attorney, he would have made more if his clients had won, but he still made enough to put me through college. I went to Harvard at the expense of the Tee-Hit-Ton.

Turning next to my mother's side of the family, all I knew was that she had been born Gertrude Joinville in Devil's Lake, North Dakota, and later moved to Hampton, Virginia. I began by looking her family up in the North Dakota town censuses for the years before and after her birth in 1912. Finding nothing, I looked at a map of North Dakota and noticed that seven miles from the town was the Devil's Lake Sioux Indian Reservation, or Spirit Lake Dakota Nation as it was officially renamed in 1995. Maybe her parents worked there. At the National Archives in Washington, D.C., I did a long, fruitless search of Bureau of Indian Affairs personnel records, some of which happened to be catalogued along with tribal roles. Working in the archives late one night, frustrated and tired, I decided to take a break and satisfy my curiosity about what a tribal census looked like. Scrolling through a microfilmed 1929 Devil's Lake Sioux roll, my attention was suddenly arrested by the names of my mother and her parents and siblings, all listed as half-bloods assigned allotment 862 (NARG 75, Devil's Lake Sioux Censuses, M 495, 1929). Records as far back as 1880 confirmed the family's residence and/or enrollment on the reservation.

My mother was four when the family left North Dakota, for reasons she no longer remembers (she turned 90 in 2002). She put me in touch with a niece I had never met, who told me her father (my mother's brother), revealed just before he died that he had been sexually abused by a white priest at the Fort Totten Indian school on the reservation. Fort Totten Indian School Records (11) show that he and two more of my mother's older siblings attended in 1914, three years before the family moved to Hampton, Virginia. Though the Hampton Institute was mainly known for providing vocational training for ex-slaves and their descendants, at that time it was also an off-reservation Indian boarding school with a program for re-educating whole families. But there is no record of anyone in Mother's family attending. Grandmother identified herself and the children as white on the 1920 Virginia census (maybe because Jim Crow laws discriminated against all non-whites?). In North Dakota, nevertheless, she and the children continued to be enumerated on tribal rolls as Devil's Lake Sioux living off-reservation. After Grandmother's death in 1935, however, my mother and her seven siblings were disenrolled (NARG 75, Devil's Lake Sioux, Letters Received, Dec. 22, 1937).

Their file in the B.I.A. archives in Washington included another brother's letter contesting their disenrollment – "we all object, being on the rolls as long as we have" – along with notarized affidavits from their father, aunt, and a tribal member who helped the family build a house on their allotment, swearing that this was where they lived and where that brother had been born. A recommendation that he be kept on the rolls was signed by the local Superintendent of Indian Affairs and approved by the tribal council, but it was rejected by the Commissioner in Washington (NARG 75, Devil's Lake Sioux, Letters Received, Jan. 4, 1938).

Maybe because my mother had lighter skin than some of her siblings; maybe because she was only five when the family left the reservation; maybe because she never attended Indian schools – whatever the reason, she ended up being raised and thinking of herself as white, telling me she remembered almost nothing about North Dakota. She was trained as a nurse, enlisted as a first lieutenant in the Army nurse corps, rose to the rank of captain, and spent part of World War II in the South Pacific on the staff of a military hospital. There she met my white father, a lieutenant in the U.S. Navy. They married after the war and lived in a white middle-class, Washington, D.C. suburb. Neither to her husband nor to any of her children did she ever mention being Native American until my discovery. Whether she never knew she was Indian, chose to forget, or was deliberately concealing it, I have never been able to determine.

I never knew my maternal grandmother Rachel Joinville, but once I learned her maiden name *Blackbird*, I found out that she, too, had been disenrolled after her own mother's death. However, she succeeded in getting re-enrolled when adopted by the reservation's mixed-blood "boss farmer," as he was called, who taught Indians to plough like white men. Rachel's sister Adele, my great aunt, married a Turtle Mountain Chippewa and had a son Peter Zast, enrolled on that reservation, 90 miles north of Devil's Lake. Peter was my mother's first cousin. After I learned of his existence from the Turtle Mountain tribal enrollment office, and, moreover, that he was still alive, I telephoned him, and he graciously invited me to the reservation. A citified Easterner, I had never been to North Dakota. I flew to St. Paul and then in a twelve-seater to Devil's Lake, where I rented a car and drove to Turtle Mountain. From the *pave*, as the main road was called, I took a right turn past the graveyard onto B.I.A. 6, a dirt road that went up into the green hills to Adele's allotment. Waiting for me in lawn chairs outside were Peter himself, age 79, a retired bus driver for the Head Start program; his white-haired wife Dorothy, breathing with help from a small oxygen tank; and their 50-year-old daughter Donna, who had pinned a tag-board poster to the side of their little bungalow with four generations of the family tree drawn in magic marker.

Unfolded on Donna's lap was a handwritten letter, dated 1916, about our mutual great-grandmother Margaret Blackbird, from her daughter Adele to the Indian agent:

"Mama died of small pox," the letter read. "She is lying out there yet on Raphael Martin's place. Our house was burned down. Pa died when we were small. We were four boys and three girls. I was taken in at Joe Allard's place. Ma used to wash for them. ... I want my mother to be in the cemetery like the others because soon maybe Raphael Martin will be plowing up those bodies. There are two lying on his land. If they sell my grand father's land, I want to have my share. I need help. The little ones, when they see me they don't know me. They all say my goodness who is this old Indian. I don't know if you will understand my letter. I don't talk good English like you. Put the letter in the fire as soon as you read it for my bad writing." (Blackbird 1916)

Later, in the cemetery, I poked through waist-high, mosquito-infested weeds to see if my great-grandmother had ever been reburied, but I never found her grave, not even among the plots reserved, according to local nuns, for Christian Indians who had not performed their Easter duties. I gave up when I saw a six-foot-long black snake with a yellow stripe: not poisonous, the nuns assured me, it'd just raise a good size welt.

To find out more about my Indian relations, I was advised by Donna and her parents to go to Fort Totten, the Devil's Lake Indian Agency town. Driving back to Devil's Lake, I took a short cut the nuns gave me past flooded fields and an abandoned farmhouse with a scarecrow on the roof holding a "for rent" sign. The road to Fort Totten was washed out, so I had to detour up to a plateau where some buffalo were grazing. When I finally got to the little town, I passed Seven Dolors Catholic church, the powwow grounds, and the tribal court before coming to a one-story blue brick building, the tribal council and local Bureau of Indian Affairs. Inside a tribal cop in jeans with a gun on his hip directed me down the hall to the B.I.A. Realty Office, a counter with a push-bell, which I rang for service. When the clerk, a large Indian woman smoking an extra long Pall Mall, appeared, I said I was Rachel Blackbird's grandson and asked to see her probate file, listing all her relations and property. Opening a file cabinet, the clerk took out an inch-thick folder. "We've seen your kind before," she remarked in passing. "Your folks chose to leave. You don't have blood here any more." She sat down and started to turn the loose pages so quickly I had to lean and eventually kneel down by her elbow to make out the faded handwriting. I asked her to stop at the record of my grandmother's 80-acre allotment.

"She wasn't supposed to have that allotment," the clerk said. "She got it cause she knew someone."

"The boss farmer adopted her," I said.

"Then you'll have to go to Social Services," the clerk said, shutting the file. "They keep all the adoption records."

In fact, Social Services didn't keep records before it began in 1970, I was told by current director Vernon Lambert, a fit-looking tribal elder in his early sixties with a tattoo on his forearm. Unlike the Realty clerk, he offered me a chair in his office and heard me out. He didn't seem surprised by anything I told him. When I finished, he looked down, chuckled, and then picked up and dialed the telephone. *Ma*, he spoke loudly into the receiver, *Them Blackbirds?* He listened, said something in Dakota – *mitakuya owas* – and hung up. His 96-year-old mother, he said, reminded him she had a cousin named Flo Langer, whose husband Charlie Blackbird used to coach fast-pitch softball. Fifty years ago Vernon Lambert played third base.

"We're related," he said.

"You and Charlie?" I asked.

"Yeah, me and Charlie, and you and Charlie, and me and you. We're all related. That's what *mitakuya owas* means."

Vernon and I met again Sunday at Seven Dolors Church. He went to mass; I sat in the parish record office going through birth, death, and marriage announcements. Then we drove out to a blue knob overlooking the prairie, where the Sun Dance had ended the night before. Vernon mentioned the place was off-limits to the white man. Before I could ask what on earth he thought I was, he started telling me his whole life story: how he hated being Indian as a child, living in a one-room, dirt-floor cabin with his parents and eight brothers and sisters. How he *wanted* to go to Indian boarding school because it had heat and indoor plumbing instead of an outhouse when it was 40 degrees below. How his mother stopped speaking Dakota at home in order to keep him from getting punished for speaking it at school. How, after high school, he left the reservation, joined the Air Force and went to Japan, and when he got out, moved to Chicago. How much he loved Chicago, taking his wife on the el to the hospital to have their first baby, but since they couldn't raise the seven children that followed without the help of aunties and uncles, grandparents and cousins, they moved back home to the rez. How he became a teacher, got his master's in education when he was 30, and then spent ten years learning to apply it to the tribal schools. How, when his kids went to school, his mother began a 25-year career teaching them and their schoolmates the same Dakota language she had weaned her own children of in the days when it was outlawed in school. How his children learned to take pride in Dakota culture, several of his daughters becoming such good traditional dancers that they were selected to go on a cultural exchange abroad. How Vernon went along as a chaperone and, in Germany, in order to answer foreigners' questions, started studying his own culture. How for a while after that he wore long hair and the ribbon shirts his mother made him. How in 1993 the Sun Dance was allowed on the reservation for the first time since the 1920s, and he went through the year-long preparation, was pierced, and given a naming ceremony.

From the Sun Dance grounds we could see for miles across fields of blue flax that rolled like waves in the sun and wind. "In the old days," Vernon said, laying his hand on my shoulder, "you would have been welcomed back with open arms."

At Vernon's urging, Monday morning, in the blue building, I visited Spirit Lake Tribal Enrollment, where I learned that, according to the tribe's constitution, all current members had to be listed by name on a 1944 tribal census or else be lineally descended from someone who was. My grandmother died in 1935, and in 1944, when the so-called "base roll" was taken, my mother was in the Army overseas – an extenuating circumstance which the enrollment officer suggested I explain to the tribal chairman in his office across the hall. The tribal college was named after a World War II veteran, and Mother had won a military commendation.

Tall and straight, in his late fifties or early sixties, a thin braid down his back, wearing cowboy boots, western jeans, and a white ten-gallon hat at his desk, the chairman examined documentation I had found of Mother's blood quantum, prior tribal enrollment, and military record. In order for me to become enrolled in the tribe, he said, Mother needed to be re-enrolled, something I assumed she wouldn't want, having lived her whole life in ignorance or denial of being Indian, but, as it turned out, when I got home, she was so excited to hear I had found a first cousin of hers she never knew existed – the last surviving relative her own age – that she wrote the chairman saying she planned to visit the reservation herself and enclosing the enrollment application I had given her to fill out, attached to all the documents I just mentioned, plus a 1898 declaration I unearthed in the National Archives, signed by chief Tiyowaste and his tribal council and conferring on my grandmother "all the rights and privileges which have heretofore and may hereafter accrue to any other member" of the tribe (NARG 75, Devil's Lake Agency, Special Cases 147, Feb. 17, 1899).

While we were waiting for a response, Vernon Lambert changed jobs to director of tribal education and started sending me articles he'd written or collected about tribal sovereignty, history, and culture. From this material I learned that in 1862, 540 Dakota women, children, and old men were removed by freight car from Minnesota. Their "lands and rights of occupancy," declared Congress, had been "forfeited" "by their most savage war upon the United States" (*Stat. Large* 12: 652–4, 819.) It began when four young Dakota warriors killed seven settlers over a couple of eggs to feed starving families. Hundreds of white settlers died in a conflict that eyewitness George Doud, Company F, 8th Minnesota Volunteers, in his diary, blamed on abusive traders and violent soldiers. The same week that the Emancipation Proclamation was signed, President Lincoln commuted death sentences of 303 Indian "hostiles," but left 38 sentences to be carried out – the largest mass execution in American history (*History and Culture of the Mni Wakan Oyate*, 1997: 14). Sixty-six hundred Indians survived the conflict, including Christian Dakota who had sheltered settlers during the war.

Many fled to Canada. Many were imprisoned. The 540 removed from Minnesota in freight cars were accompanied by missionary Thomas S. Williamson and his son John, who wrote to his mother during the trip: "I thought they would suffer a great deal, but up came a rain and cooled off the air." The train took them to the Mississippi River, where John said "they ... put us all on the boat to St. Louis" – a freighter called the *Northerner*, whose manifest listed the 540 Indians along with 30 horses. "It will be nearly as bad as the middle passage for the slaves on the lower deck," John wrote, "but then folks say they are only Indians" (Williamson 1918: 423–4). Their destination Vernon called a concentration camp: the Crow Creek reservation in South Dakota. When it proved untenably arid, the five hundred forty and an equal number of their compatriots were further removed down the Missouri River to a site now known as the Santee Reservation. Other Dakota eventually settled near Devil's Lake.

Among the items Vernon himself had written was a project proposal:

> I have observed the Holocaust Museum in Washington, D.C. After the initial shock and anger, I came away with full knowledge that this is a tremendous learning experience, whether negative or positive. The losses on this continent far surpass the European Holocaust. There were over 30 million Indian people living in what is now called North America when Columbus came. Today there are less than 2 million. (Lambert 2001)

But rather than "focusing on how bad our ancestors were treated by the United States and ... using this treatment to bargain for more welfare-type programs," Vernon proposed to create a Dakota Survival Institute, an archive of written treaties and oral traditions, that would "teach us to trace the evolution of our tribe back to the philosophy and standard our ancestors lived by in being self-sufficient survivors." Concluding that "we can begin to educate not only our people, but also the general public," he submitted the proposal to a Minnesota foundation, which responded by encouraging him to flesh out his concept into a planning proposal with a budget, timeline, and board of directors (Lambert 2001).

Vernon asked me to help write the planning grant. It was awarded, but the funder rightly preferred everyone involved to be tribal members. When I brought my mother back to the reservation to meet her first cousin, Vernon took me before the tribal council to explain this additional reason for our reaffiliation with the tribe. Examining our documentation, one of those present remarked about chief Tiyowaste's proclamation: "This ain't no white man paper."

A week after returning home, I received an official letter:

SPIRIT LAKE TRIBE

TRIBAL ENROLLMENT

P.O. Box 359 • Fort Totten, ND 58335 • Phone 701-766-1219 • Fax 701-766-1284

APPLICATION REVIEWED

JOHN HUNT PEACOCK JR
Spirit Lake Sioux Tribe Member

Your application for enrollment as a member of the Spirit Lake Sioux Tribe of the Spirit Lake Sioux Reservation has been appropriately reviewed for compliance with constitutional membership provisions and as provided in the tribal enrollment ordinance. You meet the criteria for membership. You were officially accepted into the Spirit Lake Sioux Tribe on ___AUGUST 09, 2001_____ and your

Date

name is being added to the official membership roll of the Spirit Lake Sioux Tribe by resolution No. ___A05-01-195_____.

Your enrollment number is ___303 U0 8833_____, with a blood degree of ___1/4___ Spirit Lake Sioux Indian blood. Date of birth ___02/20/1949_____.

Regards,

Tribal Chairman,
Spirit Lake Sioux Tribe

Figure 1   Official Tribal Enrollment Letter

If this could happen to me at the age of 52, I realized there must be others whose Indian relations, for good historical reasons, were unknown to them. Adoption, Indian boarding school, relocation, and intermarriage have probably led others to lose their cultural identity, either forgetting or denying being Indian as my mother did for so long, or growing up, like me, in complete ignorance. Among thousands who switched their ethnic self-identification to Native American on the 2000 U.S. census, some no doubt were legitimately reclaiming their heritage, while unfortunately adding to the number of those eligible for correspondingly scarcer federal and tribal benefits to Indians. Unlike me, some will no doubt need and avail themselves of such benefits.

To solve the problem of distributing increasingly limited material resources to poor people requires far greater experience of Indian affairs than I will ever have. I still am not sure about my evolving practice for handling sensitive cultural resources: I no longer read aloud and explain to my students the Laguna origin story that Leslie Marmon Silko put in writing in *Ceremony*. All I do now, when we come to that novel, is give students the already published resources for understanding the origin story on their own. I teach the conflict that led me to this unusual reticence. I tell the story recounted here of how that conflict led me to my own Dakota origins. I mention that I am continuing to work for the day when there will be a Dakota Survival Institute, where natives and non-natives alike will be able to hear and watch a tape of tribal elder Alvina Alberts telling the traditional Dakota origin story. Unlike at Laguna, there are no cultural sanctions I am aware of against anyone telling it at any time, in any place. It has been published in the tribally produced *History and Culture of the Mni Wakan Oyate (Spirit Lake Nation)* (1997: 42). I read it to my students. Here it is:

> There was a band of people who lived under the earth, even under the water. There was a young brother and sister, who always played together in the same area. One day, the young boy went exploring. But this time, he went a little farther than he ever did before, until he came to a very different area. When he looked up, he could see something blue. So he reached up and it took him. It was a whirlpool. It took him up to the surface of the earth. He couldn't swim, but he did his best to stay on the surface of the water. When he got to the shore, he was very tired. The water threw him up onto the shore. He did not know where he was or how he even got there. He began looking around. He found this was a very beautiful place. He wandered away from where he surfaced. As he did, he lost this place. He again began to wander around.
>
> Meanwhile, his sister was looking for him. After many days, she went where he usually went, but he was not there. She noticed there were tracks and followed them. She hoped to find her brother. The tracks kept going and she kept following. She came to the same whirlpool. She was also very curious. So she reached up and the whirlpool took her. Just as her brother, the water put her on shore. She looked around, but she did not see her brother. She did see trees and hills. This was a very different place. But she thought to herself, "how beautiful!", because it was not much different from where she had come. She began to walk in the direction that she thought he might have gone. She was also looking for shelter. As all young people

of this time, she knew the skills of survival. She did not need much to eat for there were berries and roots. The weather was warm.

After many, many days, she came to a stony ridge. From walking for so many days, she became very thirsty. To keep from getting too thirsty, she put a small stone into her mouth. By accident, she swallowed the stone. This stone traveled through her body and developed into a child.

When the boy child was born, she named him "STONE BOY." This is how the Dakota people began on the surface of the earth. This is why the Dakota honor a stone. ... We began from a stone.

Mitakuya Owas.

REFERENCES

Allen, Paula Gunn, 1990. "Special Problems in Teaching Leslie Marmon Silko's *Ceremony*", *American Indian Quarterly*, 15, pp. 379–86.

Attendance Records. Fort Totten Indian School. Heritage Center. Fort Totten, North Dakota.

Blackbird, Adele (Mrs. Elzear Zast), 1916. Letter to Indian Agent R.G. Craige. Turtle Mountain, Belcourt, North Dakota, 18 December.

Bureau of the Census. Fourteenth Census of the United States: 1920 – Population. State: Virginia. County: Augusta. City: Staunton. Enumeration District No. 135. Sheet No. 17.

Doud, George, 1863. "Diaries of George Doud, 8th Minnesota Volunteers, Company F. September 13, 1862 – October 15, 1864," *Minnesota Historical Society*, Vol. I. Quotes are for 16 and 29 December.

Fitzgerald, James, 1980. "Interview: Leslie Silko, Storyteller," *Persona*, University of Arizona Student Literary Magazine, pp. 21–39.

Garcia, Reyes, 1983. "Senses of Place in *Ceremony*", *Melus*, 10.4 (Winter), pp. 37–48.

Graff, Gerald, 1992. *Beyond the Culture Wars: How Teaching the Conflicts Can Revitalize American Education*, New York: W.W. Norton.

Hampton Institute Archives. Hampton, Virginia.

The History and Culture of the Mni Wakan Oyate (Spirit Lake Nation), 1997. Prepared by a committee of writers and informants, including Louis Garica, Lenore Alberts, Vernon G. Lambert, Paul Little, Douglas W. Sevigny, Ila McKay, and Lorraine Greaybear. Bismark: North Dakota Department of Public Instruction.

Ingram, Helen M., Lawrence A. Scaff, and Leslie Marmon Silko, 1984. "Replacing Confusion with Equity: Alternatives for Water Policy in the Colorado River Basin," *New Courses for the Colorado River*, eds Gary D. Weatherford and F. Lee Brown, Albuquerque: University of New Mexico Press, pp. 177–99.

LaDuke, Winona and Ward Churchill, 1985. "Native America: The Political Economy of Radioactive Colonialism," *Journal of Ethnic Studies*, 13.3, pp. 107–32.

Lambert, Vernon G. 2001. "Dakota Survival Institute," unpublished proposal, 24 May.

Littlefield, Dan, 1997. "American Indians and American Scholars: Some New Directions." Native American Literature Conference. Eugene: University of Oregon,15 May.

Longie, Phillip, 2001. Tribal Chair, Spirit Lake Sioux Tribe. Letter of Tribal Enrollment to the author. August 9.

NARG 75. National Archives Record Group. Records of the Bureau of Indian Affairs. National Archives and Records Service. General Services Administration. Washington, D.C.

Peacock, James C., 1989 (Counsel for Tee-Hit-Ton Band). March 2, 1955. "Petition for Rehearing." *Records & Briefs.* U.S. Supreme Court.

Peacock, John, 1996a. "Leslie Marmon Silko", *Post-war Literatures in English*, 32 (June), pp. 1–8.

Peacock, John, 1996b. "The Problem with Psychological Readings of *Ceremony*", *Literature and Psychoanalysis*, ed. Frederico Pereira, Lisbon: Instituto Superior de Psicologia Aplicada, pp. 51–7.

Piatote, Beth Hage, 1997, panel chair. Woman's Research Interest Group. Panel discussion. National American Literature Conference. Eugene: University of Oregon, 17 May.

Sequoya, Jane, 1993. "How (!) Is An Indian?" A Contest of Stories," *New Voices in Native American Literary Criticism*, ed. Arnold Krupat, Washington: Smithsonian Institution, pp. 453–73.

Silko, Leslie Marmon, 1977. *Ceremony*, New York: Penguin.

Silko, Leslie Marmon, 1979. "An Old-Time Indian Attack Conducted in Two Parts," *Shantih*, 4 (Summer/Fall), pp. 3–5.

Silko, Leslie Marmon, 1980. "Leslie Silko, Laguna poet and novelist," *This Song Remembers: Self-Portraits of Native Americans in the Arts*, ed. Jane Katz, Boston: Houghton Mifflin, pp. 186–94.

Silko, Leslie Marmon, 1981. *Storyteller*, New York: Seaver Books.

Stat. Large. Statutes at Large, Treaties and Proclamations of the United States of America. Vol. XII. From Dec. 5, 1859 to Mar. 3, 1863. Ed. George P. Sanger. Boston: Little Brown & Co., 1863.

Tee-Hit-Ton Indians v. United States, 348 U.S. 272 (1955).

Toelken, J. Barre, 1997. "Returning the Gifts to the Givers: Who Owns Thirty Years' Worth of Recorded Navajo Stories?" Native American Literature Conference. Eugene: University of Oregon, 15 May.

Warrior, Robert, 1997. "Freedom of Expression and Cultural Survival: A Basic Conflict." Native American Literature Conference. Eugene: University of Oregon, 16 May.

Williamson, John, 1918. Letter to his mother, quoted in Steven Riggs, *Dakota Portraits, Minnesota History Bulletin*, 2.8 (November), pp. 423–4.

4

Counter-Discursive Strategies in Contemporary Chicana Writing

Deborah L. Madsen

The term "counter-discourse" is now a commonplace of post-colonial theory. Helen Tiffin argues, in her seminal essay "Post-colonial Literatures and Counter-discourse" that it is the counter-discursivity of post-colonial literature, rather than any shared style or theme, that is the definitive quality of this category of writing: "Post-colonial literatures/cultures are ... constituted in counter-discursive rather than homologous practices, and they offer 'fields' or counter-discursive strategies to the dominant discourse" (Tiffin 1995: 96). The "post" in post-colonial therefore does not designate a period in time after colonialism but instead signifies the extent to which colonialism affects all cultural production after the moment of colonization. In this essay, I want to explore the ways in which this key concept of "counter-discursivity" can profitably be used to discuss aspects of contemporary Chicana writing.

The experience of colonization for Chicanos has been prolonged, complex, and many-layered, and has produced a literature that has always contested the colonized status of Mexico. Chicana writing is a form of resistance literature that uses the language of empire to contest the dominant ideologies of colonialism. Yet Chicanas are twice oppressed: first by the master discourse of colonialism (mobilized within Anglo-American culture) and then by the colonizing effect of patriarchy (within both Anglo and Chicano cultures). These effects combine to produce the *mestiza*, the mixed-blood woman, who occupies a cultural, historical and psychological borderland. Gloria Anzaldúa describes the *mestiza* as situated in a dialectical relationship with the three cultures – white, Mexican and indigenous – that have formed her. In the essay, *"La conciencia de la mestiza*: Towards a New Consciousness" (1987) Anzaldúa writes: "Cradled in one culture, sandwiched between two cultures, straddling all three cultures and their value systems, *la mestiza*

undergoes a struggle of flesh, a struggle of borders, an inner war"
(Anzaldúa 1987: 78). What this alienation from any one cultural group
lends the *mestiza* is openness to pluralism or what Anzaldúa calls "a
tolerance for contradictions, a tolerance for ambiguity." She goes on
to argue that the *mestiza* "learns to be Indian in Mexican culture, to be
Mexican from an Anglo point of view. She learns to juggle cultures"
(1987: 79). In post-colonial terms, the *mestiza* articulates a counter-
discursive strategy: she does not simply contradict the oppressive
discourse of colonialism but rather contests the dualistic thinking that
empowers this discourse. Anzaldúa argues:

> The answer to the problem between the white race and the colored,
> between males and females, lies in healing the split that originates in
> the very foundation of our lives, our culture, our languages, our
> thoughts. A massive uprooting of dualistic thinking in the individual
> and collective consciousness is the beginning of a long struggle, but
> one that could, in our best hopes, bring us to the end of rape, of
> violence, of war. (80)

A poem that demonstrates the *mestiza* assault on dualistic logic is
Anzaldúa's "We Call Them Greasers." In this poem, Anzaldúa uses the
binary oppositions between center and margin, colonizer and colonized,
masculine and feminine, civilization and nature, to deconstruct the
official history of American westward expansion. She adopts the voice
of the white male colonizer to describe an encounter with a rural
Chicano community. She goes on to list the means used to dispossess
these people of their land. "He" – the speaker of the poem – uses a false
demand for taxes; he chases off their cattle; and when some appeal to
the law, he uses their inability to speak or read English to defeat them.
The poem ends with a deliberately shocking description of the rape
and murder of one of the women, and the lynching of her husband.

In this poem, the narrative of systematic westward expansion into
uninhabited "virgin" territory is exposed as a lie that masks a history
of brutal conquest. Anzaldúa sets on the side of the white colonizer
the values of civilization, law, masculinity, but also injustice, violence,
rape, and death. The colonized are passive, feminine, and close to nature
(the juxtaposition of "chickens children wives and pigs" without even
punctuation to set the human apart from the animal). The colonized
are indigenous (the speaker claims, "I found them here when I came")
– part of the landscape and waiting to be possessed. Anzaldúa enacts the
moment of colonial possession, which is simultaneously territorial,
sexual, and ideological. Legal and sexual domination is only part of

the exercise of power through language that achieves the dispossession of the natives. The written word ("a piece of paper with some writing") and the spoken word alike invest the colonizer with the power to reduce the colonized to an inarticulate silence. The raped woman "whimpers" while her husband "keens like a wild animal"; they are placed in a passive and powerless subject position (again, akin to animals) in relation to the brutality and ruthlessness of their oppressor. What disrupts this representation of the colonial enterprise is Anzaldúa's adoption of the voice of the colonizer. The title of the poem announces that this poem, written by a woman of color, articulates through the point of view of a white man the racial values of U.S. colonialism (using the abusive term "greasers"). The story of western settlement, which is based upon the concepts of virgin territory, the civilizing mission, and Anglo-American exceptionalism, is still told by the Anglo-American voice but the story is appropriated for a Chicano historical perspective. Anzaldúa tells the story as a part of the Chicano history of annexation, dispossession, and colonization. She balances Anglo and Chicano perspectives such that the poem tells two stories at once: a story of colonial dispossession and a counter story of the westward advance of American civilization. The poem then articulates what Paul de Man called an "aporia" – an irresolvable contradiction between two logical positions. Anzaldúa does not attempt to resolve this contradiction; the contradiction itself is an expression of her *mestiza* consciousness.

Like this poem, Chicana literature in general is situated within a discursive field constituted by both the white settler discourses of Anglo-America and the discourses of a neo-colonial Chicano culture. Both of these discourses marginalize the Chicana. In the United States, Chicanas form a marginalized gender group within a marginalized racial group. The concept of colonial margins versus the metropolitan center is at the heart of much post-colonial theory, and counter-discourse is often understood as a literary enactment of this problematic relation. In these terms, counter-discourse refers to a style of expression whereby the colonized is "writing back" to contest specific narratives that articulate the ideology of colonialism. There are examples of this counter-discursive strategy to be found in contemporary Chicana literature. A powerful example is offered by Helena María Viramontes's novel, *Under the Feet of Jesus* (1995). Here, Viramontes "writes back" simultaneously to Anglo and Chicano narratives. This narrative reads at first like a Chicana version of the *Grapes of Wrath*, as it describes the coming of age of an adolescent itinerant farmworker – who comes, in the course of the narrative, to understand the true source of oppression. But, significantly,

Viramontes's protagonist is a girl. Viramontes is responding not only to the racial exclusions of the Anglo literary canon but also to the gender exclusions of the Chicano canon. The canon of Chicano literature was self-consciously created in the 1970s by a group of writers who wanted to create a cultural branch of the Chicano civil rights struggle. That struggle was rooted in the activism of agricultural workers and so the newly-created canon reflected the values of politicized Chicano masculinity. Classics of the Chicano Renaissance like Rudolfo Anaya's *Bless Me, Ultima* and Tomas Rivera's *... y no se lo trago la tierra (... The Earth Did Not Devour Him)* tell the story of the coming of age of a Chicano adolescent, as the dawning awareness of cruel social injustice and the discovery of a political consciousness. Viramontes describes the coming to political consciousness of a farmworker who is female.

The protagonist Estrella's growing sense of personal and political maturity is defined by a single act of resistance against racism, economic exploitation and her own marginal status. Much of the narrative concerns her attempts to heal a young man who has been poisoned by the pesticides sprayed upon crops. Estrella prevails upon her stepfather to drive Alejo to the nearest clinic where a nurse tells them that he requires hospital treatment. However, the money that might have bought gas to get them to the hospital, 20 miles away, has just been given to the clinic nurse, for this information that they already knew. Outraged at this latest injustice, Estrella takes up a crowbar and violently demands the return of their money:

> Estrella counted nine dollars and seven cents. She lowered the crowbar, unable to catch a breath and showed the nurse what she had taken. She did not feel like herself holding the money. She felt like two Estrellas. One was a silent phantom who obediently marked a circle with a stick around the bungalow as the mother had requested [to keep out evil], while the other held the crowbar and the money. The money felt wet and ugly and sweaty like the swamp between her legs. ... But it was then that Estrella realized the nurse was sobbing into her hands, her lipstick smeared as if she tried wiping her mouth away. (Viramontes 1995: 150)

The new sense of empowerment Estrella experiences through violence is in contradiction to her earlier sense of herself as passive, marginal, someone to whom events happen; her experiences are disjointed and recalled as images that lack logical connection. Women like Estrella are alienated from the grand explanatory narratives that lend unity and meaning to experience. Viramontes, however, appropriates one of the grand patriarchal narratives of adolescence and maturity and, using the discourse of the oppressor, she adapts this narrative to the perspective of the marginalized. In this way, Viramontes "writes back" to Steinbeck, as well as Anaya and Rivera. Like Anzaldúa, Viramontes writes from the margins to address the oppressive discourses of the metropolitan center. In this way, Chicana writers offer what Edward Said, in *Culture and Imperialism* (1993), calls a "contrapuntal perspective" upon the history of colonized peoples – a history that is usually told by and from the center.

This "contrapuntal perspective" is not "anti-colonialism" – it does not simply contradict the dominant ideology; rather, it is a process or dialectic. As Tiffin argues, "[p]ost-colonial cultures are inevitably hybridised, involving a dialectical relationship between European ontology and epistemology and the impulse to create or recreate independent local identity" (Tiffin 1995: 95). In these terms, then, the *mestiza* consciousness described by Anzaldúa engages in a deconstructive relationship with the categories of European epistemology and ontology. *Mestiza* consciousness issues a challenge to Anglo-American hegemony over the categories of being and knowing, endorsing the power of Native and folk knowledge. For example, in her novel *So Far From God* (1993) Ana Castillo moves between the techniques of realistic fiction and those of magic realism in order to challenge the logical categories of Anglo-American realism. The novel begins with the death of three-year-old La Loca and the story of how, on the day of her funeral she sat up in her coffin before flying up to the roof of the church in order to escape the priest's grasp. The spectacle of characters rising from the dead, the reporting of the activities of the dead within the everyday life of the community, instances of miraculous healing, spiritual visions – these aspects of the narrative upset the ontological assumptions about what is real and what is not that underlie the practice of novelistic realism. It is within the context of the belief in magic, practiced by the traditional *curandera*, as a cure for everyday afflictions that Castillo uses the techniques of magic realism in *So Far From God*. Throughout the narrative Castillo offers a sustained contrast between high-tech Western medicine and the traditional folk healing of the *curandera*. Conventional realism belongs to conventional attitudes towards illness and health. The hospital fails the characters of this novel repeatedly. As a child, La Loca is wrongly declared dead by a doctor at the local clinic; her eventual death from AIDS is postponed and the symptoms of her illness eased by the efforts of traditional healers who succeed in a limited way when modern medicine is powerless to act for her. La Loca's sister Caridad heals

herself after she is horribly mutilated in a sexual attack and conventional medicine gives up on "what is left of her." It is Caridad's capacity
for healing through the force of her will, combined with her power of
prophecy, that mark her as a *curandera* in the perception of the ancient
curandera, doña Felicia. In the same way that doña Felicia operates both
outside and within the domain of the Church, so the practice of *curan-
derismo* uses a combination of traditional religious symbols with
massage, herbal remedies and folk treatments to restore a patient's
spiritual and physical equilibrium. Caridad, the intern *curandera*, is also
a hybrid, but of Mexican and Pueblo ancestry; so it is not surprising that
her true spiritual powers are realized in the place, Tsimayo/Chimayo,
that is sacred to the Catholic Church as it also was to the Native peoples
long before. Powerful characters such as Caridad and doña Felicia are
able to move dialectically between European and Native values and
beliefs, transcending both and giving allegiance to neither. The integration of the marvelous or miraculous or physically impossible within
the realistic textures of mundane daily life reflects the hybrid cultural
milieu – Anglo, Chicano, native – with its multiple perspectives and
explanations of experience within which the characters move. Castillo's
refusal to privilege one perspective over the others, but to move dialectically among them, represents her allegiance to the hybridity and
diversity that characterize the condition of the *mestiza*.

The hybrid literary style of writers like Castillo demonstrates the characteristic of counter-discursivity that Helen Tiffin describes as not
"simply 'writing back' to [a] canonical text, but to the whole of the
discursive field within which such a text operated and continues to
operate in post-colonial worlds" (1993: 98). The discursive field in
which Chicana literature is situated is, as I have said, comprised of
misogynistic Chicano discourses of feminine sexuality and the
oppressive racial discourses of the American mainstream. Chicana
writers use these discourses to expose the complex subject positioning
that these discourses negotiate; but how does this discursive radicalism,
this deconstruction of European ontology and epistemology in the
interests of "independent local identity" actually take shape? Castillo
uses magic realism to disrupt Western ontological assumptions;
Viramontes appropriates or "writes back" the narrative of maturity to
represent a Chicana coming-to-consciousness. The deconstructive nature
of Anzaldúa's "We Call Them Greasers" is another counter-discursive
strategy. Vijay Mishra and Bob Hodge address this question as part of
a larger issue in their essay, "What is Post (-) colonialism?" They argue
that by articulating a response simultaneously to distinct subject

positions, "[t]he post-colonial text persuades us to think through logical categories which may be quite alien to our own" (Mishra and Hodge 1994: 282). So the disruption of Western epistemological modes is key to the counter-discursive quality of post-colonial texts.

The Chicana challenge to Western epistemological modes extends to the narratives of Chicana subjectivity that are represented by stereotypes of Chicana femininity. Writers such as Castillo, Viramontes, and Anzaldúa contest the essentialist epistemology that underlies the stereotypical identification of Chicanas with passivity, submissiveness, and their feminine sexuality. These essentialist narratives of race and gender are subjected to what bell hooks calls the "ethnographic gaze" as the gendered ethnic subject self-consciously revisits the subject position into which she is placed by cultural role models.

The stereotypes to which Chicanas are subject have powerful historical origins. I want to focus upon one: La Malinche, an iconic feminine figure who represents the ongoing impact of colonization upon the construction of Chicana femininity. The story of La Malinche begins early in the sixteenth century when the Spanish, led by Hernán Cortés, invaded Mexico. Tribes that had been subjugated by the Aztecs supported the invaders against their old enemy and eventually Mexico was conquered for Spain. Among those associated with Cortés, it is his Indian courtesan La Malinche who has entered into Chicano/a mythology. Some doubt attaches to her willingness to assist the conquistadors – whether she was raped or seduced or gave herself willingly – and her motives are also ambiguous – whether she acted to preserve her people by forging an alliance with the invaders or whether she acted more purely from self-interest. Her status as the mother of the Chicano is unquestioned; from her there issued the *mestizo*, the people of mixed Indian and Spanish blood whose descendants in the United States call themselves Chicano. La Malinche therefore represents the conquered, colonized woman. Her conquest is sexual, cultural, and territorial all at once. She has been possessed by the Spaniard Cortés, just as her children and their descendants have been possessed and colonized by the Spanish. The meaning of La Malinche is therefore inseparable from the colonization of Mexico.

The single most controversial interpretation of the significance of the Malinche figure for modern Mexico is Octavio Paz's discussion in *The Labyrinth of Solitude* (1961). "The Sons of La Malinche" describes Mexicans, mestizos, as the offspring of the rape victim (*la chingada*). The cry "¡Viva México, hijos de la chingada!" affirms the positions of Mexicans in relation to the raped indigenous woman but it also inscribes a number of gender positions as well. Paz says of the verb "chingar" that it is

> masculine, active, cruel: it stings, wounds, gashes, stains. And it provokes a bitter, resentful satisfaction. The person who suffers this action is passive, inert and open, in contrast to the active, aggressive and closed person who inflicts it. The chingón is the macho, the male; he rips open the chingada, the female, who is pure passivity, defenseless against the exterior world. (Paz 1961: 77)

La Malinche, in this interpretation, is seen as the origin of macho violence and Chicana passivity; her original betrayal of her people and her abandonment by Cortés has left them fatherless and motherless, endlessly repeating the original trauma of colonization. The consequence of this national trauma is succinctly described by Debra Castillo: Mexicans

> find themselves victims of the evil betrayer, and so have no recourse but to commit violence, including sexual violence, against women and against their fellow man so as to shore up a sagging and threatened identity as the possessor of a powerful and inviolable male body. (Castillo 1999: 193)

The narrative of La Malinche therefore places women, the daughters of La Malinche, in the position of victims and men in the position of machos: asserting their dominance of women through violence and sexual violence specifically. La Malinche's story provides the basis for a cultural meta-narrative that encompasses individual self-knowledge along with historical understanding of the nation. Within the terms of this story, categories of self and nation, gender and racial identity are blurred and confused. Chicanas use this confusion to contest the power of the stereotypes by "writing back" to them.

It is not surprising then that the figure of La Malinche appears repeatedly in Chicana writing and contributes importantly to key definitions of, or prescriptions for, Chicana femininity. Writers like Ana Castillo, Sandra Cisneros, and Alma Villanueva use these figures to represent a feminist revision of inherited Chicano/a gender roles by upsetting the logical construction of gender categories under patriarchy. So Cherríe Moraga, in *Loving in the War Years* (1983), concludes her discussion of La Malinche and the guilt for her transgression that is still borne by Chicanas by confessing:

> As a Chicana and a feminist, I must, like other Chicanas before me, examine the effects this myth has on my/our racial/sexual identity

and my relationship with other Chicanas. There is hardly a Chicana growing up today who does not suffer under her name even if she never hears directly of the one-time Indian princess. (Moraga 1983: 100)

This kind of analysis is precisely what Moraga sees as the urgent work of Chicana feminism; liberating feminine consciousness from the invisible shackles of inherited definitions and stereotypes by challenging the way in which they are interpreted and understood within the culture of Anglo-Mexican patriarchy.

The figure of La Malinche echoes through Castillo's novel *Sapagonia* (1990), particularly the episode in which the anti-hero, Máximo, tells of the circumstances of his *mestizo* inheritance: his grandfather's rape of an Indian girl who becomes his wife and Máximo's grandmother. This initiates a pattern of sexual use and abuse of women by the men in Máximo's family: Mamá Grande tells the young Máximo that he has an old soul by which she means he has inherited precisely this sexual compulsion. The figure of Mamá Grande offers a contrast with that of Castillo's heroine: Pastora chooses to accept Máximo's fantasy construction of her as the mysterious and sexually passive *mestiza*. Mamá Grande, the raped *indita*, had no choice to make, no choice beyond the passive subject position into which she was forced by sexual violence.

Máximo's machismo is represented in part by his obsessive desire for unity and control in the world around him, including the subjective unity of Pastora. While he insists upon his own individuality, he struggles to maintain his own separateness from others. Initially he sees Pastora as sexually voracious or as a lesbian to whom he is sexually irrelevant, later as passive, accepting and undemanding; either way, he cannot see her either on her own terms or on terms that are not sexual. Máximo both fears and desires Pastora; he needs her and in the end he murders her. This is an obsessive relationship; he thrills at Pastora's refusal to allow herself to be conquered by holding something of herself aloof from him in every encounter they share. She enjoys playing out aspects of her femininity that are not engaged in her other relationships while she revels in the sexual power game that teases Máximo with the deferred promise of her complete surrender to him.

It is within this framework of male desire that Pastora struggles to define her sense of herself and it is in terms of this expression of masculine desire that we are invited to view what Norma Alarcón calls Pastora's complicity in her own objectification and ultimately in her own destruction. The ambiguity of Pastora's participation in the power games she plays with Máximo is allusive of La Malinche's ambiguous complicity in the colonial conquest of her people. Pastora's is not a passive complicity, a surrender to masculine fantasy, but a choice deliberately to transgress the prohibition against feminine sexual freedom. She chooses to submit to Máximo, she chooses to participate in and thereby subvert his patriarchal fantasy for her own intellectual pleasure. She shares Máximo's powerful attraction to the image of her as a mysterious object of desire. It is her subversion of the ideology of feminine submission that is the occasion of her death: Pastora transforms passivity into an aggressive act to which Máximo responds by murdering her. In their final encounter Pastora forces Máximo to acknowledge that his need for her is greater than her need for him; this is an inversion of the power relationship that Máximo, or any machismo, cannot tolerate and so he is compelled to destroy her. It is this destructive act that reconfirms his separation and individuation. Early in the novel, Máximo tells of his compulsion to conquer women who do not want him and to destroy those who reject him: "somehow it occurred to me to choose this [girl] and once I realized that she didn't love me, that she didn't even like me, it was too late. I was committed to having her" (Castillo 1990: 13–14). Sexual relations are, in his view, power relations and Máximo's responses are determined by this power struggle. His willful creation and destruction of relationships or patterns of personal connection express the triumph of his ego, and Máximo generalizes this behavior as something all men know and understand. Violence against women is then placed in the context of masculine gender identity. The confirmation of the male self that arises from the act of violence is then in some ways the same confirmation that is obtained through sexual conquest: in either case, sexuality and violence are conjoined in Máximo's experience of masculinity and in Pastora's recreation of La Malinche's destructive femininity. Pastora uses the essentialist notions of femininity to assert power over Máximo and to assert her own right of self-definition. Nonetheless, the transgression or transcendence of patriarchal gender categories, while it offers an epistemological freedom, can offer no protection from the violence that is the reality of conquest. Pastora, then, finds herself victim of the conquest of her sex, and her people, that began with Cortés's conquest of La Malinche.

If, in *Sapagonia*, Castillo represents the figure of La Malinche as a victim, in the poetry of Sandra Cisneros she is represented as a rebel. In Cisneros's work La Malinche is reinterpreted from Octavio Paz's negative figure of La Chingada, the woman who has been violated. Instead, she appears as the figure of the sexually empowered woman. The sexual woman, rather than being a traitor to her people, her sisters, uses her sexuality to express the full reality of her defiant femininity.

It is patriarchy she betrays in the interest of her gender. Cisneros devotes much of her work to the effort of fracturing powerful inherited narratives of femininity, such as La Malinche's story. This is the significance of Cisneros's "wicked, wicked ways": the title of her 1987 volume of poems. She is "wicked" in that she has taken control of her own sexuality and the articulation of it – a power forbidden to women under patriarchy. Her wickedness is that of transgressing a patriarchally constructed boundary separating that which is legitimate for a woman from that which is not. In this way Cisneros rejects essentialist definitions of femininity. She uses the language of essentialist gender definitions to deconstruct essentialist epistemological and ontological categories. The "Loose Woman," described in the poem of the same name, assumes mythological proportions as a consequence of her subversive powers: "They say I'm a beast. ... a bitch. / Or witch. .../ They say I'm a *macha*, hell on wheels,/ *viva-la-vulva*, fire and brimstone,/ man-hating, devastating,/ boogey-woman lesbian" (Cisneros 1995: 112). Cisneros uses the language of machismo to coin new gendered words for which there has been no feminine equivalent – "macha," "la desperada," and later she calls herself Pancha Villa – the outlaw woman. She likens herself to La Malinche, declaring "I am the woman of myth and bullshit./ (True. I authored some of it.)/ I built my little house of ill repute./ Brick by brick. Labored,/ loved and masoned it" (1995: 113). Cisneros creates a complex identification between subjectivity and place. The house that is metaphorically her reputation is her creation and her life. For La Malinche, the loss of home through sexual and territorial conquest marked the beginning of her reputation as a betrayer and destroyer; for Cisneros, the defiant transgression of sexual boundaries, through her conquest of men, marks the beginning of her freedom and her self-expression. Cisneros "writes back" to the image of La Malinche as a passive victim of Mexican colonization and creates a counter-model of Chicana femininity that is empowered and in control of her own discursive being.

Counter-discursive strategies allow Chicana writers to articulate modes of being and knowing for which there are no words in the colonizer's vocabulary. The language of white patriarchy – or, indeed Mexican patriarchy – does not allow for the expression of Mexican-American feminine experience. Chicana writers "write back" against the values of the literary canon (Anglo and Chicano); against the ongoing colonizing pressure exerted by European ontological and epistemological modes; and against the role models and stereotypes that perpetuate inauthentic narratives of Chicana subjectivity. Contemporary Chicana literature does not simply offer counter-narratives: the *mestiza* inheritance of all Chicanas is Native, Mexican, and Anglo. The hybrid Chicana subjectivity transcends both Anglo and Mexican America, even as it incorporates Anglo and Chicano cultures. Accordingly, the consciousness of the Chicana moves dialectically among the racial and gender discourses that have constituted her since the sixteenth century. The ongoing legacy of that colonizing moment is a *mestiza* consciousness and a hybrid cultural identity, expressed in complex Chicana counter-discourses.

REFERENCES

Anzaldúa, Gloria, 1987. *Borderlands/La Frontera: The New Mestiza*, San Francisco: Aunt Lute.

Castillo, Ana, 1990. *Sapagonia*, Tempe: Bilingual Press.

Castillo, Ana, 1993. *So Far From God*, London: Women's Press, 1994.

Castillo, Debra, 1999. "Border Theory and the Canon" in *Post-Colonial Literatures: Expanding the Canon*, ed. Deborah L. Madsen, London: Pluto Press, pp. 180–205.

Cisneros, Sandra, 1995. "Loose Woman," in *Loose Woman*, New York: Knopf, pp. 112–15.

hooks, bell, 1994. *Outlaw Culture: Resisting Representations*, New York: Routledge.

Mishra, Vijay and Bob Hodge, 1994. "What is Post(-)colonialism?" in *Colonial Discourse and Post-Colonial Theory*, eds Patrick Williams and Laura Chrisman, New York: Columbia University Press, pp. 276–90.

Moraga, Cherríe, 1983. *Loving in the War Years*, Boston: South End Press.

Paz, Octavio, 1961. *The Labyrinth of Solitude: Life and Thought in Mexico*, New York: Grove Press.

Said, Edward, 1993. *Culture and Imperialism*, New York: Knopf.

Tiffin, Helen, 1995. "Post-colonial Literatures and Counter-discourse" in *The Post-Colonial Studies Reader*, eds Bill Ashcroft, Gareth Griffiths, and Helen Tiffin, New York: Routledge, pp. 95–8.

Viramontes, Helena María, 1995. *Under the Feet of Jesus*, New York: Penguin.

5

"At Least One Negro Everywhere": African American Travel Writing

Alasdair Pettinger

That's right, the airport. We came over here steerage, but we're going back first class. Let's climb onboard that silver bird. (Jackson-Opoku 1998: 320)

I

The past two decades have seen a remarkable growth of scholarly interest in travel literature, much of it informed by a "post-colonial" sensibility. Since Edward Said's *Orientalism* (1978), studies of the "rhetoric of empire" in the writings of explorers, traders, missionaries, and colonial officials have appeared with some regularity (Pratt 1992; Spurr 1993). In a related and parallel development, critical perspectives were brought to bear on more scientific, particularly anthropological, writings of the modern period (Fabian 1983; Clifford and Marcus 1986).

Both approaches focused on European and North American authors, showing how they tended to legitimate the colonial project by representing it as essentially benign, by figuring the colonized as peoples without history. This scholarship has produced valuable studies ranging from archaeologies of stereotypes to reconstructed etymologies of key words, and has developed a new vocabulary in order to dissect, say, "monarch-of-all-I-survey" scenes (Pratt 1992: 201–27) or "allegories of salvage" (Clifford 1986b).

While some of this work was criticized for its tendency to treat colonial discourse as monolithic and inescapable, with travel writing as its inevitable servant, attention has since shifted. It is now more usual to try and tease out the ways in which travel writings might challenge rather than exemplify this discourse. Typically, scholars have gone about this in one of two ways.

First, they have identified and explored a certain crisis of authority in ethnography. One may find signs of this in, for instance, the diaries and notes of anthropologists which hint at dimensions of the fieldwork experience repressed in their published work: anxieties and frustrations of the author, the intricate relationships between researcher, informants, interpreters, host governments and so on. There may be evidence of it in the published texts themselves, as authors – having previously enjoyed an apparently exclusive relationship with the people they study – obliquely acknowledge that their descriptions might be questioned by the people they write about, people who must increasingly be counted among their readers. No longer feeling confident enough to repeat the imperious generalizations of the past, contemporary travelers often hide behind a screen of self-parody (Holland and Huggan 1998: 27–47). Some writers have responded to this crisis more directly and reflexively by experimenting with the form of the travel narrative or anthropological monograph itself, producing de-centred, polyphonic texts that mix genres and intentionally make it difficult for old, imperial certainties to take hold (Holland and Huggan 1998: 157–85; Clifford 1988: 21–54; Marcus and Fischer 1986).

Second, there has been a growing interest in travel writings by authors from colonized and formerly colonized countries, especially those which recount journeys to Europe and North America. A few of these writings take the form of what are recognizably travel books, which have been rediscovered through reissues in modern critical editions, sometimes translated for the first time into English (for two recent examples see Mukasa 1998; Sayyah 1999). Much valuable work, however, is to be found in diaries, letters, articles and memoirs, often reaching a wider public through republication in anthologies and special issues of journals (Handlin and Handlin 1997; Pettinger 1998; *Wasafiri* 2001). However, the "writing back" that has, arguably, attracted most attention are the contemporary, self-consciously post-colonial travel narratives of Caryl Phillips, Jamaica Kincaid, Pico Iyer, Amitav Ghosh and others: authors born in countries which a few generations ago Western publishers imagined were inhabited by people who were only written *about* (Holland and Huggan 1998).

The search for travel writing that challenges the Eurocentric legacy of the genre has been undertaken with some caution. Colonial discourse may not be monolithic and all-embracing, but it is not easy to identify a straightforward alternative. There may be gaps, uncertainties, revisions, inversions, and yet the continuing presence of colonial assumptions remains. As Patrick Holland and Graham Huggan suggest in a chapter entitled "After Empire" in their recent survey of contemporary travel writing (Holland and Huggan 1998: 27–65), the self-deprecation of the (typically) English gentleman diverts attention from serious questions of power and privilege, while the "counter-travel" of cosmopolitan writers of color cannot help perpetuating the long-standing Western investment in the "exotic." Every attempt to subvert the tradition runs the risk – it seems – of being co-opted by it.

II

African American travel writing has been largely ignored by these developments. (For some exceptions see: Gruesser 1990; Griffin and Fish 1998.) No doubt this is because it doesn't easily fit the categories that they created. After all, the situation of slaves and their descendants in the United States is not readily amenable to a colonial or post-colonial analysis. As an oppressed minority, their travel writings might be expected to be oppositional in some way; yet, when describing journeys overseas, it would not be surprising if they began to resemble those of white Americans visiting those parts of the world over which the United States exerts formidable economic, political and cultural influence.

A sense of its anomalous status may be glimpsed from the confused assessment of the one African American author who has received more than passing reference in recent studies of the genre: Zora Neale Hurston. The claim by James Clifford that "feminist ethnography ... has not produced either unconventional forms of writing or a developed reflection on ethnographic textuality as such" (1986: 20–1) came in for much criticism, and Hurston was often cited as a counter-example (hooks 1991: 143; Behar 1993: 318; Visweswaran 1994: 32–6).

Mules and Men (Hurston 1978), the innovative presentation of her research into the vernacular folk culture of Florida, where she grew up and spent most of her life, has been widely praised for the way it challenged the objectifying tendencies of the academic monograph; for some, offering a privileged "insider's" perspective (Adams 1991); for others, anticipating later developments in post-modern anthropology (Boxwell 1992). On the other hand, the chapters on Haiti in *Tell My Horse* (Hurston 1990), have been treated as something of an embarrassment, one author claiming that they offer a "dismaying apology for the [American] Occupation" as well as "a number of alarming and racist references to the weaknesses of Haitian character" (Dash 1988: 59). To complicate matters further, however, it is also possible to find interpretations of the former work as evidence that Hurston shared with other contemporary travelers and explorers a "romantic, and, it must be said, colonial imagination" (Carby 1990:80) as well as reappraisals of the latter as an example of "decolonizing ethnography" (Meehan 2001: 245).

To be sure, this difficulty in placing Hurston's work is partly due to its unusually playful and provocative character, but it also suggests that the usual parameters of "post-colonial" theory might not be entirely adequate to deal with African American travel writing. With this in mind, I propose to change tack and consider the fairly specific role that travel has played in the African American literary tradition; for, if we can speak of such a tradition, among its founding texts are the antebellum slave narratives.

Much has been made of the way these narratives "arose as a response to and refutation of claims that blacks *could* not write" (Gates 1985: xv). Less attention has been paid to the way they also challenged the assumption that they could not *travel*. As slaves, many of them were forced to travel hundreds of miles on foot in the company of traders. As fugitives, they covered a lot of ground too, perhaps especially after crossing to the "free" states (working as abolitionist agents, or simply moving to keep ahead of kidnappers – from Philadelphia to New York to Boston, and thence often to Canada or Europe) or sometimes returning to the South because recaptured or voluntarily to aid the escape of other family members.

Their narratives herald the emergence of African American travel writing. On one level, they function as "a response to and refutation of" the travel writings of white Americans and Europeans that represented them as static objects of observation and pity or scorn. On the other hand, they represent a challenge to the legal restrictions that prevented blacks from traveling voluntarily without papers in the South and consigned them to separate accommodations on the railroads and steamships of the North. Many fugitive slave narrators celebrate overcoming such restrictions, either through their descriptions of clandestine flight, campaigns against segregation, or pointedly dwelling on the pleasures of moving and mixing freely in public places beyond the borders of the United States.

Subsequent African American travel writing has inherited this frame of reference. To some extent these barriers continue to exist at the level of cultural expectations. In a recent anthology, one writer suggests that the very *idea* that black people might actually travel for the sake of it is hard for some to accept. "Are you visiting relatives?" "Do you work here?" (Lazard 1997: 223); but then, as a contributor to the same collection half-answers, "former share-croppers do not teach their children to travel for pleasure" (Nayo 1997: 232). Even if they learn some other way, their options still appear to be restricted, as a third author discovered when her travel piece was turned down by her editor. "With pity in his voice he blurted, 'Black people don't go to Iceland'" (Bolden 1997: 312).

Nevertheless, other, more tangible, obstructions have continued to exist. Some travelers tell of the difficulty in obtaining passports because of a lack of documentation of date and place of birth that would satisfy the authorities. Passports are sometimes denied altogether: W. E. B. Du Bois, Paul Robeson and Richard Wright were just three leading African Americans who were deprived of the right to travel by the State Department. Above all, perhaps, African American travel writing remains haunted by the ancestral memory of the Middle Passage, the enforced journeys of the slave ships. Every subsequent journey is liable to be measured against it, a gauge of how much "the race" has progressed since, as perhaps the epigraph to this paper suggests.

In the circumstances, then, it might be expected that African American travel writing is different. It tends to foreground the fact and experience of travel itself, celebrating a freedom that is at best only grudgingly permitted at home, and thus typically set in an autobiographical frame, in which the validation of "self" is of central importance. Much more rare are those books that claim to offer authoritative observations of the people and customs of a single country or community. Accordingly, in the following section, I will briefly consider several peripatetic African American narratives, from the 1850s to the 1990s, which describe travels outside the United States. Read against the background of the cultural significance of geographical mobility in the African American (literary) tradition, these texts suggest ways in which post-colonial approaches to travel writing may need to be reconfigured in order to make sense of them.

III

A Colored Man Around the World (Dorr 1999) was published by David Dorr in Ohio in 1858, after escaping from Louisiana lawyer Cornelius Fellowes, who failed to keep his promise of freeing him on their return from a three-year tour of Europe and the Middle East. This extraordinary account of their journey (only recently rediscovered and reprinted) makes only passing (and usually disparaging) reference to Fellowes. For the most part, the first person singular predominates, and the voice is typically that of the leisured upper-class traveller: "Drive me to the national assembly, I said to the coachman" (Dorr 1999: 34). It is almost as if Dorr himself were the slaveholder, traveling alone.

This voice is perhaps most evident in his frank and obsessive sexual interest in working-class women, such as from the "half-bending posture" of the maid at his London hotel (1999: 15) to the dancing girls he observes at a dinner hosted by the British and American consul in Cairo:

> Such a jingling; such screwing in and out of bodies; such a gesturing; and such a quivering of the bodies from their necks to their knees, is only to be imagined. One girl stuck her head between her legs in front, whilst another done the same over backwards. (1999: 177–8)

The slip into the Southern vernacular in the last clause may not be accidental. Although he adopts an aristocratic persona, Dorr makes no secret of his race, as the title of his book suggests. Indeed, he offers a stout defence of "the doctrine of the unity of man" (192), against the proponents of the new American ethnology, whom he would have antagonized with his bold assertion that the ancient Egyptians were black (11) and that therefore "the black man was the first skilful animal on the earth" (134).

It is presumably as "a colored man" – rather than Southern slave-holder – that he mocks the "worthless trash" that appears in the section devoted to American Arts and Sciences at the Great Exhibition in London (20); and takes carnivalesque pleasure in portraying the high and mighty in an unflattering or humiliating light: a "broken down princess," paid by her husband to stay away from him (32); two Americans ruined by the Casino at Baden-Baden (52); the atrocious manners of a "Mr Bullion from California" (1999: 156); an English "lady of rank" "prostrated on the floor, kissing ['our Savior's tomb'] with great devotion" (184). The pithy one-line captions he provides for cities and nationalities – Zurich is "the prettiest city in Switzerland" (47); Naples "yet the most wicked city on the face of the globe" (104); the Dutch "a reasonable, just and inoffensive people ... the last people I am acquainted with to count unhatched chickens" (57–8) – are a strange mix of guidebook descriptions and down-home humor that undercuts the pretensions of the cultured traveler, as if Dorr hasn't quite mastered the idiom, adding to its satirical force.

Over fifty years later, the eminent educator Booker T. Washington also traveled to Europe with a white companion, his secretary, Robert E. Park, later to achieve fame on his own account as a sociologist. Park effectively co-wrote *The Man Farthest Down* (Washington 1912), but

Washington's name appears on the title page. The object of the trip was to acquaint themselves with "the condition of the poorer and working classes in Europe, particularly in those regions from which an ever-increasing number of immigrants are coming to our country each year" (1912: 3). Washington wanted to know *why* so many Europeans were leaving their homelands; he discovers that the highest levels of emigration were to be found where agricultural conditions were at their worst, and vice versa (5–6).

In some ways his conclusions are comforting for conservatives in the United States, reinforcing the claim that Southern Negroes are no worse off – indeed better off in some cases – than the poorest classes in Europe (a claim used to defend slavery, and subsequently to defend the racial stratification of the South after Reconstruction). (On the other hand the image of a former slave on an eight-week vacation in Europe, accompanied by a white secretary would be unlikely to endear him to them.) But as a travel book it is interesting for other reasons. "In order to carry out the plan I had in mind," he writes, "it was necessary to leave the ordinary beaten track of European travel and to plunge into regions which have not been charted and mapped, and where ordinary guides and guide-books are of little or no avail" (9–10). To this extent his project does not differ much from those social explorers of "darkest England" of the late Victorian period, who turned the conventions of the African travel narrative on the domestic urban poor. What is novel is not the standard condemnation of mass tourism but the rejection of the aestheticization that romantic travelers so often embraced:

> Most people who travel in Europe seem to me to be chiefly interested in two sorts of things: they want to see what is old, and they want to see what is dead. The regular routes of travel run through palaces, museums, art galleries, ancient ruins, monuments, churches, and graveyards.
>
> I have never been greatly interested in the past, for the past is something that you cannot change. I like the new, the unfinished and the problematic. My experience is that the man who is interested in living things must seek them in the grime and dirt of everyday life. (13)

Washington counterposes the perspective of the romantic traveler with that of the peasant whom that traveler exoticizes: "I have found that the places in which the life of the peasants is most interesting to tourists are usually the places that the peasants are leaving in the largest numbers" (325). *The Man Farthest Down* breaks with the convention of the social explorer narrative to the extent that the people he meets "and shake[s] hands with" (320) are not naturalized objects of observation but subjects who respond to their conditions: emigrating overseas, sending part of their income back home, sometimes returning with new skills and ideas, or establishing voluntary associations as a way of improving housing, education, and other amenities, that would render emigration unnecessary.

In a village near Cracow, Washington "noticed that our guide and interpreter seemed to be quite as interested in learning about America as I was interested in getting acquainted with Galicia" (250). This chiastic formulation anticipates more role reversal, for it turns out the man has a cousin in New York and Washington offers to look him up on his return (251). In this way, the conventional division between the mobile travel writer and the static "travelee" gives way to a more reciprocal relationship, where knowledge and favors are exchanged.

Like many autobiographies of leading public figures, Langston Hughes' *The Big Sea* (Hughes 1986) and *I Wonder As I Wander* (Hughes 1993), which cover his life through to his late thirties in 1938, reinforce the author's claim to national standing by demonstrating how well-traveled he is. The first volume begins with his experiences as a merchant seaman, which take in West Africa, the West Indies, and Rotterdam, where he leaves the service. After some time in Paris, working as a doorman, then assistant cook, and on vacation in Italy, he works his passage back to the United States, where his talents as a poet begin to be recognized and he becomes a leading light in what later became known as the "Harlem Renaissance." In the second volume he resumes his travels, which take him to the Caribbean, the Soviet Union, Japan, Hawai'i, Mexico, ending in Paris, on his way back from reporting on the Spanish Civil War. Yet he foregrounds his journeying to such an extent that it does not enhance or embellish his life but actually is his life. He traverses the United States as if it were just another country. In Paris, in the early hours of 1938, he reflects that

> [t]he year before, I had been in Cleveland. The year before that in San Francisco. The year before that in Mexico City. The one before that at Carmel. And the year before Carmel in Tashkent. Where would I be when the next New Year came, I wondered? (1993: 405)

As a child his family moved frequently, and when as an adult he hears his mother is sick, he decides to head "home – home being Oberlin, where I had never been" (309). There is little sense of Hughes being *from* anywhere: *The Big Sea* opens with him throwing his college text books overboard, as he sails out of New York harbor on his first ocean voyage (the story of his upbringing is significantly inserted as a flashback after the first chapter); and *I Wander* ends that New Year's Day in the French capital.

But it is in this closing chapter that Hughes' deceptively light-hearted cosmopolitanism is juxtaposed sharply with the less fortunate and more circumscribed wanderings of others. Bumping into a Japanese theatre director he met several years before, they catch up over drinks in an empty cafe.

> Seki Sano said, "I read a year or two ago in the Moscow papers about your being expelled from Japan. I'm sorry that happened to you in my country. But I am expelled, too. I cannot go back."
>
> "I'm sure someday you can go back," I said, " and I, too, if I want to go."
>
> But Seki Sano was not so optimistic. "There are too many people wandering around the world now who can't go home," he said. "Lots of them are in Moscow. More are in Paris – people from the Hitler countries, from the South American dictatorships, from China, from my own Japan. No exiles from America – though I wouldn't be surprised if the day didn't come."
>
> "That's one nice thing about America," I said, "I can always go home – even when I don't want to." (1993: 403–4)

The barriers to recreational travel encountered by African Americans – only alluded to indirectly in Hughes' autobiographies (and yet at the same time all too evident in the way he feels the need to make so much of his success in overcoming them) – are addressed in the introduction to Colleen McElroy's *A Long Way from St Louie* (McElroy 1997).

> Accounts of great travels never included black people, so I had no role models. In fact, until I escape the airport red tape of each new destination, my traveling companions more than likely will be white. (1997: iv)

Yet she never imagines that once separated from those companions she becomes "one of the people": "I am a Western woman, and I must always, always be aware of how that life has affected my vision, my ability to see myself as akin to and different from the people I meet" (1997: vi).

Subtitled "Travel memoirs", the form of the book – which organizes its material thematically rather than by place or time – is well suited to capture her double existence as both an intrepid black woman traveler and a regular Western tourist. Each chapter gathers anecdotes and impressions unified by a single motif: her love of Latin dance, taxi rides, border crossings, foreign languages, romantic encounters, and so on. There is no beginning or end to anchor her in one identity or another.

If closing scenes of travel books often promise a kind of resolution – of conflicts that have dominated the narrative hitherto – this is not the case here. The last piece, "No Stops Till Darwin," offers subtle reflections on an Australian tour, exploiting the pun that links the capital of the Northern Territory and the Victorian scientist. Marking her distance from the rest of the group that visits Ayers Rock, she remarks how her difference of "vision" makes it impossible for her not to notice the absence of black people in what often purport to be realistic movie scenes set in downtown New York; the same perspective forces her to challenge the similar attempt to edit out the existence of real (rather than symbolic) Aboriginals in Sydney, Melbourne, and Brisbane, working in "banks, hospitals, law offices and schools": not victims of natural selection on the verge of extinction, but adapting, surviving, through "continuous variations," just like African Americans back "home" (225). Yet, McElroy chooses to end her book, not here – with a potentially glib assumption of cross-cultural solidarity – but a few pages later, turning the Darwinian metaphor on herself, figuring her travels as "the evolution of me" (241), a process that is far from over:

> I return home to replenish my friendships, to touch base with my family and snuggle down in my own bed, but the sound of jets streaking overhead fills me with longing. There's something out there beckoning me – I don't know what; I don't know where. But I can hardly wait for my ticket to get there. And I don't plan to stop until I find it. (241)

IV

One motif found in the work of all four authors is the chance encounter with a fellow African American on their travels abroad. Two of them comment on the likelihood of this happening. Hughes writes: "Having since been around the world, I have learned that there is at least one Negro everywhere" (1993: 104), echoing McElroy's grandmother's "belief that there are black folks everywhere on this earth" (1997: v). In mainstream travel writing the encounter with a fellow traveler is likely to provoke a certain defensiveness: in order to preserve the effect of the narrative revealing the unique experiences of an individual, the other traveler is likely to be portrayed in a way that suggests his or her experiences are inauthentic or irrelevant. Typically they will be dismissed as tourists: and this can function as a useful reminder to readers that the book in their hands is an authoritative account. (These days it is almost as common, however, to find authors inverting the relationship, casting themselves as incompetent tourists and allowing themselves to be mocked by serious travelers: thus attempting to win over the reader with an apparently refreshing honesty. The narrator's uniqueness is nevertheless preserved.)

When authors such as those discussed above meet other African Americans, the response is usually somewhat different. In Constantinople David Dorr comes across Frank Parish, a "very large," free colored man in his forties, who owned property in Nashville, and is impressed as Parish declines to give way as the Sultan ("a weak looking man" of 22 who has never left the land of his birth) approaches and instead walks up to his carriage and shakes his hand (Dorr 1999: 126–7). Parish seems to embody or act out that sense of cultural superiority (of West over East) that Dorr can only timidly inscribe on the written page once back home, although when the author meets him later in Athens, impressing a young "scotchwoman" by quoting Byron, he is careful to remind his readers that the big man from Tennessee was a mere barber (1999: 140).

Booker T. Washington quotes from a letter he received from a "coloured man who was born and raised in the South," who had been unemployed in London for over a year, his attempts to find work frustrated by racist employers ("It seems to me that all Britain are against the Negro race") (Washington 1912: 34). The man appeals for help in obtaining a ticket to return home. "The winter is coming on," he writes, "and I like to get home to shuck corn or to get to Maryland for a oyster draggin. It is a long time since I had watermelon, pig's feet and corn" (1912: 35). Here, Washington appears to make use of this – rather minstrelized – compatriot in order to voice criticisms of British society he might have been reluctant to make himself.

In Moscow Langston Hughes makes the acquaintance of Emma from Kentucky, who had been in Russia nearly forty years. "I'm sure glad to see some Negroes," she said as Hughes and his companions arrived in the city. "Since I am always hankering to see more and more Negroes myself, right off I took a liking to Emma" (Hughes 1993: 83). Cheerfully deriding the Soviet regime and making full use of the black market, she nevertheless sincerely denounced lynch law in the United States on the public platform, while privately conceding, "I wish I was back home" (83). Hughes (whose own cowardice before the House Un-American Activities Committee lost him many friends on the Left) wryly notes that "the nonpolitical foreigners loved her," and concludes, somewhat patronizingly: "Certainly Emma added a big dash of color all her own to the grayness of Moscow" (86).

At a conference in Dubrovnik Colleen McElroy is pleased to meet several other African American women delegates. "We greeted each other as if we'd been lost in the desert and found an oasis" (McElroy 1997: 123). About town together they attract a good deal of attention, and at a cafe they are approached by a waiter, who, they gradually realize, is convinced one of them must be Alice Walker. He holds out a book to be signed, and – eager to get on with ordering their meal – the others nominate McElroy as the one to pass herself off as the author of *The Color Purple*. "I signed the book: LJUBAV, ALICE, in scrawling letters," she writes. "And let me tell you, that dinner was the best one I had in Dubrovnik" (1997: 124). McElroy is not suspicious of her fellow-travelers; on the contrary she welcomes them and shares a conspiratorial moment with them at a local's expense. If Dorr, Washington and Hughes seem to prefer the conventional distancing of theirs – by undermining their authority or dignity to a greater or lesser degree – they nevertheless identify with these compatriots, allowing us to glimpse slightly exaggerated versions of themselves, living on their wits, in a potentially hostile world. But note that this solidarity is national as much as racial. One finds very few examples of this connection when meeting people of color from other countries which do not end with an anticlimactic recognition of how little common ground they share. (This is particularly marked in narratives of travel to Africa. See, for example, Wright 1954.)

To this extent, then, the encounters with other African Americans disclose less a diasporan, "black atlantic," perspective so much as a black version of the American urge to feel at home in the world, interpreting it in resolutely American terms. Struggling against the material obstacles and expectations that make it difficult to travel and write about travel, black authors from the United States – it would seem – only find the confidence to do so by adopting a (white) American persona, albeit a self-critical one. This is certainly not because "travel writing" as such is an inherently colonialist medium or genre (although, in rejecting this claim, I think we should hesitate before classifying the texts we have examined as "post-colonial"). Their perspectives cut across those of the two most familiar guises of the traveler in post-colonial studies, as the "global/local" axis begins to displace the "metropole/colony" axis: the elite and the vernacular cosmopolitan.

As an oppressed minority within the United States, whose freedom and opportunity to travel abroad have only been won through generations of struggle, and only precariously maintained, African Americans are unlikely to share the insouciance of cosmopolitan elites who can boast their world citizenship and scorn patriotism only because they can cross borders freely and (are made to) feel "at home" anywhere (unless, of course, they impersonate someone who does). On the other hand, they would not normally belong with those vernacular cosmopolitans – migrants, refugees, exiles – who must "make a tryst with cultural translation as an act of survival" (Bhabha 2000: 139) – although they will certainly encounter some on the way: Washington's London correspondent, and Emma in Moscow, being prime examples. As Langston Hughes admitted to his Japanese friend, African Americans (at least those who publish travel books) can (nearly) always "go home," even if they don't want to. As such they might be better described as occasional cosmopolitans – traveling in defiance of those forces that would keep them at home, and yet unwilling to risk surrendering the right to belong. For that reason their books, as well as the travels they describe, begin and end in the United States.

REFERENCES

Adams, Amelia Maria, 1991. "Zora Neale Hurston: Native Anthropologist," in Alice Morgan Grant, ed. *All About Zora*, Winter Park: Four-G.

Behar, Ruth, 1993. "Introduction: Women Writing Culture," *Critique of Anthropology* 13, pp. 307–25.

Bhabha, Homi, 2000. "The Vernacular Cosmopolitan" in Ferdinand Dennis and Naseem Khan, eds *Voices of the Crossing: The Impact of Britain on Writers from Asia, the Caribbean and Africa*, London: Serpent's Tail, pp. 133–42.

Bolden, Tanya, 1997. "In the Land Up Over" in Elaine Lee, ed. *Go Girl! The Black Woman's Book of Travel and Adventure*, Portland: Eighth Mountain Press, pp. 307–12.

Boxwell, D. A. 1992. "'Sis Cat' as Ethnographer: Self-Presentation and Self-Inscription' in Zora Neale Hurston's *Mules and Men*," *African American Review*, 26: 4 (Winter), pp. 605–17.

Carby, Hazel, 1990. "The Politics of Fiction, Anthropology, and the Folk: Zora Neale Hurston" in Michael Awkward, ed. *New Essays on "Their Eyes Were Watching God"*, Cambridge: Cambridge University Press, pp. 71–93.

Clifford, James, 1986a. "Introduction: Partial Truths" in Clifford and Marcus (1986), *Writing Culture: The Poetics and Politics of Ethnography*, Berkeley and Los Angeles: University of California Press, pp. 1–26.

Clifford, James, 1986b. "On Ethnographic Allegory" in Clifford and Marcus (1986), *Writing Culture: The Poetics and Politics of Ethnography*, Berkeley and Los Angeles: University of California Press, pp. 98–121.

Clifford, James, 1988. *The Predicament of Culture: Twentieth-Century Ethnography, Literature, and Art*, Cambridge and London: Harvard University Press.

Clifford, James and George E. Marcus, eds, 1986. *Writing Culture: The Poetics and Politics of Ethnography*, Berkeley and Los Angeles: University of California Press.

Dash, J. Michael, 1988. *Haiti and the United States: National Stereotypes and the Literary Imagination*, London: Macmillan.

Dorr, David, 1999. *A Colored Man Round the World*, Ann Arbor: University of Michigan Press. [Orig. 1858.]

Fabian, Johannes, 1983. *Time and the Other: How Anthropology Makes Its Object*, New York: Columbia University Press.

Gates, Henry Louis, Jr., 1985. "Introduction: The Language of Slavery" in Charles T. Davis and Henry Louis Gates, Jr., eds *The Slave's Narrative*, Oxford and New York: Oxford University Press, pp. xi–xxxiv.

Griffin, Farah J. and Cheryl Fish, eds, 1998. *A Stranger in the Village: Two Centuries of African-American Travel Writing*, Boston: Beacon Press.

Gruesser, John C., 1990. "Afro-American Travel Literature and Africanist Discourse," *Black American Literature Forum*, 24.

Handlin, Oscar and Lilian Handlin, eds, 1997. *From the Outer World: Perspectives on People and Places, Manners and Customs in the United States, as Reported by Travelers from Asia, Africa, Australia, and Latin America*, Cambridge and London: Harvard University Press.

Holland, Patrick and Graham Huggan, 1998. *Tourists with Typewriters: Critical Reflections on Contemporary Travel Writing*, Ann Arbor: University of Michigan Press.

hooks, bell, 1991. *Yearning: Race, Gender and Cultural Politics*, London: Turnaround.

Hughes, Langston, 1986. *The Big Sea*, London: Pluto. [Orig. 1940.]

Hughes, Langston, 1993. *I Wander as I Wonder*, New York: Hill and Wang. [Orig. 1956.]

Hurston, Zora Neale, 1978. *Mules and Men*, Bloomington: Indiana University Press. [Orig. 1935.]

Hurston, Zora Neale, 1990. *Tell My Horse*, New York: Harper & Row. [Orig. 1938.]

Jackson-Opoku, Sandra, 1998. *The River Where Blood is Born*, New York: One World.

Lazard, Dorothy, 1997. "Finding Myself in the World" in Elaine Lee, ed. *Go Girl! The Black Woman's Book of Travel and Adventure*, Portland: Eighth Mountain Press, pp. 221–26.

McElroy, Colleen, 1997. *A Long Way from St Louie: Travel Memoirs*, Minneapolis: Coffee House Press.

Marcus, George E. and Michael M. J. Fischer, eds, 1986. *Anthropology as Cultural Critique: An Experimental Moment in the Human Sciences*, Chicago and London: University of Chicago Press.

Meehan, Kevin, 2001. "Decolonizing Ethnography: Zora Neale Hurston in the Caribbean" in Lizabeth Paravisini-Gebert and Ivette Romero-Cesareo, eds *Women at Sea: Travel Writing and the Margins of Caribbean Discourse*, New York: Palgrave, pp. 245–79.

Mukasa, Ham. 1998. *Uganda's Katakiro in England*, ed. Simon Gikandi, Manchester: Manchester University Press. [Orig. 1904.]

Nayo, Lydia A., 1997. "A Sharecropper's Daughter Goes to Paris" in Elaine Lee, ed. *Go Girl! The Black Woman's Book of Travel and Adventure*, Portland: Eighth Mountain Press, pp. 232–34.

Pettinger, Alasdair, ed., 1998. *Always Elsewhere: Travels of the Black Atlantic*, London and New York: Cassell.

Pratt, Mary Louise, 1992. *Imperial Eyes: Travel Writing and Transculturation*, London and New York, Routledge.

Said, Edward W., 1978. *Orientalism*, London: Routledge & Kegan Paul.

Sanjek, Roger, ed., 1990. *Fieldnotes: The Makings of Anthropology*, Ithaca and London: Cornell University Press.

Sayyah, Muhammad Ali, 1999. *An Iranian in Nineteenth Century Europe: The Travel Diaries of Haj Sayyah, 1859–1877*, trans. Mehrbanoo Nasser Dehim, Bethesda, Maryland: Ibex.

Spurr, David, 1993. *The Rhetoric of Empire: Colonial Discourse in Journalism, Travel Writing, and Imperial Administration*, Durham and London: Duke University Press.

Visweswaran, Kamala, 1994. *Fictions of Feminist Ethnography*, Minneapolis: University of Minnesota Press.

Wasafiri, 2001. Special issue: "Travellers" Tales: Alternative Traditions," 34 (Autumn).

Washington, Booker T., 1912. *The Man Farthest Down: A Record of Observation and Study in Europe*, Garden City: Doubleday, Page & Co.

Wright, Richard, 1954. *Black Power*, London: Dennis Dobson.

6

Unsettling Asian American Literature: When More than America is in the Heart

Rajini Srikanth

no idiom has yet emerged to capture the collective interests of many groups in translocal solidarities, cross-border mobilizations, and postnational identities. Such interests are many and vocal, but they are still entrapped in the linguistic imaginary of the territorial state. (Arjun Appadurai, "Patriotism and Its Futures," 1996)

One of the dangerous consequences of paying undue attention to diasporas is that it distances the so-called diasporic populations from their immediate environments, rendering these populations into foreigners in the context of everyday life. (Arif Dirlik, "Asians on the Rim," 1999)

A binary paradigm is *not* the most useful way to conceptualize the complicated realities of the lives of Asian Americans. Presenting the local (or domestic) and diasporic (or transnational) as oppositional states of being sets up a needless dichotomy within Asian American communities. It misrepresents the highly intricate maneuvers people make, on the one hand, to be active locally in their neighborhoods and towns in the United States and, on the other, to be connected transnationally to ancestral countries and to others who are part of the diaspora of these original homelands. This essay does not judge the relative merits of one type of sensibility over the other, but it does operate from the premise that many Asians in the United States do not see the local and the diasporic as contradictions. Increasingly, Asian American writers deploy a multiple geographical perspective in their literary narratives, de-centering the United States and making it "one node in a ... network of diasporas" (Appadurai 1996: 171). More than "America" is in the hearts, minds, and words of these writers, and such a sensibility is not limited to Asia-born authors but appears to transcend generations, finding expression in Asian American writers who were born in or arrived early in their life to the United States.

"Diaspora" is a term that no longer applies only to the Jewish or African peoples. Colonial dictates, labor migrations of the nineteenth and twentieth centuries, wars, and the globalization of capital have resulted in the wide dispersal of Asians (such as the Indians, Chinese, or Vietnamese) to various regions of the globe – East Africa, the Caribbean, Fiji, Latin America, England, Canada, and the United States, for example; at the same time, rapid technological advancements have made it possible for these dispersed peoples to establish and maintain global communities of shared interest. This essay speaks to the ramifications of such a global and transnational perspective on the teaching of Asian American literature, with specific reference to writings by Filipino/a, South Asian, and Vietnamese Americans (the three most rapidly increasing populations within Asian America). Questions that frame the analysis include: What nurtures the transnational imaginations of these writers? How do the elements of diaspora and multiple homelands affect the portrayal of the United States in the writings? What is the nature of "belonging" in these works? What can we learn about citizenship from these writings? The relevance of such an approach, given the times in which we live, is indisputable. Additionally, the paradox of such a transnational focus is that it yields rich insights into how to practice a critical local multiculturalism, a multiculturalism that moves past the vacuous celebration of diversity to a grappling with substantive issues of power – why and how certain ethnic and racial groups are denied power – and the inequitable availability of resources and opportunity.

A word about the term "Asian American": coined in the late 1960s in California by students who modeled their demands for ethnic empowerment on the Civil Rights movement, it is a label that is being actively contested today. The influx of large numbers of South and Southeast Asians into the country is forcing a reassessment of the hitherto East Asian (primarily Chinese and Japanese) orientation of the label (Filipino/a Americans have long held that the term's groundedness in the notion of yellow power has marginalized their membership in the collective, and South Asians push against the "Mongolian" racial dimension implicit in how the term is popularly understood in the United States).[1] Just as certain groups are challenging the limits of the "Asian" in "Asian American," so also are neighboring countries challenging the appropriation of "America" by the United States (Rustomji-Kerns 1999). The result is that the scope of the term "Asian American" is steadily expanding to include other nation states in the Americas. Below, I briefly discuss the complexity of Asian experiences in the Americas. However, this essay's primary focus is on the writings of individuals of Asian descent living in the United States, and, unless I indicate otherwise, any reference to "Asian American literature" denotes this body of texts.

Virtually all scholars of Asian American literature are familiar with the two fundamentally different perspectives articulated by Frank Chin *et al.* and Lisa Lowe. Chin, considered even by his detractors as a pioneer of Asian American literature, declared along with his co-editors, in 1974, that Asian American means "Filipino-, Chinese-, and Japanese-Americans, *American born and raised*" (1974: vii, emphasis added). The collection they released at the time was titled *Aiiieeeee! An Anthology of Asian-American writers.* In 1991 the same editorial collective of Frank Chin, Jeffrey Chan, Lawson Inada, and Shawn Wong, published the *Big Aiiieeeee! An Anthology of Chinese American and Japanese American Literature.* But this time they narrowed the focus of the anthology, subtitling it *An Anthology of Chinese American and Japanese American Literature.* In what seems almost a perverse move, Chin *et al.* emphatically restricted the sphere of Asian American literature at a time when the demographics of Asian America was undergoing enormous change with the influx of immigrants from all parts of Asia, and, most particularly, South and Southeast Asia. Although there is nothing in the title of the 1991 collection to suggest that it represents the full range of Asian American writing (notice that the word "Asian" does not appear anywhere in the title), it cannot but help evoke the earlier *Aiiieeeee!*, which did announce itself as a collection of Asian American writing; in having the title of the 1991 collection refer back to the 1974 anthology, the editors seem to imply that only Chinese and Japanese American Literature is authentically Asian American.

Lisa Lowe, in her essay "Heterogeneity, Hybridity, Multiplicity: Marking Asian American Differences," originally published in 1996 and referenced frequently within Asian American studies, provides an alternative and more inclusive vision of Asian America, and by extension, Asian American literature:

> from the perspectives of Asian Americans, we are extremely different and diverse among ourselves: as men and women at different distances and generations from our "original" Asian cultures – cultures as different as Chinese, Japanese, Korean, Filipino, Indian, Vietnamese, Thai, or Cambodian – Asian Americans are born in the United States and born in Asia, of exclusively Asian parents and of mixed race, urban

and rural, refugee and nonrefugee, fluent in English and non-English-speaking, professionally trained and working-class. As with other immigrant groups in the United States, the Asian-origin collectivity is unstable and changeable, with its cohesion complicated by inter-generationality, by various degrees of identification with and relation to a "homeland," and by different extents of assimilation to and distinction from "majority culture" in the United States. (1991: 66)

Although very few Asian American scholars and educators today subscribe to Frank Chin's Chinese- and Japanese-defined Asian America, the issue of local versus transnational – literature centered in the United States versus literature encompassing other geographies – is still an area of active debate. It is not that Asian Americanists deny the occurrence of transnational themes in the fiction, poetry, and memoirs being written; rather, the struggle revolves around the extent to which such themes ought to be foregrounded in the pedagogy of Asian American literature. Sau-ling Wong provides a thought-provoking critique, in her 1995 essay "Denationalization Reconsidered: Asian American Cultural Criticism at a Theoretical Crossroads," of what she sees as a misguided celebration of diasporic and transnationalist perspectives. She warns that such a stance leads many Asians to de-politicize themselves within a U.S. context and train their sights on "home" country politics and emergencies. Moreover, she questions, of what use is diasporic sensibility to American-born Asian Americans?

Wong's essay is of critical importance to any discussion of Asian American studies. Her cautionary objections to a mindless embracing of "chic" theories of diaspora is a necessary reminder that we examine the lure of new approaches in light of the impact they have on the positions of Asians within the United States. I object to Wong, however, on two fronts: first, that a diasporic or transnational perspective results in de-politicization in a domestic (U.S.) context, and, second, that American-born Asian Americans have a limited use for diasporic connections.

Let me address the charge of de-politicization first. "Asians for Mumia" is a recent example of Asian American activism in the cause of social justice set squarely within the United States. Mumia, an African American reporter on death row, is believed to have been falsely sentenced for a crime he did not commit. Many participants in "Asians for Mumia" are of the immigrant generation with active interest in the politics of their homelands (I use the term "immigrant" merely to indicate individuals born in countries other than the United States and not to suggest, as some immigration scholars do, their greater investment in and assimilation to something called "the American way of life" than that exhibited by sojourners and those in exile). Yet, these Asian-born Asian Americans are deeply committed to the cause of social justice in the United States and participate with vigor in protesting, among other things, unfair imprisonment, police brutality, racial profiling, the use of sweatshop labor, and discrimination in housing.

The relationship between American-born Asians and their ancestral homelands is complex and not unproblematic. American-born Asians attending college during the years following the ethnic studies and multiculturalism movements have been encouraged to find their ethnic and racial "roots." American-born Asians are thus deeply interested in their ancestral histories and heritage; some even make the trip back to ancestral homelands (sansei David Mura's visit to Japan, for example, that he records in *Turning Japanese* or Jhumpa Lahiri's trips to India resulting in some stories in her collection *Interpreter of Maladies* being set in India; one might even include in this pattern of "return" Indiana-born and Texas-raised Susan Choi's setting of a portion of her novel *Foreign Student* in Korea).

While ethnic studies programs were initially started as fronts of political resistance and challenge to European American dominance in all areas of civic life, these oppositional movements have quickly become co-opted into a state-sanctioned multiculturalism divested of political overtones and shaped into a harmless celebration of cultural difference (Lowe 1996: 39–42). One could argue that this attraction for the homeland of one's parents or grandparents weakens the already com-promised position of Asian Americans as American citizens. A cynical but not invalid view of multiculturalism is that it has furthered divisions among Americans of color by reifying difference, and that it has reinforced the foreignness of Asians, regardless of their having been born in the United States. Diaspora and transnationalism have been readily, if in some instances uncritically, accepted by American-born Asians. The task for educators, then, is not to bemoan the phenomena but to teach students to engage analytically with the trend toward diaspora and transnational issues in Asian American literature and, through the analysis, to direct students to understand the complex interaction between local and transnational concerns.

WEN HO LEE, MUSLIM AMERICANS, AND IMPOSED OUTSIDER-ISM

In March 1999, there was an eerie replay of Cold War rhetoric and per-spective. Taiwan-born Chinese American scientist Wen Ho Lee was suspected of espionage when he was found to have mishandled sensitive computer files at the Los Alamos National Laboratory. A near-hysteria gripped the nation's security establishment; vital national interests were said to have been compromised. The U.S. District Court in Alburqueque, New Mexico ordered him held without bail. It was this move that jolted Asian Americans to respond in outrage. They realized that they were witnessing a situation reminiscent of the internment of 120,000 Japanese Americans following the bombing of Pearl Harbor in 1941. Lee sued the FBI and Justice and Energy Departments for violating the Privacy Act and for wrongly portraying him as a Chinese spy. Ultimately, the government's case against Lee was found to be so tenuous and predicated on FBI prevarications that, in September 2000, all but one of the 59 charges against him were dropped and the presiding judge apologized to Lee for the wrongdoings of the Executive branch (Lee and Zia 2002).

Both Lee's and the World War II Japanese Americans' experiences make starkly clear to Asian Americans that their membership within the United States is a fragile affair, that regardless of the longevity of their rootedness in the country, there is always some doubt about the strength of their allegiance to the nation state. In the post-September 11 climate of extreme national suspicion and paranoia, the branding of certain American citizens as perpetual outsiders has extended to cover those of Muslim faith and Middle Eastern or South Asian ancestry (these, because they are perceived to "look like" Middle Easterners). The Asian Pacific American Legal Consortium (APALC) and South Asian American Leaders of Tomorrow (SAALT), both Washington, D.C.-based organizations, have compiled extensive documentation on hate crimes against Asian Americans following the September 11, 2001 attacks on the World Trade Center buildings and the Pentagon. Being Asian American is no guarantee of being American. Kandice Chuh has pointed out that some groups are forcibly transnationed, that is, deemed to have loyalties to a country other than the United States (1996: 94). Such was the case with the Japanese Americans and Wen Ho Lee, and such is the case with Muslim Americans, Arab Americans, and South Asian Americans. Luis Francia conjectures that this awareness of one's tenuous membership within the body politic of the United States leads many Asian Americans to retain ties with ancestral homelands and to preserve memories of past histories and heritages in countries other than the United States (1999: 213).

In the pages that follow, I turn to selected Filipino/a, South Asian and Vietnamese American writings to examine the ways in which they employ a split vision (with one eye on the United States and the other on the world beyond the borders of the U.S.): an experience not unlike the double consciousness that W. E. B. Du Bois claimed was common to all African Americans. Asian American writers know that even while they may consider themselves theoretically to be Americans, they will always be also seen as Asians, individuals outside the U.S. body politic, with allegiances elsewhere. In the past, Asian American writers were careful to distance themselves from attachments to ancestral homelands in Asia (a stance best exemplified by Frank Chin and his ilk); today, however, increasing numbers of Asian American writers are drawing strength and creative inspiration from the influences of multiple geographies.

THEY DON'T THINK MUCH ABOUT US IN AMERICA: FILIPINO/A AMERICAN WRITING

San Juan's reading of Carlos Bulosan's writing demonstrates the pervasiveness of a split vision in Bulosan's texts. Bulosan came from the Philippines to the United States in 1931, when he was 17. His memoir *America is in the Heart* (1946) when it first appeared was seen as evidence of immigrant success (an unschooled young man had, within a short time in the United States, become a published author); it is curiously marked by a faith and idealism in the possibilities of the United States even as it relentlessly exposes the grim existence of Filipino migrant workers in the country. San Juan, however, sees it as a text that negotiates the local (United States) and the global in powerful ways, critiquing the much-vaunted ideals of American individualism and enterprise. San Juan writes:

> Charting in America the evolution of his life from his childhood to the outbreak of World War II, Bulosan succeeds in establishing connections between the multiracial proletarian movement in the United States and over four hundred years of dissidence, protests, and revolts against colonial impositions in the Philippines. His mosaic of Filipino lives pays homage to the grassroots initiative found, for example, in the 1931 uprising of peasants in Tayug, Pangasinan, which may be interpreted as an anticipatory emblem for the strikes of the multiethnic farm workers in Hawaii and the West Coast. This nexus in turn ruptures U. S. jingoist patronage. *America [is in the Heart]*, now a classic text of vagrancy and failure, becomes implicitly a critique of the official assimilationist ideology, the paradigm of immigrant success, that apologists of free-enterprise individualism continue to uphold. (Juan 1995: 16)

The tension evident in *America is in the Heart* between a longing for the ideal of America and a rejection of its harsh realities is echoed in much of Bulosan's other writings. A transnational pedagogical trajectory in teaching Filipino American literature would be to view the writing for its connections with Philippine writing in English and the deep ambivalence in both literary bodies to the cultural influences of the United States and the resistance against all forms of colonization. Writing in English enables an expression of the rage that writers on both sides of the Pacific would like the colonizer to hear –unmediated through translation.

Much Filipino/a American writing appears to be a corrective to the sentiment captured in Alfredo Navarro Salanga's poem:

> The only problem is
> they don't think much
>   about us
> in America.
>   That's where Manila's
> just as small as Guam is:
>   dots
> on a map, points east. (Salanga 1996: 251)

The politics of Filipino/a American writing is, by and large, a move to re-inscribe the Philippines in the consciousness of all Americans, who, because of the erasure from officially disseminated history of the United States' colonial and expansionist exploits in the Philippines, have no understanding of the imperial aspirations of the United States. The takeover of the Philippines marked the United States' entry into world politics and set it on the path to seeing itself as a global power. Because the United States could not reconcile its colonization of the Philippines with its image of itself as the champion of democracy and freedom, there was a selective release of information to the public, creating an impression among the American people that it was the United States' moral duty to take over the Philippines. The importation of labor from the Philippines for the sugarcane plantations of Hawai'i and the extraction of raw materials from the Philippines marked the typical power relationships characterizing colonizer and colonized interactions. Like all colonizing nations, the United States was able to justify its subjugation of the Filipino people by casting them as savages in need of enlightenment and civilization.[2] One can read Filipino/a American literature as a case of the empire writing back, that is, using the language of the colonizer and forcing the reader, as it were, to lock his/her attention onto the Philippines to see just how its residents both suffer and subvert the economic and cultural influences of the United States.

In the next few years Filipino Americans are expected to become the largest Asian minority in the United States. The umbilical cord between the two nations is still strong, despite the gradually receding U. S. military presence from the Philippines in recent years. Because the consciousness of most Filipino/as is still shaped so markedly by American influences, there is a thematic correspondence between the writings of Filipino/a American authors and those of Filipinos in the Philippines writing in English. Eric Gamalinda's writing presents an example of this confluence of Filipino and American influences. Born and raised in the Philippines, Gamalinda now lives and writes in New York, when he is not in other parts of the world on writing residencies. His fiction and poetry partake easily of both the United States and the Philippines, making seamless transitions from one to the other and, in the process, showing how inextricably intertwined the two countries are, at least in the consciousness of Filipinos and Filipino Americans. His short story "Elvis of Manila" is a case in point. In it, Gamalinda effects a skillfully ironic ricocheting of the United States and the Philippines off each other. A group of middle-aged immigrant Filipino Americans in California is putting on a Nostalgia Night "talent show" to raise money for the victims displaced by the eruption of Mount Pinatubo in the Philippines. The program consists of a series of acts in which the immigrant performers, including one Eddie Valdez, render with strict fidelity to the smallest bodily gesture and vocal detail the songs of famous American artists: "The Everly Brothers were to open the show, followed by Shirley Temple, then Simon and Garfunkel, Matt Monroe, the Four Tops, Barbra Streisand, Bob Dylan, and John Travolta. Carmen Miranda would follow, and the show would close with Elvis" (1996: 115). Back in the Philippines, Valdez had been known as the Elvis of Manila and had been immensely popular, enjoying what he believed to be a kind of immortality.

On Nostalgia Night in California, Eddie Valdez resurrects his Elvis of Manila act to a rousing audience of Filipino Americans of all generations. After the show, several youngsters crowd around Eddie Valdez for his autograph. It is in this intergenerational encounter that Gamalinda delivers a most skillful critique of the Philippines' obsession with American cultural icons:

"Man, that was *awesome*," one of the kids told him. "How long have you been doing that act?"

"A long time," he said. "Long before you were born."

"It's *great*, man," the boy continued. "Like, me and my friends, we were rolling down the aisles, you know? Like it was *wild*."

"Glad you liked it," Eddie said.

"Hey," the boy continued, "I don't mean to put anybody down. I mean, I thought everyone was funny and shit, but you were the funniest of them all, man. Like, you were hysterical, man. You got real talent." (117–18)

On the stage earlier that same night, Valdez had reproduced his Elvis act spurred on by the thought that "People miss us." The young boy's comment, with its harsh reduction of the performances to comedy, provides a sobering corrective to Valdez's nostalgic revival of a time in the Philippines when he was celebrated as an American rock idol.

The same kind of satirical scalpel cuts through Jessica Hagedorn's novel *Dogeaters* (1991), which is set almost entirely in Manila. The ubiquity of American culture, piped through television signals and radio waves to the Philippines, is unmistakable. Young girls, grown women, military leaders, gay club owners and bartenders, every conceivable type of Philippine urban resident, turns to American pop culture, American matinee idols, and American images of urban life to fashion his/her consciousness. Hagedorn is unflinching in her portrayal of the characters' dependency on these influences, and through the juxtaposition of several narrative voices and experiences, draws a parallel between the characters' inhalation of these tawdry symbols and drug addiction.

Born and raised in the Philippines, Hagedorn moved to the United States as a teenager in the 1960s, having imbibed a large dose of American culture. Hagedorn challenges conventional notions of Asian American, both in terms of the ethnicities she includes in the "Asian" category and the manner in which she pushes outward with "American," going beyond the nation state boundaries of the United States. The collection of Asian American short fiction that she has edited, *Charlie Chan is Dead: An Anthology of Contemporary Asian American Fiction* (1993), is remarkable for the range of Asian ethnicities it includes and the geographies it evokes. Of the 48 writers anthologized in *Charlie Chan is Dead*, Hagedorn writes:

> Some were born in the Philippines, some in Seattle. A few in Hawai'i. Others in Toronto or London. Some live in San Francisco. Oakland.

Stockton. Los Angeles. New York City. Santa Fe. Family in Panama. Singapore. Tokyo. Manila. Pusan. Chicago. Hayward. Boston. Brooklyn. Beijing. Mindoro. Washington, D. C., Seoul. Greeley, Colorado. India. Penang. Moscow. Idaho.

Asian American literature? Too confining a term, maybe. World literature? Absolutely. (1993: xxix–xxx)

Hagedorn tells us in her preface that Frank Chin declined to be included in her anthology, a decision that is not surprising when we consider that Frank Chin's early definition of Asian American literature made a sharp distinction between Asia and America.

THE GLOBAL REACH OF SOUTH ASIAN AMERICAN LITERATURE

The term "South Asia" encompasses Bangladesh, Bhutan, India, the Maldives, Nepal, Pakistan, and Sri Lanka. Meena Alexander perhaps best articulates the increasingly visible extra-U. S. strand in Asian American literature when she says, "the prose of my world [is] unfixed" (1996a: 53). She forces us to encompass worlds outside of the United States, to attend to lives other than our own, and to begin to see the interconnectedness of nations:

I think of the terrible bombardment of Iraq during the Gulf War, the countless quick and slow deaths, the massacres of children from on high under the gleaming aegis of the latest fighter-bombers.

... For this was also an Asian war and there were thousands of men, women, and children in the refugee camps set up in the Jordanian desert. I heard of a woman from Kozencheri who gave birth in the sand, then was airlifted, with others from neighboring villages, back to Kerala, in a wide-bodied plane, hundreds cramped together, cast out of Kuwait and Iraq, thrust back into India, into overcrowded houses, into temporary shelters. (Alexander 1996b: 78)

Alexander undoes constricted notions of what constitutes Asian America and the purview of its literature. For instance, her use of the term "Asia" to refer to the area typically called the Middle East – "For this was also an Asian war and there were thousands of men, women, and children in the refugee camps set up in the Jordanian desert" – means two things: that she is conceiving of the Middle East as West Asia (imagining the globe from a non-Eurocentric perspective) and that she is referring specifically to the numerous South and Southeast Asian laborers living in Kuwait and other areas of the Middle East whose lives were dramatically disrupted by the Gulf War and whose means of livelihood brought to a cruel halt. In both cases, she links the United States not only with Iraq, Kuwait, and other areas of the Middle East, but also with the small town of Kozencheri in Kerala and to other regions of Asia. Alexander globalizes Asian American literature; her vision ranges the world – Beirut, Bosnia, New York, the Sudan, Egypt, Tiananmen Square, India, England; and wherever the syllables of her "poems" cluster, she voices a powerful critique against injustice.

That metaphors of space and location play a prominent role in the imaginations of South Asian American authors is evident from the titles of three recent works: *A Map of Where I Live* (1997), *Falling off the Map: Some Lonely Places of the World* (1993), and *A Nostalgist's Map of America* (1991), by S. Shankar, Pico Iyer, and Agha Shahid Ali, respectively. Many South Asian American writers, though they live permanently in the United States, reach beyond the boundaries of the U. S. nation state to situate their narratives in places as diverse as Sri Lanka, Trinidad, the Sudan, Pakistan, India, Guyana, Canada, and Britain. Whether of the immigrant first-generation or of the U.S.-born second generation, these writers are producing work at prolific rates, some of it set solidly in the United States, some spanning several geographies.

Given that the United States' involvement in Asia has centered largely on East and Southeast Asia, South Asian American writing with its narrative and poetic locus in South Asia, historically the purview of British colonialism, poses a particularly difficult academic terrain for students and educators of Asian American literature. Thus, the adoption of South Asian American writing into courses on Asian American literature is gradual and a phenomenon of relatively recent occurrence. Pakistani American writer Bapsi Sidhwa's short story "Defend Yourself Against Me" (1996) illustrates the challenge of a pedagogy that engages with South Asian American literature. Although set in Houston, Texas, this story demands a knowledge of South Asian subcontinental history for a full appreciation of its impact. The history that forms an undercurrent to this narrative is the Partition of 1947, a bloody rending of the Indian subcontinent into two countries, India and Pakistan and the carnage shadowing that event. The mass migration of people (about 6 million, approximately) in both directions across the border between the two newly formed nations was accompanied by the brutal massacre of over half a million people; Muslims slaughtered Hindus and Sikhs, Hindus and Sikhs slaughtered Muslims.

The narrative's setting is a South Asian dinner party in Houston, at which members from several different South Asian nationalities and communities are present – Indian, Pakistani, Hindu, Muslim, Parsi,

Sikh, and Christian. The climax of the story occurs when two Sikh gentleman who have been invited to the gathering burst into the room in dramatic fashion, their beards undone and clad in extremely humble garb. They fling themselves on the floor before an older Muslim woman visiting from Pakistan and beg her forgiveness for what the Sikhs did to her and to other Muslims in the partition riots of 1947: "Maajee! Maajee! Forgive us"(Sidhwa 1996: 416), they implore, reaching out to touch the hem of her garment and "[g]rasping her ankles [as] they lay their heads at her feet in the ancient gesture of surrender demanded of warriors" (419).

The story makes a point about atonement and forgiveness. Such atonement and forgiveness would be hard to contemplate in the current climate of India–Pakistan hostilities; but here, in Houston, thousands of miles away from the geographies in which the tensions between the two countries continue to play themselves out, the extraordinary gestures become possible: both on the part of the Sikh men and on the part of the elderly Muslim woman, who initially declares that she can never never forgive their fathers and grandfathers but who ultimately consoles the two men by acknowledging that she forgave their fathers a long time ago, because how else could she go on living? Does this mean, then, that the United States is the site of reconciliation? Perhaps. However, in order to appreciate the extraordinary quality of this reconciliation both the instructor and the student must embark on a journey, however cursory, of the events surrounding the independence from British rule of the Indian subcontinent. In the global politics of the post-September 11 era, knowledge of subcontinental history by residents of the United States would seem to be almost a necessity of responsible citizenship. Such knowledge would presumably inform a willingness to engage with the complexities embedded in the writings of South Asian American authors and inhibit the tendency to make reductive conclusions about South Asians and South Asian Americans alike.

IMAGINING VIETNAM IN AMERICA: VIETNAMESE AMERICAN LITERATURE

At the heart of the challenge faced by Vietnamese American writers is the task of how to create a literature that is not a mere addition to the surfeit of existing representations of Vietnam, albeit in the context of the war. Le Thi Diem Thuy's words are both bold and poignant as she declares,

let people know
VIETNAM IS NOT A WAR
but a piece
us,
sister
and
we are
so much

more. (Duffy 1997: epigraph)

In the conversations I have had with second-generation and twenty-something Vietnamese Americans, what becomes apparent is the strength of their desire to learn about the homeland that their parents were forced to leave.[3] Until recently, the Communist government in Vietnam made it difficult for diasporic Vietnamese to visit, and this obstacle further fueled the sense of urgency that many young Vietnamese Americans felt about imagining their ancestral country. Thus, because much Vietnamese American writing in English is being produced by those of the second generation and those who came as children to the United States, the content of this literary output is and will continue to be marked by a strong thrust of inventing, conceptualizing, and fashioning Vietnam either from their memories or from the memories of their parents and relatives.

Andrew Lam's short story "Show and Tell" (1998) is a compelling case of this tendency. A show-and-tell exercise in an eighth-grade classroom becomes the occasion for the newly arrived student Cao Long Nguyen to inscribe his version of Vietnam over that of the classroom bully, Billy Baxter. Billy initially succeeds in making Cao cry, by bringing in his father's U.S. military uniform and other props to tell his story of Vietnam:

> He [Billy] unfolded the uniform with the name Baxter sewed under U. S. ARMY and put it on a chair. Then he opened one magazine and showed a picture of this naked and bleeding little girl running and crying on this road while these houses behind her were on fire. That's Napalm, he said, and it eats into your skin and burns for a long, long time. (Lam 1998: 119)

Cao, however, exhibits enormous courage, given that it is his second day at school and that he cannot speak English. He is an excellent artist, and with the help of the sympathetic Robert Mitchell, who is the story's narrator as well as Cao's assigned buddy, Cao grabs some colored chalk from the teacher's desk and sketches his vision of Vietnam on the blackboard:

> First he drew a picture of a boy sitting on this water buffalo and then he drew this rice field in green. Then he drew another boy on another water buffalo and they seemed to be racing. He drew other kids running along the bank with their kites in the sky and you could tell they were laughing and yelling, having a good time. Then he started to draw little houses on both sides of this river and the river ran toward the ocean and the ocean had big old waves. Kal [Robert's pronunciation of Cao] drew a couple standing outside this very nice house and holding hands and underneath them Kal wrote *Ba* and *Ma*. (120)

As the images emerge on the blackboard, Robert fashions a narrative from them, at Cao's urging. Dan Duffy not inaccurately likens Robert to a "ventriloquist's dummy" (9) who, even though he speaks for Cao, does so at Cao's bidding. The other significant fact about Robert is that because he lives with his mother and has no knowledge of his father, he, too, is the butt of Billy's ridicule. It would appear that Lam was careful to ensure that Robert not be seen as more privileged than Cao. To have done so would have been to reproduce the unequal power relations that Truong describes in the interviewer–respondent relationships found in the collections of Vietnamese American oral histories. Cao is the "author" of his Vietnam.

The narrator of Monique Truong's short story "Seeds" (1998) recounts his experiences in Paris as he looks for work as a cook. "Like a courtesan, forced to perform the dance of the seven veils," he finds himself having to answer question after question to explain his presence in Paris:

> "In Paris. Three years."
> "Where were you before?"
> "Marseilles."
> "Where were you before that?"
> "Boat to Marseilles."
> "Boat? Yes, well, obviously. Where did that boat sail from?"
> "Alexandria."
> "Alexandria?"
> "Yes, Egypt." ...
> "Hmmm ... you say you've been in Paris for three years? Now, let's see, if you left Indochine when you were twenty, that would make you ...". (Truong 1998: 24–5)

Not only does Truong remind us that France is one of the other diasporic locations of the Vietnamese but she also hints at the relentlessly peripatetic life of refugees cast out from their homeland.

Andrew Pham's extraordinary memoir *Catfish and Mandala: A Two Wheeled Voyage Through the Landscape and Memory of Vietnam* (2000) marks the bold attempt by a second-generation Vietnamese American to rediscover, on his own terms, the land that he left as a young child. Pham is not a nostalgically romanticizing "lost son" of Vietnam; in fact, quite the opposite. His reactions to his relatives in Vietnam frequently border on the comic, so Western is he in his perspective. However, this is a book that is notable for its deft combination of the United States and Vietnam and its double allegiance to both nations. Given the United States' heavy involvement in the politics of their home country, being in the United States is at one level a constant reminder to the Vietnamese of loss, destruction, and departure even as their new home becomes the site of renewal and hope. In depicting this hope, writers may temper it to render the collision of expectations with the realities of making a home in a new location.

WHO ARE WE?

Asian American literature poses a question of profound importance to Asians in the United States: who are we? It is a critical question for all Asians in the country – first- through fifth-generation – not only because they are frequently assumed to be "foreign" and "other" but also because they must understand the ways in which their supposed/perceived familiarity with Asian *and* American cultures leads to their being deployed as mediators and bridges in the service of U.S. economic interests. Reminding us of the egregious exploitation of overseas labor that makes possible the huge profits of U.S.-based companies, Evelyn Hu-Dehart cautions that Asians in the United States should guard against "the risk of being reduced to *compradores* for non-Asian American global capitalists, who merely use Asian Americans, with their cultural capital, as conduits and instruments to penetrate the Asian market [and] as subcontractors to manage production and labor relations at the floor level" (1999: 19). Who are we? In attempting to answer that question imaginatively through fiction, poetry, and memoir, Asian American authors challenge readers to approach their writings with a necessary complexity of perspective. In reading their works, the worst that a reader can do is to reduce the interpretative framework to binary opposites – American or not? Asian or not? Local or Transnational? Citizen or foreigner? Such polarities do nothing to engage the difficulties of creating and maintaining a civic society in these complicated times and neglects the complex of web of interlocking and inter-related themes explored in contemporary Asian American literature: nostalgia, memory, hope, rebuilding, journeying, erasure, family, gender relations, voice, neighborhood, place, belonging, comfort, refuge, departure, arrival.

NOTES

1. For Filipino/a American dissatisfaction with their position in Asian America, see Yen Le Espiritu, *Asian American Panethnicity: Bridging Institutions and Identities* (Philadelphia: Temple University Press, 1992), especially 103–09. Filipino/a American frustration came to a head at the 1998 annual conference of the Association of Asian American Studies (AAAS), when the Filipino/a American caucus forced a vote on a resolution calling for the revocation of the association's literary award to Lois-Ann Yamanaka for her novel *Blu's Hanging*. The caucus declared that the association's honoring of Yamanaka (this was the third year that Yamanaka had either won or been nominated for the literary award) despite her continued racist depictions of Filipino Americans indicated the AAAS's disregard for the concerns of Filipino/a American members. For a discussion of South Asian Americans and their past limited engagement with the Asian American category, see Lavina Shankar and Rajini Srikanth, eds, *A Part, Yet Apart: South Asians in Asian America* (Philadelphia: Temple University Press, 1998), especially their introduction "Closing the Gap? South Asians Challenge Asian American Studies" and Nazli Kibria's essay "The Racial Gap: South Asian American Racial Identity and the Asian American Movement"; Lavina Shankar's essay "The Limits of (South Asian) Names and Labels: Postcolonial or Asian American?"; Rajini Srikanth's essay "Ram Yoshino Uppuluri's Campaign: The Implications for Panethnicity in Asian America"; Sandip Roy's "The Call of Rice: (South) Asian American Queer Communities"; Sumantra Tito Sinha's "From Campus to Community Politics in Asian America"; and Anu Gupta's "At the Crossroads: College Activism and Its Impact on Asian American Identity Formation."
2. A selection of texts on the Philippine American War and colonization of the Philippines includes: *Amerasia Journal* 24.2 (1998) and 24.3 (1998) special issues on Essays into American Empire in the Philippines; Eric Gamalinda's "Myth, Memory, Myopia: Or, I May Be Brown But I Hear America Singin'," in *Flippin': Filipinos on America* (New York: Asian American Writers Workshop, 1996), eds Eric Gamalinda and Luis Francia; Luis Francia's "The Other Side of the American Coin," also in *Flippin'*; Thomas Peyser, *Utopia and Cosmopolis: Globalization in the Era of American Literary Realism* (Durham: Duke University Press, 1998), especially 142–51; Daniel B. Schirmer, *Republic or Empire: American Resistance to the Philippine War* (Cambridge, MA: Schenkman Publishing Company, 1972); Ephraim K. Smith, "William McKinley's Enduring Legacy: The Historiographical Debate on the Taking of the Philippine Islands," in *Crucible of Empire: The Spanish-American War and Its Aftermath*, ed. James C. Bradford (Annapolis, MD: Naval Institute Press, 1993); Richard E. Welch, Jr., *Response to Imperialism: The United States and the Philippine-American War, 1899–1902* (Chapel Hill: University of North Carolina

Press, 1979); Marilyn Blatt Young, ed., *American Expansionism: The Critical Issues* (Boston: Little Brown, 1973); *Mark Twain's Weapons of Satire: Anti-Imperialist Writings on the Philippine-American War*, ed. Jim Zwick (Syracuse, NY: Syracuse University Press, 1992).

3. The Coalition of Asian Pacific American Youth (CAPAY), a Boston, Massachusetts-based organization, is the largest organization of Asian Pacific American high school and college youth. Conversations in the 1998–9 academic year with CAPAY members have contributed enormously to my observations on Vietnamese American literature.

REFERENCES

Alexander, Meena, 1996a. *River and Bridge*, Toronto: TSAR Publications.

Alexander, Meena, 1996b. *The Shock of Arrival: Reflections on Postcolonial Experience*, Boston: South End Press.

Ali, Agha Shahid, 1991. *A Nostalgist's Map of America*, New York: Norton.

Appadurai, Arjun, 1996. "Patriotism and Its Futures," *Modernity at Large: Cultural Dimensions of Globalization*, Minneapolis: University of Minnesota Press, pp. 158–77.

Bulosan, Carlos, 1995. "If You Want to Know What We Are," *On Becoming Filipino: Selected Writings of Carlos Bulosan*, ed. E. San Juan, Jr., Philadelphia: Temple University Press, pp. 166–8. [Orig. 1946.]

Chin, Frank, Jeffrey Paul Chan, Lawson Fusao Inada and Shawn Wong, eds, 1974. *Aiiieeeee! An Anthology of Asian-American writers*, Washington: Howard University Press.

Chin, Frank, Jeffrey Paul Chan, Lawson Fusao Inada and Shawn Wong, eds, 1991. *The Big Aiiieeeee, An Anthology of Chinese American and Japanese American Writers*, New York: Meridian Books.

Chuh, Kandice, 1996. "Transnationalism and its Pasts," *Public Culture* 9, pp. 93–112.

Dirlik, Arif, 1999. "Asians on the Rim: Transnational Capital and Local Community in the Making of Contemporary Asian America," *Across the Pacific: Asian Americans and Globalization*, ed. Evelyn Hu-Dehart. Asia Society, New York: Temple University Press, pp. 29–60.

Duffy, Dan, 1997. "Editor's Note: The Dummy Speaks," *Not a War: American Vietnamese Fiction, Poetry and Essays*, ed. Dan Duffy, Yale University Council on Southeast Asia Studies, pp. 7–10.

Francia, Luis, 1999. "Inventing the Earth: The Notion of 'Home' in Asian American Literature," *Across the Pacific: Asian Americans and Globalization*, ed. Evelyn Hu-Dehart. Asia Society, New York: Temple University Press, pp. 191–218.

Gamalinda, Eric, 1996. "Elvis of Manila," *Flippin': Filipinos on America*, eds Eric Gamalinda and Luis Francia, New York: Asian American Writers Workshop, pp. 110–18.

Hagedorn, Jessica, 1991. *Dogeaters*, New York: Penguin Books.

Hagedorn, Jessica, 1993. Introduction: "Role of Dead Man Require Very Little Acting," *Charlie Chan is Dead: An Anthology of Contemporary Asian American Fiction*, New York: Penguin Books, pp. xxi–xxx.

Hu-Dehart, Evelyn, 1999. "Introduction: Asian American Formations in the Age of Globalization," *Across the Pacific: Asian Americans and Globalization*, ed. Evelyn Hu-Dehart, Asia Society, New York: Temple University Press, pp. 1–28.

Iyer, Pico, 1993. *Falling off the Map*, New York: Vintage.

Juan, San E. 1995. "Introduction," *On Becoming Filipino: Selected Writings of Carlos Bulosan*, Philadelphia: Temple University Press., pp. 1–44

Lam, Andrew, 1998. "Show and Tell," *Watermark: Vietnamese American Poetry and Prose*, eds Barbara Tran, Monique T. D. Truong, and Luu Truong Khoi, New York: Asian American Writers Workshop, pp. 111–21.

Lee, Wen Ho and Helen Zia, 2002. *My Country Versus Me: The First-Hand Account by the Los Alamos Scientist Who Was Falsely Accused*, New York: Hyperion.

Lowe, Lisa, 1996. *Immigrant Acts: On Asian American Cultural Politics*, Durham: Duke University Press.

Pham, Andrew, 2000. *Catfish and Mandala: A Two Wheeled Voyage Through the Landscape and Memory of Vietnam*, New York: Picador.

Rustomji-Kerns, Roshni, 1999. *Encounters: People of Asian Descent in the Americas*, Boulder, CO: Rowman and Littlefield.

Salanga, Alfredo Navarro, 1996. "They Don't Think Much About Us in America" in *Flippin': Filipinos on America*, eds Eric Gamalinda and Luis Francia, New York: Asian American Writers Workshop.

Shankar, S. 1997. *A Map of Where I Live*, New York: Heinemann.

Sidhwa, Bapsi, 1996. "Defend Yourself Against Me," *Contours of the Heart: South Asians Map North America*, eds Sunaina Maira and Rajini Srikanth, New York: Asian American Writers Workshop, pp. 401–20.

Truong, Monique T. D., 1998. "Seeds," *Watermark: Vietnamese American Poetry and Prose*, eds Barbara Tran, Monique T. D. Truong, and Luu Truong Khoi, New York: Asian American Writers Workshop.

Wong, Cynthia Sau-ling, 1995. "Denationalization Reconsidered: Asian American Cultural Criticism at a Theoretical Crossroads," *Amerasia Journal*, 21. 1, 2, pp. 1–27.

7

Forging a Postcolonial Identity: Women of Chinese Ancestry Writing in English

Mary Condé

From its beginnings, the tradition of fiction in English by women of Chinese ancestry has been entangled with ideas of disguise and fabrication, and with the deliberate appropriation of the exotic. Edith Eaton, one of the founders of the tradition, was the daughter of a Chinese mother and an English father, born in England in 1865. Her sister Winnifred was born in Canada in 1875, and each adopted another writing "self," Edith choosing a Chinese identity by writing under the name "Sui Sin Far" ("Water Fragrant Flower") and Winnifred a Japanese identity by writing under the name "Onoto Watanna."

There is no doubt that there was widespread English and American prejudice against the Chinese in the Eaton sisters' lifetimes, evident, for example, in the work of the traveler Mary Kingsley and of J.A. Froude, a prolific writer on empire (Kingsley 1899: 385; Froude 1886: 176). It was, too, a good marketing decision for Onoto Watanna to become Japanese rather than Chinese in turn-of-the century America, because, as S.E. Solberg points out,

> The Chinese were commonly perceived as mysterious, evil, nearby, and threatening, while the Japanese were exotic, quaint, delicate ... and distant ... the general fascination with the exotic (Japanese) was able to transcend racist ideas so long as distance was a part of the formula. (Solberg 1981: 29)

Amy Ling, reflecting as late as 1999 on "the white man's world" of her girlhood in the U.S., remarks that she is relieved that "aliens" are now extraterrestrials rather than Chinese (1).

Sui Sin Far, unlike her sister, is praised simultaneously for the accuracy of her writing and her racial loyalty, for example by Lorraine McMullen (1990: 150). Similarly, Frank Chin, in his polemic "Come All Ye Asian

American Writers of the Real and the Fake," congratulates Sui Sin Far
not only on fighting the "rampant stereotype and antiyellow racism that
were encouraging the passage of exclusion laws," but on her "contemporary portraits of Chinatowns from Toronto to Seattle" (Chin 1991: 12).
"Contemporary" here, however, means "1912," the year of Sui Sin Far's
short story collection *Mrs. Spring Fragrance*. Frank Chin is less comfortable with later Asian American women writers, and, as Elaine H. Kim
has suggested (1982: 198), has gone so far as to argue that the masculinity of Asian American men today is threatened by their
comparatively large number; David L. Eng has commented recently on
the gender imbalance of Asian American Studies (2001: 15). Many of
the works by women do decisively signal in their titles or subtitles their
female focus of interest: Jade Snow Wong's *Fifth Chinese Daughter*, Su-
Ling Wong's *Daughter of Confucius*, Maxine Hong Kingston's *The Woman
Warrior*, Katherine Wei's *Second Daughter*, Li Lienfung's *A Joss Stick for My
Mother*, Yang Gang's *Daughter*, Alice Murong Pu Lin's *Grandmother Had
No Name*, Jung Chang's *Wild Swans: Three Daughters of China*, Amy Tan's
The Kitchen God's Wife and *The Bonesetter's Daughter*, Anchee Min's
Katherine, Yan Li's *Daughters of the Red Land*, Gish Jen's *Mona in the
Promised Land*, Catherine Lim's *The Bondmaid*, Adeline Yen Mah's *Falling
Laves Return to Their Roots: The True Story of an Unwanted Chinese Daughter*,
Meihong Xu and Larry Engelmann's *Daughter of China*, Annie Wang's
Lili: A Novel of Tiananmen, and so on. It is noticeable how many titles
or subtitles also signal an interest in family relationships, although,
according to one critic, Henry Zhao, the intricacies of these are ironed
out for their target audience by women writing in English, who tend
to follow a neat chronological order and avoid complex questions
(quoted by Stanford 2002: 13). This list of titles has also jumbled together
novels and autobiographical accounts, and indeed the dividing line is
not always very clear. *Fifth Chinese Daughter*, for example, is always
taken as an autobiography even though it is narrated in the third person,
whereas *Lili* announces itself as fiction even though it draws on firsthand
experience of the suppression of the Tiananmen uprising of 1989. Joan
Chiung-huei Chang says of *Fifth Chinese Daughter* that it

> is widely read as the story of a daughter's desire to be free of patriar-
> chal control, her intention to be independent from traditional Chinese
> codes, her pursuit of female autonomy, and her efforts to claim indi-
> viduality as a Chinese American in American society. (2000: 65)

This could be taken as a fairly accurate description of the Chinese
American woman's novel in English, especially if we factor in a highly

developed consciousness of marketing. In her autobiographical essay of 1909, "Leaves from the Mental Portfolio of an Eurasian," Sui Sin Far had written,

> They tell me that if I wish to succeed in literature in America I should dress in Chinese costume, carry a fan in my hand, wear a pair of scarlet beaded slippers, live in New York, and come of high birth. Instead of making myself familiar with the Chinese-Americans around me, I should discourse on my spirit acquaintance with Chinese ancestors. (1909: 105)

Although she did try to make herself familiar with the Chinese Americans around her, Sui Sin Far did effectively dress in Chinese costume and carry a fan in her hand in her relocation of herself as Chinese and in her choice of heroine. In the story "Mrs. Spring Fragrance" when she writes home to her husband, she puns on *fudge* (she is going to make fudge and also fudge the issue of a marriage), but there is also an element of fudge in sentences like

> Greetings from your plum blossom, who is desirous of hiding herself from the sun of your presence for a week of seven days more. (1912: 234)

Is this the way a Chinese American of 1910 would write? Are we to understand that Mrs. Spring Fragrance is writing in a Chinese language and Sui Sin Far is translating? Mrs. Spring Fragrance is capable of speaking perfectly brisk, conventional English to other characters. As educator of her audience, Sui Sin Far is still the purveyor of a rather vague and unfocused exoticism.

Sui Sin Far, because she could have passed for English, is consistently congratulated on passing for Chinese. However, since she grew up speaking no Chinese language and never visited China, and her mother was an Anglicized Chinawoman, educated by British missionaries, this was essentially a flowery fabrication. Praise for Sui Sin Far and blame for Onoto Watanna surely arise more from the fact that the former aligned herself with a vilified ethnic minority than from any concept of "authenticity."

Wittman Ah Sing, the irascible hero of Maxine Hong Kingston's novel *Tripmaster Monkey*, who is modeled on Frank Chin, is characteristically obsessed with the idea of conferring authenticity on Chinese Americans as a valid and viable social group. Also characteristically, as he harangues his "loving community" of friends (Kingston 1989: 331), he begins to muddle himself:

When I hear you call yourselves "Chinese", I take you to mean American – understood, but too lazy to say it. You do mean "Chinese" as short for "Chinese-American", don't you? We mustn't call ourselves "Chinese" among those who are ready to send us back to where they think we came from. But "Chinese-American" takes too long. Nobody says or hears past the first part. And "Chinese-American" is inaccurate – as if we could have two countries. We need to take the hyphen out – "Chinese American". "American", the noun, and "Chinese", the adjective. From now on: "Chinese Americans". However. Not okay yet. "Chinese hyphen American" sounds exactly the same as "Chinese no hyphen American". No revolution takes place in the mouth or in the ear. (Kingston 1989: 327)

In the work of many women writers of Chinese ancestry the emphasis is precisely on the revolution which does take place in the mouth and in the ear: that is, on the transformations which occur when a bond is forged between speaker and listener. Storytelling, above all, is presented as a powerful transaction which is difficult to monitor or control. An example is the dangerously loaded story of the narrator's aunt, which opens, and colors the whole of, Maxine Hong Kingston's *The Woman Warrior* (1976). This aunt, made pregnant outside marriage, brings disaster on her whole family and is hounded into the murder of her new-born baby and her own suicide. This is certainly intended to be a terrible warning, and is accordingly retailed to the daughter as soon as she begins to menstruate; it transfers to the younger generation the bitter but necessary knowledge of retribution and shame (Kingston 1976: 13). Its power depends on the fact that it tells of a real event, but at the same time this undermines its impact as a warning. The aunt, unlike the characters in deliberately manufactured anecdotes, is a real person whose situation demands the daughter's imaginative immersion in it, so that the story, meant to ensure the survival of the clan, ironically reveals the clan as treacherous and contemptible. In *Tripmaster Monkey*, Wittman Ah Sing, ardently believing in the power of the story, tells his girlfriend Taña that

"I'm going to tell you a wedding story from the tradition of the Heroic Couple on the Battlefield that will turn you into a Chinese." (Kingston 1989: 172)

Unfortunately for him he has not properly studied the unreliable nature of an audience:

> Wittman thought that with this story he was praising his lady, and teaching her to call him Beloved. Unbeknownst to him, Taña was getting feminist ideas to apply to his backass self. (175)

He is right only in his realization that it is with stories that he pays his way in their relationship: "Got no money. Got no home. Got story" (175). Bette Bao Lord in her novel *Spring Moon* (1982) places even more emphasis on the role of storytelling as currency. Her heroine Spring Moon tells stories to help earn her keep among the peasants she joins before the secret birth of her son (Lord 1982: 274). At an emotional crisis a private story of the clan is the only gift with which she can repay her aunt Golden Virtue's gift of 52 gold coins (1982: 246). Stories have to be exchanged with absolute fairness between herself and Enduring Promise, even though he is never allowed to know that she is his mother (295).

Stories may convey truth, but once the truth is openly acknowledged, it becomes dangerous. Chinese emigrants, and the delicate balance of their stories, are accordingly threatened by their American-born children, as Kingston says,

> always trying to get things straight, always trying to name the unspeakable. (Kingston 1976: 13)

For example, in Amy Tan's *The Joy Luck Club* (1989) the little girl Lena is told by her Chinese-born mother Ying-Ying that

> my great-grandfather had sentenced a beggar to die in the worst possible way, and that later the dead man came back and killed my great-grandfather. Either that, or he died of influenza one week later. (Tan 1989: 102)

This is a story typically exasperating to a listener who likes to get things straight. Was the great-grandfather's death natural or supernatural? The anti-climactic conclusion is like the final revelation in Amy Tan's second novel *The Kitchen God's Wife* (1991) that the hateful Wen Fu is Pearl's real father – or that maybe he is not. But Lena is especially fascinated by the phrase "in the worst possible way." What is that? Her mother, in Chinese, condemns her daughter as one of "you Americans" for her morbid curiosity; Lena justifies herself by explaining to the reader,

> I always thought it mattered, to know what is the worst possible thing that can happen to you, to know how you can avoid it, to not be drawn by the magic of the unspeakable. (Tan 1989: 103)

This argument for the explicit is borne out by Tan's own narrative. Ying-Ying never relates to her daughter Lena, but only to the reader, the worst possible things that have happened to her. She does not tell the stories of her own misery which would have given Lena the strength to avoid her disastrous marriage to the odious Harold and the degrading nonsense of her work, itself a corruption of stories, which she loves only "when I don't think about it too much" (1989: 159). Within the time-span of the novel the revolution never takes place in Ying-Ying's mouth or Lena's ear which could have transformed Lena's view of her mother from "a small old lady" to "a tiger lady" (248).

When another of the American daughters, June, balks at explaining her Chinese mother to her half-sisters in China, Ying-ying poignantly advises her, "Tell them stories she told you, lessons she taught, what you know about her mind that has become your mind" (40). However, like Lena, June has known very little of her mother's mind, her baffling explanations making her feel that "My mother and I spoke two different languages, which we did. I talked to her in English, she answered back in Chinese" (33–4). Although this mother did tell her daughter of her own experiences, June mistook this for "a Chinese fairy tale" because the endings always changed (25), to the American-born June a mark of fiction, not of fact. Only when June goes to China after her mother's death and meets her half-sisters for the first time does the fairy tale finally come true, as the novel closes with the accomplishment of her mother's "long-cherished wish" (288). The transactions between teller and listener are completed only at length and after many false starts. Rose, the fourth daughter represented in the novel, thinks for years that her mother An-mei believes in fate rather than faith because she cannot pronounce the "th" sound in "faith." By the time Rose realizes her mistake An-mei has shifted her allegiance from faith to fate in any case (131). In *The Hundred Secret Senses*, unfortunately, this suggestive confusion has degenerated into a "joke" about the difference between death in Auschwitz or in "Auto in ditch" (Tan 1996: 94).

In Amy Tan's *The Kitchen God's Wife*, our suspicions should be aroused by Winnie's smoothly telling her grandchildren that the Kitchen God is "only a story" (Tan 1991: 53), since her life's experiences have taught her to dread the power of stories. When the Kitchen God was a man, he ill-treated and ejected his good wife; later, when he is in well-deserved misery, this good wife takes pity on him. In shame he leaps into the fire and is burnt to ashes. As a reward for his humility he is made into a celestial talebearer who watches over each household and flies back up the chimney each year to report on everyone's behavior. Winnie's (and

Tan's) moving of the Kitchen God's wife to center-stage illustrates the tussle with what Elaine H. Kim in her study *Asian American Literature* identifies as central: the contradictory messages of Chinese tradition for a woman. Is she to be a slave or a woman warrior?

Gish Jen opens her novel *Typical American*: "It's an American story" (Jen 1991: 3). It's also a typical Chinese American woman writer's story in its emphasis on a correct protocol for telling and listening, and on the impossibility of ever limiting a narrative's meaning. As Kae, the Chinese Canadian writer-figure in Sky Lee's *Disappearing Moon Café*, exclaims: "No wonder no one writes family sagas any more!" (Lee 1990: 128). *Disappearing Moon Café* is of course precisely a family saga, but, as Kae's friend Hermia so shrewdly diagnoses, it is not a story of several generations, but of one individual thinking collectively (189) – and that individual is the ancestor Gwei Chang. Sky Lee's novel may be contrasted with *Empire of Heaven* (1990) by the Chinese American writer Linda Ching Sledge, which was, she says, inspired by a family legend about her own great-grandfather. Sledge's great-grandfather occupies a fixed point in history: *Empire of Heaven* is "A Novel of Nineteenth-Century China"; Gwei Chang extends across the centuries through his search for the bones of Chinamen who have died constructing Canada, in the form of the Canadian Pacific Railway. He is chosen by the Benevolent Associations for this task because, as they tell him, "... you have been reincarnated many times. You have lived many lives fruitfully ... " (Lee 1990: 2).

It might be argued that, nevertheless, the strongest challenge to Gwei Chang as the controlling presence in the novel is made by Kae, since as a writer, who diligently researches her family's history by visiting China (40), she would also appear to wield time beyond a single human life-span. Yet, Kae remains a weak and ineffectual figure, not least because she dreams of a vulgar marketing of her ethnicity, evinced by the trivializing "movie poster" titles she concocts for her work, *House Hexed by Woe* and *Temple of Wonged Women* (208–9). Kae has been sufficiently infantilized by the psychic domination of her great-grandfather and its tragic repercussions, for her to be incapable of distinguishing a genuinely affecting history from a cheaply manufactured story which merely panders to the box office.

Just as many narratives by Chinese women, for example Jung Chang's *Wild Swans* (1991), Anhua Gao's *To the Edge of the Sky* (2000), Anchee Min's *Red Azalea* (1993) and Ting-xing Ye's *A Leaf in the Bitter Wind* (2000), end at the point that China is left behind, for Britain, the U.S., or Canada, so Sky Lee's work opens in Canada, offering no workable idea of life in China. This is hardly surprising in view of the fact that Sky

Lee was born in Canada, but in *Disappearing Moon Café* the tragedy is not only that Kae has no valuable links with China, but that she is successful as a Canadian only by selling a Chinese identity she does not really possess.

Sau-Ling Cynthia Wong complains of Amy Tan that she "Privileges a version of mother-daughter cultural conflict premised on the same static conception of Chinese American culture that first turned Chinatown into a sideshow," and remarks acidly of *The Joy Luck Club* that:

> what the Chinese mothers do in the course of their mothering is always heavily fraught with cultural significance. Being bearers of traditional Chinese values appears to be their only preoccupation and occupation: as what might be called "professional ethnic mothers", they are constantly demonstrating some ancestral wisdom or other to their daughters, and indirectly, to the readers. (Wong 1994: 257)

This is precisely the kind of scenario Sky Lee mocks: her women are linked together only as "women wailing around a timeless circular table" (1990: 187) as Kae later realizes, and only as sharing the same fate of obliteration. They have no "traditional Chinese values" nor "ancestral wisdom," and China exists for them only as a blank, a denial. The great wall of China which they build together is merely "the great wall of silence and invisibility we have built around us" (180). Ironically, in demolishing this wall of silence and invisibility, and attempting to demolish myths of the strength and endurance of women, Sky Lee is building another exotic "ethnic" edifice; what the novel itself contains and deploys brilliantly is a consciousness of its own marketability.

Larissa Lai, born in La Jolla, California, and now living in Vancouver, a Chinese Canadian who used to be a Chinese American, examines in her novel, *When Fox Is a Thousand* (1995) the implications of disguise for ethnic identity. It is narrated in the first person by the mythical character of the Fox – who takes on a series of disguises as a woman – and by a ninth-century Chinese woman poet, and in the third person by a narrator describing the lives of Chinese Canadians in late twentieth-century Canada: Canadians disguised as Chinese. It is significant that Lai draws attention in her title to the possibilities for a magical animal that dons a series of disguises. Yet, here she is still firmly at the heart of the tradition, founded as it was by Edith Eaton, who could have passed for English, but instead chose to pass for Chinese under the fabricated name of Sui Sin Far, and in this disguise became, as Amy Ling and Annette White-Parks put it, "a writer of multilayered visions, all frequently operating at once" (Ling and White-Parks 1995: 6).

The reasons for the multilayered visions of Asian American women writers are in themselves multilayered. First, they often live, as Amy Ling puts it in the title of her study of women writers of Chinese ancestry, "between worlds" (Ling 1990). As Victoria Chen, for example, recalls in her essay on "The Construction of Chinese American Women's Identity":

> Before moving to Canada, I was educated in a Chinese school for six years. ... I often find myself struggling between two sets of cultural realities, each with its own beauty and coherence. (Chen 1992: 226)

Second, they are constantly in danger of being read as representative. Jinqi Ling in *Narrating Nationalities* comments that

> whether Asian American writers consciously assume the role of spokesperson for their communities or warily guard against the limitations imposed by that role, readers tend to measure their works as either confirming or resisting the ethnic group's culturally assigned status. (1998: 226)

A female writer, Merle Woo, complains that this danger goes well beyond being read, writing bitterly:

> I get so tired of being the instant resource for information on Asian American women. Being the token representative, going from class to class, group to group, bleeding for white women so they can have an easy answer. (1981: 143)

Woo's activism, of course, depends on her physical appearance in a way that Sui Sin Far's did not; when the Chinese Canadian writer Evelyn Lau remarks in an interview that she might change into being a Chinese American, although she has lived in Canada all her life, she is clearly identifying herself through physical appearance (Condé 1995: 105).

Even critics become unusually aware of their physical appearance when writing about Asian Americans. Phillipa Kafka in her preface to her study *(Un) Doing the Missionary Position: Gender Asymmetry in Contemporary Asian American Women's Writing* is anxious to establish that her own is a kind of disguise:

> As a first generation American child of Polish Jewish parents who fled from the pogroms that preceded the Holocaust and therefore survived while all our relatives who remained behind perished, I am without prior knowledge of, complicity with, or connection to American culture and history. I am therefore inwardly unlike my mainstream sisters from whom I appear indistinguishable outwardly,

while I am inwardly more like women of color from whom I appear different outwardly. (Kafka 1997: xiv)

This heightened awareness of physical appearance is a third reason for Asian American women writers' "multilayered visions," since social realism for them already has an element of the fantastic, and interweaving the socially realistic with the fantastic is a way of conferring equal importance on each. They forge, in the double sense of making and faking, a postcolonial identity, by playing on the ideas of disguise and fabrication on which their fictions pivot.

REFERENCES

Chang, Joan Chiung-huei, 2000. *Transforming Chinese American Literature: A Study of History, Sexuality, and Ethnicity*, New York: Peter Lang.

Chang, Jung, 1991. *Wild Swans: Three Daughters of China*, London: HarperCollins.

Chen, Victoria, 1992 . "The Construction of Chinese American Women's Identity," *Women Making Meaning: New Feminist Directions in Communication*, ed. Lana F. Rakow, New York and London: Routledge, pp. 225–43.

Chin, Frank, 1991. "Come All Ye Asian American Writers of the Real and the Fake," *The Big Aiiieeeee! An Anthology of Chinese American and Japanese American Literature*, eds Jeffery Paul Chan, Frank Chin, Lawson Fusao Inada and Shawn Wong, New York: Meridian, pp. 1–92.

Condé, Mary, 1995. "An Interview with Evelyn Lau," *Etudes Canadiennes/Canadian Studies*, 38, pp. 105–11.

Eng, David L., 2001. *Racial Castration: Managing Masculinity in Asian America*, Durham, N.C., & London: Duke University Press.

Far, Sui Sin (Edith Eaton), 1909. "Leaves from the Mental Portfolio of an Eurasian," *Independent*, 66 (21 January).

Far, Sui Sin (Edith Eaton), 1912. *Mrs. Spring Fragrance*, eds Amy Ling and Annette White-Parks, Urbana & Chicago: University of Illinois Press.

Froude, J.A., 1886. *Oceana, or England and Her Colonies*, London: Macmillan.

Gang, Yang, 1986. *Daughter: An Autobiographical Novel*, Beijing: Phoenix; London: Macmillan.

Gao, Anhua, 2000. *To the Edge of the Sky*, New York: Viking.

Jen, Gish, 1996. *Mona in the Promised Land*, London: Granta, 1998.

Jen, Gish, 1991. *Typical American*, London: Granta, 1998.

Kafka, Phillipa, 1997. *(Un)Doing the Missionary Position: Gender Asymmetry in Contemporary Asian American Women's Writing*, Westport & London: Greenwood Press.

Kim, Elaine H., 1982. *Asian American Literature: An Introduction to the Writings and Their Social Context*, Philadelphia: Temple University Press.

Kingsley, Mary, 1899. *West African Studies*, London: Macmillan.

Kingston, Maxine Hong, 1976. *The Woman Warrior: Memoirs of a Girlhood Among Ghosts*, New York: Alfred A. Knopf.

Kingston, Maxine Hong, 1989. *Tripmaster Monkey: His Fake Book*, New York: Alfred A. Knopf.

Lai, Larissa, 1995. *When Fox Is a Thousand*, Vancouver: Press Gang.

Lee, Sky, 1990. *Disappearing Moon Café*, Seattle: Seal Press.

Li, Yan, 1995. *Daughters of the Red Land*, Toronto: Sister Vision.

Lienfung, Li, 1985. *A Joss Stick for My Mother*, Singapore: Federal Publications.

Lim, Catherine, 1997. *The Bondmaid*, London: Oriel.

Lin, Alice Murong Pu, 1988. *Grandmother Had No Name*, San Francisco: China Press.

Ling, Amy, 1990. *Between Worlds: Women Writers of Chinese Ancestry*, Oxford: Pergamon Press.

Ling, Amy, 1999. "Introduction: What's in a Name?" *Yellow Light: The Flowering of Asian American Arts*, ed. Amy Ling, Philadelphia: Temple University Press, pp. 1–8.

Ling, Amy and Annette White-Parks, eds 1995. *Mrs Spring Fragrance and Other Writings by Sui Sin Far*, Urbana: University of Illinois Press.

Ling, Jinqi, 1998. *Narrating Nationalities: Ideology and Form in Asian American Literature*, New York & Oxford: Oxford University Press.

Lord, Bette Bao, 1982. *Spring Moon: A Novel of China*, London: Book Club Associates.

Mah, Adeline Yen, 1997. *Falling Leaves Return to Their Roots: The True Story of an Unwanted Chinese Daughter*, London: Michael Joseph.

McMullen, Lorraine, 1990. "Double Colonization: Femininity and Ethnicity in the Writings of Edith Eaton," *Crisis and Creativity in the New Literatures in English: Canada*, ed. Geoffrey Davis, Amsterdam & Atlanta: Rodopi, pp. 141–51.

Min, Anchee, 1993. *Red Azalea: Life and Love in China*, London: Victor Gollancz.

Min, Anchee, 1995. *Katherine*, London: Hamish Hamilton.

Sledge, Linda Ching, 1990. *Empire of Heaven: A Novel of Nineteenth-Century China*, New York: Bantam.

Solberg, S.E., 1981. "Sui Sin Far/Edith Eaton: First Chinese-American Fictionist," *MELUS*, 8 (Spring).

Stanford, Peter, 2002. "The East is Read – All Over Again," *Independent on Sunday*, 27 January, p. 13.

Tan, Amy, 1989. *The Joy Luck Club*, New York: Ballantine.

Tan, Amy, 1991. *The Kitchen God's Wife*, New York: G.P. Putnam's Sons.

Tan, Amy, 1996. *The Hundred Secret Senses*, London: Flamingo.

Tan, Amy, 2001. *The Bonesetter's Daughter*, New York: G.P. Putnam's Sons.

Wang, Annie, 2002. *Lili: A Novel of Tiananmen*, London: Macmillan.

Wei, Katherine and Terry Quinn, 1984. *Second Daughter: Growing up in China 1930–1949*, Boston: Little, Brown.

White-Parks, Annette, 1995. *Sui Sin Far/Edith Maude Eaton: A Literary Biography*, Urbana & Chicago: University of Illinois Press.

Wong, Jade Snow, 1945. *Fifth Chinese Daughter*, New York: Harper and Row.

Wong, Sau-Ling Cynthia, 1994. "Ethnic Subject, Ethnic Sign, and the Difficulty of Rehabilitative Representation: Chinatown in Some Works of Chinese American Fiction," *Yearbook of English Studies*, 24, pp. 251–62.

Wong, Su-Ling and Earl Herbert Cressy, 1952. *Daughter of Confucius: A Personal History*, New York: Farrar Strauss.

Woo, Merle, 1981. "Letter to Ma," *This Bridge Called My Back: Writings by Radical Women of Color*, eds Cherríe Moraga and Gloria Anzaldúa, New York: Women of Color Press, pp. 140–7.

Xu, Meihong and Larry Engelmann, 1999. *Daughter of China: The True Story of Forbidden Love in Modern China*, London: Headline.

Ye, Ting-xing, 2000. *A Leaf in the Bitter Wind*, London: Bantam.

8

Border Crossings: Filipino American Literature in the United States

Angela Noelle Williams

The 1990 U.S. census revealed Filipino Americans to be the second-largest Asian ethnic population in the United States. Filipinos are currently the largest Asian Pacific ethnic group in California (Nakanishi 1996). The 2000 census is expected to show that the Filipino population in America has outgrown the Chinese American population, a community with a much larger country of origin, to become the largest ethnic Asian population in the United States. The first Chinese and Filipino immigrants seem to have arrived at approximately the same time in the seventeenth century, aboard Manila galleons plying the trade between the Spanish colonies in the Philippines and the Americas. The first Filipino in what would later be the United States was reportedly a sailor who jumped ship in San Francisco in the 1660s. Filipinos also settled in Louisiana in the eighteenth century (Cordova 1983: 1–7). However, Filipinos arrived in large numbers only after the Philippine–American war in 1903 (see Sucheng Chan 1991: 192–9). Yet, Filipino and Filipina American literature is among the least known and the least taught of ethnic American literatures in the U.S. academy and the connection between the Philippines and the United States is even less familiar to most American college students today at its centennial. The relatively recent controversy within the Association of Asian American Studies over the proposed awarding of Japanese American author Lois-Ann Yamanaka – whose representations of Filipinos have been called into question by some members – reveals the surprising invisibility of Filipino concerns even within relatively specialized segments of the academy such as the AAAS.

Despite their growing presence in both America and American cultural production, Filipinos are most often noteworthy for their apparent *lack* of presence in the institutions of the American press and academy. In "The Other Side of the American Coin," Luis Francia asserts:

> [I]t has become commonplace among Filipinos to talk resignedly about being forgotten even in a secular "paradise." But that tells only half the story. To forget implies an unconscious process, absent volition. Our insistence on forgetfulness lets America off the hook, as though we were making excuses for a doddering but essentially benevolent uncle. Ignoring and denying: not quite the same as forgetting. (Francia and Gamalinda 1996: 7)

Oscar Campomanes cites a number of texts that alliteratively attach the adjective "forgotten" to Filipinos, and asserts that "the spectre of 'invisibility' for Filipinos is specific to the immediate and long-term consequences of American colonialism" (1992: 53). As Amy Kaplan remarks, "The invisibility of the Philippines in American history has everything to do with the invisibility of American imperialism to itself" (cited in Campomanes 1992: 53). Overcoming this willed national amnesia when it comes to American colonialism is a primary necessity in the teaching of Filipino American literature in the United States. To read Filipino American texts requires not only students but the American academy as a whole to remember America's past and current forms of colonialism.

The denial of history when it comes to America's past in the Philippines and its impact on Filipino Americans is no doubt related to the fact that America's history of colonialism abroad is at such odds with American ideals. How can a nation founded in revolution be active in resisting revolution elsewhere? It is as if one national story, such as one featuring George Washington and Paul Revere, obviates any contradictory future national stories. While America's engagement in this paradox is certainly not limited to relations with the Philippines, as other essays in this collection reveal, U.S. intervention in and administration of that one-time colony is one of the most sustained examples of this paradox.

The fact that many of the American military officers assigned to fight in the Philippines were veterans of the Indian Wars in the western United States reveals a link with a much older form of American colonialism. Yet, the American era in the Philippines was a period of extended imperial control of a population that was consciously – albeit not very self-consciously – viewed by Americans as wholly distinct from the United States. After U.S. and Filipino forces simultaneously and successfully fought against the Spanish during the Philippine Revolution and the Spanish–American war, the Spanish surrendered to American forces in 1898. In explaining his decision to annex the Philippines rather than allow it to be self-governing or under an American protectorate, President McKinley famously pointed to America's duty to "Christianize" the largely Catholic nation ("Remarks to Methodist Delegation" in Schirmer and Shalom 1987: 22–3). Filipinos were assigned to the category of U.S. nationals, a category that simultaneously obscured Filipinos' status as indigenous inhabitants of a foreign land taken by force, and prohibited them from claiming United States citizenship. A year after the bloody Philippine–American war was declared officially over in 1902 (although some areas of the Philippines were never quite pacified), the United States began the *pensionado* program. This sent many Filipinos to the United States to continue their education and to further Filipino assimilation to American culture and ideology. The American-designed educational system in the Philippines and the *pensionado* program together led to the production of a whole canon of English language literature. The first year in which a course was taught at the University of the Philippines in any language other than English was 1962 (Gaerlan 1998: 98). Filipinos' unique status allowed them to avoid the exclusion acts that were aimed at keeping out Asian immigrants and to immigrate relatively freely with American passports until 1934 when the Tydings-McDuffy Act imposed a limit of 50 Filipino immigrants per year and set the date for independence as ten years away. Anti-Filipino forces also mounted a repatriation campaign, finally passing a bill in 1935 that offered Filipinos a paid trip to the Philippines provided that they gave up the right of reentry. As fewer than 5 percent of the Filipinos living in the United States took the offer, repatriation could be seen as a failure. However, the restrictions of the Tydings-McDuffy Act achieved some of the same goals (see Melendy 1977: 56–7). In the neo-colonial era that followed independence, education, economics, and other forces continued to bring migrants from the former colony to the former metropole. Thus, the initial border crossing of American forces into the Philippines begat the later border crossings of Filipino immigration into the United States.

The odd colonial status of Filipinos as neither alien nor citizen seems to have followed Filipino artists into the present-day academy. The literary institution often works as a kind of border guard, keeping diasporic literature out of American literature classrooms, deeming it as not "American" enough in its focus. One major problem confronting would-be teachers of Filipino American literature is to find an opportunity to teach the literature at all. The discipline of English-language literary studies divides itself among fields that are defined by national borders and century-long increments of time. The institutional imperative to categorize course offerings as "English," "American," or occasionally, "World" literature, leaves very little opportunity for the study of diasporic artists who may continually cross borders in order to live and publish.

A brief glance at a list of the most canonical English-language Filipino authors reveals the problem. Authors such as Carlos Bulosan, N. V. M. Gonzales, Jessica Hagedorn, Cecilia Manguerra-Brainard, Ninotchka Rosca, Bienvenido Santos, and Linda Ty-Caspar were all born in the Philippines but moved to the United States at some point in their lives; many continue to publish in *both* the United States and the Philippines. Should each of these authors be categorized as American writers or as Philippine writers who happen to reside and/or publish in the United States?

Bienvenido Santos' biography is a good example of the border-crossing reality of many Filipino cultural producers. He was born in Manila but came to the United States in 1941 as a *pensionado* where he continued his education begun in the Philippines, worked for the Philippine government in exile in Washington D.C. during the Second World War; he went on to teach both in the Philippines and the United States, producing prose and poetry for publishing houses in both the Philippines (New Day Publishers) and the United States (University of Washington Press), retiring to a life in which he divides each year between Colorado and the Philippines. While Santos is more privileged in his mobility than many Filipino authors, the difficulty that his works present to teachers working within the surprisingly narrow structures of "Twentieth-Century World Literature" or "contemporary American" course listings is not uncommon.

The relatively new field of postcolonial studies has done much to utilize existing English department catalogue listings such as "World Literature" – course listings which were frequently synonyms for European literature in translation – for needed studies of Anglophone literature that explicitly analyze the colonial context of English language literary production. However, this wave of change has done little to bring into the academy the study of an English-language literature and culture impacted by American rather than British colonialism. This Anglo-centric focus of the major forces in postcolonial criticism is quite understandable given the longer history of British colonialism and the British or Commonwealth origins of major figures such as Homi Bhaba and Stuart Hall. Yet, a lack of focus on American colonialism can be seen not only in American course listings but also in American publications: for example, the publisher looking for "totally new perspectives on colonialism" for a planned series who clarifies that he wants totally new perspectives on Australia, Canada, Ireland, India and perhaps Africa.

To be just, one or two Filipino American texts may be taught in a course on Asian American literature (if one is offered), and maybe one in a comparative course on Ethnic American literatures. Or perhaps Bulosan might find his way into a class on California Literature or "Literature of the Western United States" – both very rare in themselves. However, even in the Asian American literature classroom – one which is seemingly highly specialized and predicated on the need for inclusion and diversity in American literature – Filipinos are often surprisingly absent. Chinese American and Japanese American literatures and cultures generally dominate syllabuses, conference presentations, and some journals devoted to Asian American or ethnic literature.

While literary theory and criticism have been moving away from essentialist approaches to race, gender, and ethnicity, essentialism has found new life in the logic of how many of our curriculums and syllabi are designed. For example, the syllabuses of multiethnic literature courses which seek to expose students to a range of cultural experiences and productions often lead students to infer that an assigned text is representative of a whole cultural group. Teachers have to be clear that, while various texts are included to "represent" experiences from a range of cultures and genders, the texts themselves must be read as individual creations and not "representative" of a whole racial or ethnic group. This dilemma of representation particularly affects Filipino literature, as instructors will often turn to high-profile Chinese American texts such as *The Woman Warrior* or *The Joy Luck Club* to represent the whole of Asian American experience and expression as these are well known and there are many materials available to support the teaching of such texts.

In the comparative ethnic literature classroom there is an even larger dearth of Filipino texts, yet this may be the location where there is the possibility of the greatest change. Filipino American culture has as many connections to ethnic groups outside a specifically Asian context as it does within a pan-Asian construction of ethnicity. The histories of both Spanish and American colonialism, religion, hispanicity, youth cultures, socioeconomic and geographic environments in the United States, all work to connect Filipino culture with ethnicities outside the Asian American construct. While these differences have worked to render Filipino culture somehow "unrepresentative" in certain Asian American cultural venues, they can actually be used as a strength in understanding cross-racial comparisons.

Thus, the first step in the teaching of Filipino American literature needs to be at the level of program and curricular development. Educators must cross the national borders present within our own discipline in order to teach diasporic and colonized literatures. Rather than being seen as a weakness, the diasporic aspect of Filipino culture and literature can be used as a productive site for cross-cultural comparisons and contrasts with a variety of Latino, Asian American and African American cultures.

Lisa Lowe writes,

> A national memory haunts the conception of the Asian American, persisting beyond the repeal of actual laws prohibiting Asians from citizenship and sustained by the wars in Asia, in which the Asian is always seen as an immigrant, as the "foreigner-within," even when born in the United States and the descendant of generations born here before. (1996: 5–6)

The supposed "foreignness" of Asian American subjectivity has become even more of a factor as the Asian American community has been transformed since the eradication of immigration quotas based on national origins in 1965. Prior to 1970 Asian Americans were most commonly English-speaking and the descendants of a generation or more of American citizens. Japanese Americans, followed by Chinese Americans, were the largest single ethnic group among Asian Americans. After the 1965 Immigration Act, Asian immigration expanded and half of Asian Americans were Asian-born by 1980 and two-thirds of all of Asian Americans were born in Asia and had a language other than English as their first language by 1990 (see Nakanishi 1996: 27). It is this wave of immigration that has seen the largest growth in the Filipino American population.

Despite these changes in Asian immigration, the teaching and analysis of Asian American literature in English is still primarily the realm of the descendants of earlier waves of immigrants. Consequently or merely coincidentally, teachers of Asian American literature frequently choose texts by authors from more established Asian American populations that specifically claim an American rather than Asian identity. In some ways this helps to undercut the mainstream dismissal of Asian American literature as foreign or outside of American literature and culture. This preference for texts focusing on an American versus a diasporic identity can be seen in American publications as well as classrooms. However, all of this works against diasporic Filipino American texts.

The Manong generation of pre-World War II immigration, made up mostly of single males, brought with them memories of a colonized Philippines in which many of their loved ones still lived. Thus, their homeland figures prominently in their literature. The prevalence of the Philippines in contemporary Filipino American texts can be traced to the fact that the largest wave of immigration from the Philippines occurred at the juncture of reduced barriers to Asian immigration after 1965 and the establishment of martial law in the Philippines in 1972. Many of the authors who belonged to this later generation, such as Ninotchka Rosca, were emigrating specifically to elude political oppression in the homeland and to speak and write freely about politics *in* the homeland. Thus, the Philippines – rather than America – again became a primary topic for many of the more recent migrant authors. However, even second-generation Filipino American authors, a generation largely made possible by the rise in women's and family immigration after World War II, often focus on the Philippines in their literature. The fact that the presence of the Philippines is not just evoked in texts by first-generation Filipino Americans can be seen in the work of second-generation author Peter Bacho. Most of his first novel, *Cebu* (1991), is set in the contemporary Philippines with a flashback to World War II-era Cebu and Manila.

The persistence of the Philippines in literary representations by Filipino American authors can be seen even in R. Zamora Linmark's *Rolling the R's* (1995). In its recreation of late 1970s Hawai'i, Linmark's work bears the closest kinship with that of Lois-Ann Yamanaka in its evocation of a painful and knowing adolescence, its liberal use of Hawaiian creole, and its dense references to American popular culture. The latter characteristic it also shares with the work of Jessica Hagedorn along with an adept use of pastiche to knit together a diverse number of subplots and characters. However, even in Linmark's suburban Honolulu, the seemingly inescapable homeland returns in the sections "Portraits" and "Requiem." When Vicente is invited into the home of Florante Sanchez, the child of Filipino intellectuals, we learn of the murder of Florante's missing family members and the remaining family members' escape to the United States via a portrait which Vicente notices on the wall. Florante explains simply, "Some people didn't like what my grandparents and parents were writing about" (Linmark 1995: 61).

Linmark provides character development and simultaneously critiques both the previous colonizations of the Philippines and the Marcos regime through the description of one wall of the Sanchez home:

Thumbtacked on the wall facing the typewriter are three posters. A blindfolded Jesus wearing a barbed-wire tiara is crucified at the center; his lips are stapled shut. The head of the cross is inscribed with the date 1521. To his right is a map of the Philippine archipelago that is striped in red-white-and-blue and looks like the skeleton of a dog sitting upright; to his left is a cartoon of Mount Rushmore bearing the faces of George Washington, Thomas Jefferson. Ferdinand Marcos, and Charles Manson. Above their heads, in capital letters, is the phrase ALL IN THE FAMILY. (59)

Linmark's five-sentence description summarizes nearly five centuries of Philippine history, beginning with Ferdinand Magellan's arrival in 1521. His choice of decor for the Sanchez household critiques, first, the Spanish use of religion as a means of pacification and control; second, the neo-colonial stranglehold of the United States over the Philippine economy; and third – via the juxtaposition of Marcos, a convicted murderer, and two heroes of American democracy – the United States' complicity in the Marcos regime's denial of its citizens' democratic rights and, ultimately, the regime's use of torture and murder to retain its power.

In some ways, the predicament of the Filipino/a author can be expressed by paraphrasing the statement of Marlowe's Mephistopheles: "this is hell nor am I out of it." Filipinos are within the hegemonic realm of the United States nor are they out of it when they cross the borders between the United States and the Philippines. Filipinos in the Philippines do not yet exist in a space separate from the impact of U.S. colonialism on that nation. Similarly, the subject positions and general treatment of Filipinos within the United States are shaped by the history of colonialism in their (or their ancestors') homeland. Filipino immigrants to the United States could be said to be migrants within the same hegemony rather than immigrants from one distinct realm to another. Perhaps the best example of this phenomenon can be seen in the work of Carlos Bulosan. The impact of the contradiction between American values and American reality is described by Carlos Bulosan in a 1937 letter:

Western peoples were brought up to regard Orientals or colored peoples as inferior, but the mockery of it all is that Filipinos are taught to regard Americans as our equal. Adhering to American ideals, living

American life, these are contributory to our feeling of equality. The terrible truth in America shatters the Filipinos' dream of fraternity. (Excerpted in Bulosan 1995: 173)

Bulosan describes a process of interpellation which he went through *prior* to migrating, a process which claims him as an American subject even as it denies him rights as an American citizen.

The "American paradox" as Bulosan names this disjuncture is thematized throughout his most taught work, *America is in the Heart*. This book presents a problem for students unfamiliar with the history of Philippine–American relations, as the narrator's unending quest for an idealized America is sometimes read by careless readers as a tale of assimilation, one which is especially solicitous to American readers in its focus on American ideals. This is further complicated by the way the text crosses generic borders between autobiography and novel. As Lisa Lowe warns readers of the text as a kind of "ethnic bildungsroman": "Whether the novel is read as a narrative of immigrant assimilation or even as a narrative of successful self-definition ... both characterizations privilege a telos of development that closes off the most interesting conflicts and indeterminacies in the text" (Lowe 1996: 45).

Thus, once a space has been created in which to teach Filipino American literature, one must then turn to contextualizing it. To understand the continuing border crossing of American hegemony, one must first examine the primary forms of interpellation starting with the educational system set in place during the American regime. In *The Philippine Educational System* (1949), Antonio Isidro notes that under each of the successive occupying forces in over four hundred years of colonialism, including Spain, the United States, and Japan (during World War II), education was always used as "an instrument of colonial policy": "The schools were used for the propagation and development of the ideals and culture of the sovereign nation ... . If Spain zealously spread the Catholic faith, America, with no less zeal, inculcated democratic principles and ways of life among the Filipinos" (Isidro 1949: 2–3). Writing for the 1905 Census, Prescott Jernegan made American motives explicit:

The primary reason for the rapid introduction, on a large scale, of the American public school system in the Philippines was the conviction of the military leaders that no measure would so quickly promote the pacification of the islands. General Arthur McArthur, in recommending a large appropriation for school purposes, said: "This appropriation is recommended primarily and exclusively as an adjunct to military operations calculated to pacify the people and to procure and expedite the restoration of tranquility throughout the archipelago." (Jernegan 1905: 640; MacArthur also cited in Constantino 1975: 309)

The irony of democratic ideals being used to pacify and control a populace gets to the heart of America's paradoxical colonial venture in the Philippines.

The history of English-language schooling in the islands reveals the paradox in detail. Military personnel who themselves became the first teachers knew that teaching classes in English rather than the traditional Spanish would be key to bringing the Philippines into the American fold. Thus, despite the seemingly naive and certainly ignorant manner in which McKinley and others forged ahead in the colonial enterprise, the occupying forces immediately hit upon the most powerful way to interpellate Filipinos into a long-lasting American sphere of influence.

This interpellation was in part so effective because Philippine and American desires momentarily met at the juncture of education. In her study, "The Pursuit of Modernity: Trinidad H. Pardo de Tavera and the Educational Legacy of the Philippine Revolution," Barbara Gaerlan notes three major desires at work in the Philippine Revolution and later in the resistance to United States rule: nationalism, egalitarianism, and "enthusiasm for modernity" (Gaerlan 1998: 89). Pardo de Tavera and other *Illustrados*, an elite group who had worked to reform the previous Spanish regime, saw English as a way to achieve their goals of "modernization and social mobility through education which had been a goal ... which permeated the Philippine Revolution" (Gaerlan 1998: 91). The imperial power's institution of American-style public education did indeed bring education to many more people than had ever been served by the Spanish system, which focused on religious education for the common people and confined education in Spanish, the language of rule, to an elite few. English education did, at first, provide upward mobility for many Filipinos, as English speakers were needed to fill the ranks of the American colonial bureaucracy and the educational system itself. Yet, as Gaerlan notes, "as time passed and the finite number of positions were filled, upward mobility via English slowed. Additionally, thousands, ultimately millions, of students were never able to master it. The result was that English education eventually came to contribute to increased stratification in Filipino society" (1998: 99).

This growing national stratification is depicted even within the same family in Bulosan's "The Story of a Letter." In this 1946 story, a son, who has run away to Manila at 13 and then on to the United States, writes a letter home to his father in English. After the village priest dies of overeating and the only remaining literate son himself runs away to America, the father puts his faith in the narrator's learning English and translating the letter. However, when the school that the village builds fails to teach English, the letter is forgotten until the remaining son himself runs away to America. The narrator pays for his fare by taking a job posing nude for an American painter. When he gains enough literacy he has his father send him the letter but his translation is later returned to him with the message that his father has died. The irony that the younger son's translation is a faulty attempt to express his brother's homesickness reveals the great loss connected with gaining what the imperial center had to offer, including English. Only once the younger brother has given up his homeland, his family, and even his modesty, to follow his older brother's path, can he read and translate his older brother's sorrow at having taken that path.

Despite the period of Japanese occupation of the Philippines, during which time the occupying force tried to again utilize the educational system to interpolate the populace as imperial subjects of the invading state, the American-built educational system largely survived after the Philippines gained full independence from the Japanese, and then from the Americans in 1946. In "The Mis-education of the Filipino," Renato Constantino notes the lasting impact that the American-built education-al system has had on the Philippines:

> With American education, the Filipinos were not only learning a new language; they were starting to become a new type of American ... . Our consumption habits were molded by the influx of cheap American goods that came in duty-free. The pastoral economy was extolled because this conformed with the colonial economy that was being fostered. Our books extolled the Western nations as peopled by superior beings because they were capable of manufacturing things that we never thought that we were capable of producing ... . Now we are used to these types of goods, and it is a habit we find hard to break, to the detriment of our own economy. We never thought that we too could industrialize because in school we were taught that we were primarily an agricultural country by geographical location and by the innate potentiality of our people. (Constantino 1975: 48–9)

Thus, the importation of American education produced not only English-language authors but, according to Constantino, led directly to a postcolonial dependence on American goods.

In *Dogeaters* (1991), Jessica Hagedorn examines the habits of consumption of a whole range of characters and, in doing so, presents a family similar to that depicted in "The Story of a Letter" in the way that hierarchical structures produced by colonialism have fractured familial bonds:

> my brown-skinned, gray-eyed grandmother, is not asked to sit at our dinner table. When guests inquire after her, my Rita Hayworth mother simply says *Lola* Narcisa prefers eating alone in her room. Actually, my *lola* prefers eating her meals with the servants in the kitchen. She prefers to eat what the servants cook for themselves, after everyone else in the house has been served their food. While they eat *kamayan* with their hands, she and the servants go over the intricate plots of their favorite radio serial. (9–10)

In contrast, other members of the Gonzaga clan demand that the servants heat up a can of Heinz Pork 'n' Beans "because they're expensive and imported" (62). Hagedorn focuses on consumption habits as a way of rendering the borders between races and classes that bisect the Gonzaga clan visible. More importantly for the study of literary production, the status connected with the consumption of import goods includes media productions and the status-conscious family members insist on going only to English-language films produced in Hollywood, eschewing the grandmother's Tagalog radio serials. Without an understanding of the colonial history that could make race and even class issues divide a single family, students could misread this narrative as a tale of various eccentric characters. In context, Hagedorn's detailing of her characters' consumption of various foods, plots, and mythologies ties into her analysis of the intersection of Philippine nationalist and exilic nostalgias, colonial mentalities, desires for upward mobility and equality, and various dreams of liberation. Like Bulosan, Hagedorn provides a lot of cultural context and analysis in the pages of her text, but U.S. readers need some additional information on the original border crossing at the start of colonialism, the border crossing of various migrations, and the current crossing of goods, corporations, and master narratives across the national borders of the United States and the Philippines.

English may have begun as a national language but for various reasons it has become an international language. In teaching a diasporic literature that has grown out of colonial contact, a multiply interpellated literature produced by the increasingly global economy, English teachers need to move beyond national borders, including those constructed by our own discipline. This pedagogical border crossing requires us to think outside of usual, nationally defined categories and even outside the boundaries of the literary discipline as a whole as we reach out for historical, economic, and sociological materials to contextualize the literature.

REFERENCES

Bacho, Peter, 1991. *Cebu*, Seattle: University of Washington Press.

Bulosan, Carlos, 1995. *On Becoming Filipino: Selected Writings of Carlos Bulosan*, ed. E. San Juan, Jr., Philadelphia: Temple University Press.

Campomanes, Oscar, 1992. "Filipinos in the United States and Their Literature of Exile," *Reading the Literatures of Asian America*, eds Shirley Geok-lin Lim and Amy Ling, Philadelphia: Temple University Press, pp. 49–78.

Chan, Sucheng, 1991. *Asian Americans: An Interpretive History*, Boston: Twayne Publishers.

Constantino, Renato, 1975. *A History of the Philippines: From the Spanish Colonization to the Second World War*, New York: Monthly Review Press.

Cordova, Fred, 1983. *Filipinos: Forgotten Asian Americans: A Pictorial Essay/1763–Circa-1963*, Demonstration Project for Asian Americans.

Francia, Luis H. and Eric Gamalinda, eds, 1996. *Flippin': Filipinos on America*, New York: Asian American Writer's Workshop.

Gaerlan, Barbara, 1998. "The Pursuit of Modernity: Trinidad H. Pardo de Tavera and the Educational Legacy of the Philippine Revolution," *Amerasia*, 24.2 (Summer), pp. 86–108.

Hagedorn, Jessica, 1991. *Dogeaters*, New York: Penguin.

Isidro, Antonio, 1949. *The Philippine Educational System*, 3rd edn, Manila: Bookman, Inc.

Jernegan, Prescott F., 1905. "Education: II. Under the Americans," *Mortality, Defective Classes, Education, Families and Dwellings* Vol. 3 of *Census of the Philippines Islands, Taken Under the Direction of the Philippine Commission in the Year 1903, Volume III:*, Washington D.C.: United States Bureau of the Census.

Linmark, R. Zamora, 1995. *Rolling the R's*, New York: Kaya Production.

Lowe, Lisa, 1996. *Immigrant Acts: On Asian American Cultural Politics*, Durham: Duke University Press.

Melendy, H. Brett, 1977. *Asians in America: Filipinos, Koreans, and East Indians*, Boston: Twayne Publishers.

Nakanishi, Don T., 1996. "Politics and Demographics: The New Asian Pacific American Students," *Affirmative Action and Discrimination: Asian and Pacific Americans in Higher Education: Proceedings of the 9th Annual Conference of APAHE*, Sacramento, CA: APAHE.

Schirmer, Daniel B. and Stephen Rosskamm Shalom, eds, 1987. *The Philippines Reader: A history of colonialism, neo colonialism, dictatorship, and resistance*, Boston: South End Press.

9

Reading the Literatures of Hawai'i Under an "Americanist" Rubric

Paul Lyons

If I perceive my ignorance as a gap in knowledge instead of an imperative that changes the very nature of what I think I know, then I do not truly experience my ignorance. (Barbara Johnson 1987: xi)

I. NOTES FROM THE SCENE OF "INSTRUCTION"

In 1893, following the illegal overthrow of the Hawaiian monarchy, U.S. President Grover Cleveland, after whom no high schools are named in Hawai'i, deplored the fact that:

> By an act of war, committed with the participation of a diplomatic representative of the United States and without authority of Congress, the Government of a feeble but friendly and confiding people has been overthrown. A substantial wrong has thus been done which a due regard for our national character as well as the rights of the injured people requires we should endeavor to repair. ("President's Message Relating to the Hawaiian Islands – December 18, 1893" in Scudder 1994: p. 32)

Rather than repair the wrongs, Cleveland's successor, William McKinley, after whom a high school in Honolulu *is* named, claimed the islands as a U.S. Territory. More than a century later, as Haunani-Kay Trask argues, it comes as a surprise to most Americans that Hawai'i is an American colony: "the ideology that the United States has no overseas colonies and is, in fact, the champion of self-determination the world over holds no greater sway than in the United States itself" (Trask 1993: 180). This desire to *not know* about Hawai'i in specific cultural and historical ways remains the norm on the continent (U.S.) even in the wake of Public Law 103–150, "Apology to Native Hawaiians on Behalf of the United States for the Overthrow of the Kingdom of Hawaii," a Joint Resolution of Congress signed by President Clinton in 1993 (text in Scudder 1994). The apology, it should be noted, has been followed by a decade of lawsuits attacking Hawaiian "entitlements," and on their heels the Akaka Bill, which offers Hawaiians "Native American" status and "self-determination" *under the plenary power* of the Board of Indian Affairs.

Most English teachers who arrive at the State's flagship campus (faculty at UH-Manoa are predominantly continental *haole* [whites] like myself) are initially held by the convenient ignorance through which Hawai'i is unproblematically and irreversibly assimilated into the U.S. Those who feel an ethical imperative to begin "decolonizing" their thought through study of the grounds they teach on, are led by the process to reassess pedagogical practices in ways that are not simply extensions of (post)national reconceptualizings of fields and disciplines. In Hawai'i, where the indigenous people continue to struggle for a land base, critical introspection about how one's teaching of "American literature" reproduces or creatively displaces colonial poetics involves consciousness of *place*, or *knowing one's place* in terms of the post-annexation history of education. This involved a concerted program of imparting "American civilization" to ethnic minorities (Fuchs 1961: 283) and a systematic repression of Hawaiiian ways of seeing and and knowledges (Benham and Heck 1998).

The differences in the cultural poetics of texts produced in and about Hawai'i in such an educational/political climate inform contemporary divisions among Hawai'i's famously diverse population, and can themselves be foregrounded in "American literature" (AmLit) classes. Juxtaposed with representative texts in the expanding field of American Studies, they serve as a means of turning what might be a scene of displacement into an occasion for exploring the situatedness of reading practices, as well as the problem of students' often double-consciousness inducing relation to the U.S. imaginary. Texts produced in Hawai'i may themselves in turn be illuminated by exploring their relation (or opposition) to residual or emergent U.S. paradigms. For instance, a founding "local" work like Milton Murayama's, *all i asking for is my body*, a novel in which the nisei narrator escapes the confines of a Maui sugar plantation, can be read as an embodiment of the Americanist paradigm of self/society, or as fitting models of generational paradigms for immigrant fiction, or as a text in which an oppressed settler group, in part by identifying with a competitive American ethos, elides or displaces the indigenous people.

This sort of multi-perspectival approach requires initial, reductive taxonomies, which can only be touched on here by way of establishing contexts for a located pedagogy in Hawai'i, among the following epistemo-cultural traditions:

1. *Haole* settler culture, whose heritage in the islands is largely rooted in colonial legacies, eurocentric views and/or their critique, including canny oppositional regionalisms in a reenvisioned Asia/Pacific that fractures the "nation state imaginary" (Wilson) and a turn among longtime Hawai'i residents toward "local" and Hawaiian themes (raising questions of propriety, misrepresentation, appropriation).
2. "Local" communities, in one version, Asian-led and cohesively conscious of a journey up from a plantation heritage; in other versions, rooted in an awareness of indigenous priorities (Sumida 1992), and/or "post-local" and/or bonded through alternative communities, and/or affiliated with other sites of settler creolization and resistance.
3. Indigenous Hawaiian culture, with its sometimes primordialist poetic and historiographic articulations (Trask 1999) assertions of family relations among a pan-Pacific community, and more hybrid articulations.

"Literatures of Hawai'i" (LOH) refers to all of the above, and more, and is thus a sum of contestations; Hawaiian literature refers to writings by persons tracing their genealogy to before European contact.

Among these posited divisions "local" is demographically largest, hardest to define, and most internally fissured. As products and in turn purveyors of colonial education, with its dismissive attitude toward indigenous and "local" traditions, many "locals" identify as "Americans," ambivalently or not, and pursue self-inscription within "mainland" markets or paradigms. Others assert the "local" as a linguistic group whose language has long been repressed by schools and ignored by mainland publishers (Tonouchi 2002), or as a geo-ethno-"working-class"-anti-colonial identity resistant to inscription within "mainland" subjectivities (Okamura 1996). In some versions this emergent "local" sensibility resembles "American" regionalisms (the South, with its conflicted memory, structural class shifts, oral-based storytelling, or a certain Southwest with its consciousness of a tri-cultural base). In other versions, the "local" asserts a sub-national status, analogous to the ethnic cultural nationalisms that emerged out of Civil Rights movements (Fujikane 1994). From the point of view of the latter, the regionalistic Hawai'i amounts to feel-good nostalgia that fetishizes "small-kid time" (and is thus arrested at an early stage in a developmental narrative) and feeds American reconfigurations, and the sub-nationalistic amounts to a claim upon Hawaiian lands, or legitimation of Hawai'i as Asian or multicultural settler state. The exclusion and/or stereotyping of Tongan, Samoan, Filipino (locals) and Hawaiians by local-Asians within this posited multiculturalism has itself caused much contentiousness, as is effectively discussed in *Whose Vision? Asian Settler Colonialism in Hawai'i* (eds Fujikane and Okamura 2000).

Worth noting in order to understand the present situation is the fact that, however linked Hawai'i's literary movements may be to global transformations, colonial poetics are now subject to critique and counter-narration within a range of public institutions, including the university system and its traditionally colonial English departments. The Hawaiian language, banned as a medium of instruction by the Provisional Government (1896) and long in critical condition, is being rejuvenated in immersion schools (*Punana Leo* or "language nests" and Charter Schools). The Hawaiian Renaissance that began as a spiritual, cultural and political movement in the 1960s has produced both a varied contemporary body of writing, extending the possibilities of expression (collected in several anthologies, and in the Hawaiian journal, *'Oiwi*), and a vital scholarship that refocuses attention on the richness of nineteenth-century writing, much of which first appeared in the hundreds of Hawaiian language newspapers that circulated before the overthrow among a population with one of the highest literacy rates in the world. Such newspapers, begun as a medium through which American values were imposed on the islands, became a forum for native resistance as well, so that colonialism and anti-colonialism often work through them at the same time. HCE, the first language of 700,000 people in the state, derogated for a century within Hawai'i's schools, has flourished as a literary language, and often links "local" and Hawaiian forms of expression (as in Lisa Kanae's *Sista Tongue*, Kathy Banggo's *4-Evas, Anna*, or Joe Balaz's *Electric Laulau*). Local and Hawaiian, that is, were not always as contentious as they sometimes appear in contemporary formulations (Morales 1998), and Hawaiians often assert identification with both without contradiction (Okamura 1996).

II. OF "AMERICANIST" RUBRICS

Given the contexts sketched above, and the movement from left to center to dialogize U.S. curricula, one must ask what in the line of Americanist rubrics and methods resonates in Hawai'i? Here surveys –

and the anthologies they are organized around, sustain, and are sustained by (the industry shows no signs of closing shop) – might be taken as tropes for the "field" to ask on what terms AmLit remains conceptually viable, or whether, surveyable or not, Amlit can be creatively *engaged*. In this chapter, which emerges out of personal quandries in designing core, Intro/AmLit classes, and which does not refer to courses with primarily postcolonial, regional and/or Hawai'i/Pacific-centered content, I approach the above questions by imagining AmLit surveys (as long as we are called on to teach them) as sites for subjecting "national narratives" to an anti-colonial scrutiny that acknowledges their historic and *ongoing* relevance in Hawai'i without reifying nation-building assumptions.

In this I resist the temptation to begin courses catalogued under AmLit with a statement like, *There is no such thing as American literature*, as Gregory Jay advocated a decade ago. Jay's solving of the problem of the referent "America" by dissolving it is a compelling gesture, since regarding "America" as legimate referent *does* to some degree return one to "neo-nationalist" paradigms, call them *Heath* or New Americanist, which, located nowhere in particular, are winning the field. For me, however, teaching at a university built on *not*-postcolonial, ceded Hawaiian land, the evacuation of Americanist rubrics without an actually pulling out (at least of courses labeled AmLit from the catalogue) seems, if not disingenuous or premature, then not sufficiently (de)constructive.

Such "new" paradigms are "neo" in the sense that, while insisting on "America" as a Humpty-Dumpty of a referent – and providing materials for competing and even anti-nationalist constructions to emerge – their framing implicitly reinscribes regionalist tropes (in Phillip Fisher's sense of American Studies as characterized by a shift from "myths" to "rhetorics") in which the (post)nation's exceptionalism now resides in rhizomatic cultures played out against, under, around, in spite of a common enemy, the white mythology of Schlessengeristic America and its institutional manifestations in the State. Underlying this conception is the practice of extending U.S. citizenship (with due multicultural "difference") retroactively to the arts of annexed lands so that, once a people's territory has been seized through military force, or once a border has crossed people, their arts become anthologizable as AmLit. Only through such thinking, of course, could the "Colonial Period" or the texts narrating the scramble for and establishment of what Howard Mumford Jones called the "future U.S." have ever been considered U.S. Writing. Of course, it is also importantly the case that, without such "inclusiveness," one is liable to have the sorts of exclusive,

Eurocentric anthologies that for years simply erased the workings of colonialism, and the historical complexities of cultural clash and exchange in the Americas.

Hawai'i, however, remains tellingly peripheral to all such rubrics, and thus a vantage point from which the imperial dynamics of U.S. poetics, including internal colonization of and by settler groups, are readily visible. For instance, except for a few poems by two Asian American poets (Garrett Hongo, who left Hawai'i at age nine, and Yale Younger Poet award winner, Cathy Song) there are no Hawai'i writings in the *Heath*. This cannot be attributed to a scarcity of materials that might have represented Hawai'i in ways consonant with the *Heath*'s refinements of what qualifies as "literature" and/or "American," or its reenvisioning of AmLit as multicultural from (before) its putative origins. Nearly every entry in the *Heath* could have some counterpart from Hawai'i, from explorer narratives to sermons to indigenous chants, stories, and excerpts from any of a number of nineteenth-century Hawaiian novels. The point of this observation is *not* to lobby for the inclusion in AmLit anthologies of texts "from" Hawai'i (or to criticize the *Heath*, which I regard as the best of the AmLit anthologies). Rather, the virtual erasure in the *Heath* of Hawai'i as a place rich in textual production manifests anxiety about how to think/not think about Hawai'i within the parameters of U.S. literatures. Imagining Hawai'i as naturally part of the U.S. (as in the widespread use of the word "mainland" for the U.S. continent), but culturally "American" only on certain terms, fulfills political, economic, and psychological needs, which split around "Hawaiianness."

However, while Hawaiian culture has the status of fantasy from the "mainland" U.S. position, multicultural literary Hawai'i *is* increasingly assimilable to neo-American paradigms, continuing senses in which Hawai'i, since the "drive toward statehood," has been promoted as a proto-version of American ethnic pluralism. Thus, Jamie James in *Atlantic Monthly* lauded the arrival of the "Hawaiian Bard" in the form of Asian-local Lois-Ann Yamanaka, and an essay in the "progressive" *Honolulu Weekly* invoked James as confirmation of a "renaissance of Hawaiian literature" without referring to a single work of Hawaiian literature (Coleman 1999). The diversion of multiculturalism into "safe channels," that is, as Ang and Stratton have argued of the U.S. and Australia, cannot include indigenous peoples in an "image of consensual unity-in-diversity without erasing the memory of colonial dispossession, genocide, and cultural loss and its continued impact" (155).

In short, in my view neither the attempt to "extend canon and curriculum" (Lauter *et al*. 1990: xli), which seems poised to take in a certain Hawai'i, nor Jay's desire to "uproot" AmLit's "conceptual model" (Jay 1991: 264), nor the attempt to re-"route" AmLit sufficiently engages socio-poetic conflict in Hawai'i. Global/local or "Americas cultural studies" (Cheyfitz 1995) approaches, for all their usefulness in drawing out both colonial and early Americas rhizomatic diversity, and their flexibility in describing post-modern flows of capital and identity, sacrifice purchase in Hawai'i on questions like ownership and administration of land, funding for social and cultural programs, or control of the media and school systems. To consider evictions or prison demographics in Hawai'i, for instance, is to recall continental racism, and at least consider Eliot Butler Evans' assertion that "Rodney King was beaten as a member of an American minority, not as a member of the black diaspora" (quoted in Wong 1995: 18). The point here is not in turn to minimize senses in which Hawai'i is and has been subject to globalizing forces, but to suggest that a force-field of "American" ideologies continues to attract, shape, and hold students in Hawai'i. To that extent, the *Heath*, taken as an index of structural and institutional transformations in the "Americanist" field, remains an appropriate and useful rubric under which – using supplemental LOH readings – to locate a pedagogy in Hawai'i.

III. ASPECTS OF A LOCATED PEDAGOGY

To practice a located pedagogy means to approach a given topic (here, AmLit and how it speaks in/to Hawai'i) in relation to the cultural priorities, conversations, histories, and narratives of a particular place. Implicitly or explicitly, a located pedagogy opposes the imposition of (trans)national agendas (including critical/methodological ones) upon a regional, local, and/or indigenous population. Located pedagogy prioritizes the histories of a place, and, in terms of cultural analysis, becomes *critical* by attending to ways in which these *vertical* or historical structures engage *horizontal* or contemporary movements along the evolving horizons of the regional (Asia/Pacific *or* Pan-Pacific), national-state imaginary (U.S.), and global.

My own attempt at "located pedagogy" involves three aspects, conceived of as interanimating rather than sequenced:

1. A tracking and interior critique ("inside narrative") of American institutions and self-imaginings as they emerge, are consolidated, and circulate through "American" writings and out into the Pacific

from the time of Euroamerican–Native contact through White America's "process of organizing American coherence through a distancing of African[ist]" and other "presences" and idioms (Morrison 1992: 8).

2. An exploration of how attention to the contingencies or "location" of aesthetic response, as well as an appreciation of the difficulties of reading – let alone reading interculturally – might keep one's politics in the classroom (relatively) honest.

3. The introduction of the multiple and competing traditions of the "Literatures of Hawai'i," indigenous and endemic in particular, as complicitous with U.S. hegemony, or as counter-texts to orientalist and U.S. national narratives, and/or as alter/Native poetics.

My first emphasis is based on a belief that, whether in the Western psychoanalytic sense, or in a Hawaiian sense of "ho'oponopono" (to make something right through healing discussion), creative under-standing and engagement must include an engagement of the sources of the present situation. This is not, in my view, simply the task of "Early American literature" courses; rather, the more contemporary a text the more massive the histories behind it. Most of my students *are* American and it is appropriate that we clarify our relations to U.S. tele-ologies. I have found it valuable, for instance, to begin AmLit classes with the double-edged question, "How did Hawai'i become part of the United States?" (through what political processes and military acts, and with what effects to the consciousnesses and self-narration of people in Hawai'i), and to suggest over a semester how an answer might be augmented by an assessment of both centuries of continental ideolo-gical formation, and the linked and analogous cultural dynamics through which a colonizing power's importation of labor to a native place contributed to a contentious multiculturalism and hybrid sub-jectivities, expressed textually through competing or conflicted claims upon Hawaiian locality.

Of initial value for anatomizing American Pacific Orientalism, and encouraging a located "historical sense" of U.S. imperialism long missing from the study of American culture (Kaplan 1993), are works like Edgar Allan Poe's fetishistic *The Narrative of Arthur Gordon Pym* (1838) and Herman Melville's psychosomatic *Typee* (1846). Poe's text exemplifies ways in which scientific racism underlies a nascent American capitalism linking factions of the U.S. to each other and to the Pacific islands and Asia, while *Typee* (in addition to a number of vicious swipes at Hawaiian royalty) at once perpetuates the touristic, escapist tradition of literary perceptions of the Pacific (that persists powerfully) and inaugurates a subversive, anti-imperialist critique that matures into the vision of American exploitative labor-relations in the conquest of the resources of the Pacific in *Moby-Dick*. In ideologically saturated "travelogues" like these, and subsequently elsewhere, images of islanders, African Americans, and Native Americans were increasingly interconnected, so that during the drive to annex Hawai'i, U.S. cartoons represented Queen Lili'uokalani as African American.

My second emphasis, on reading, develops connections among aesthetics, ideology, and location, while acknowledging both the anti-mimetic strangenesses and artful mobilization of culturally varied forms through which language relates the world. In one sense, I follow Barbara Johnson's recuperative aesthetics in regarding literature as a mode of language "where impasses can be kept and opened for examination, where questions can be guarded and not forced into a premature validation of the available paradigms" (Johnson 1987: 15). At the same time, the holding open of texts happens within coordinates, and one responsibility of located pedagogy is to foster vigilance about how texts position readers along outsider/insider continuums, in particular through their regimes of naming. Only with such awareness can students consciously position texts, and analyze how canons and methods disenfranchise and disorient populations by encouraging them toward semiotic grids that resist or conscript them. There is considerable force in demonstrating the workings of "rhetorical county" in literature, or the textual borders beyond which explanation becomes required, and then considering, alternatively, the possibilities of achieving a widened syntax of being through modes of textual travel.

My third emphasis involves both a comparative and multiperspectival mode, juxtaposing LOH texts with continental texts at all levels and phases of Amlit courses, while considering the positioning of LOH works themselves in relation to Hawaiian issues, forms, and expressive traditions (as in Rodney Morales's uses of Hawaiian shark tales in *When the Shark Bites* or Gary Pak's sense of Hawaiian cultural forms as underlying the healthy construction of "local" communities in *The Valley of the Dead Air*). In the multi-perspectival mode, one might approach Hawaiian writer John Dominis Holt's tri-lingual (English, HCE, and Hawaiian) novel, *Waimea Summer*, as a pastoral text in the continental coming-of-age tradition, as a more localized expression of divided subjectivity and allegiance within interlinked multi-and mixed-ethnic communities, or as a text whose heart remains steeped in the Hawaiian culture it only seems to flee from in the end.

The comparative mode emphasizes the contingency of literary status and the ethics of canons and representation. For instance, reading Jack

London's "Ko'olau the Leper" alongside Pi'ilani Ko'olau's "The True Story of Kalauiko'olau," and comparing the two in terms of even familiar Western categories like stylistic richness, emotive force, characterization, and thematics demonstrates the potential violence of teaching texts like Cooper's *Last of the Mohicans* or Hemingway's "Indian Camp" without teaching countertexts from the perspective of those represented. That many Hawai'i-educated students have read London, and few have heard of Pi'ilani, brings home the shameful dynamics of a colonial education, a point effectively argued in essays by Ku'ualoha Ho'omanawanui and Dennis Kawaharada.

Today the comparative approach seems ethically and aesthetically necessary. As Rob Wilson writes, "post-modern justice demands" a court of consciousness in which the *mo'olelo* (Hawaiian story) as expression of another system of creativity, belief and *praxis* can not only get a hearing but "be preserved, and circulated for alternative knowledge" (Wilson 2000: 210), including knowledge about the value of stories. In fact, without alternative forms of knowledge and ways of seeing, one's experience of a *mo'olelo* will be superficial. As with other indigenous literatures, each story is packed with references, each with a story behind it that alludes to further stories, so that "one story is only the beginning of many stories" (Silko 1981: 56). Such stories, as Leslie Marmon Silko puts it, are in multiple-sense "maps" (64), full of thoughts on ethical leadership, spiritual values, and stewardship of land. To start an Early American Literature class with a reading like Dennis Kawaharada's of the Hawaiian, "He Mele No Kane," suggests to students opening the *Heath* to a Native American chant some of the kinds of cultural knowledge one would need to begin, in Langston Hughes' phrase, to "listen fluently," and suggests that such knowledge surrounds Hawai'i's readers in storied landscapes. Kawaharada frames his essays with a discussion of his own departure point from realizing that he had learned nothing about "Hawaiian traditions during [his] colonial education in Hawai'i" and was thus in a sense a "third-generation tourist traveling through a tropic landscape, ignorant of [its] stories" (Kawaharada 1999: 5). Becoming aware of such stories, and of what is lost when one thinks of land by the colonial name rather than the indigenous one ("Chinaman's Hat" rather than Mokoli'i), can be a stimulus for students to rethink their relation to the land they grew up on or occupy.

The sense of Native Hawaiian literature as informed by an alternative epistemology and frame of reference, and thus requiring modified reading practices, can be initially overwhelming with a text like S. N. Hale'ole's *La'ieikawai* (1864). The novel calls in its Preface for a Native

Hawaiian literature that would look superficially "like those of the foreigners," at once claiming and modifying the form in its attempt to preserve things Hawaiian for future generations. The ways in which Hale'ole's text is embedded in its historical period are complex, and the text rewards the reader in some proportion to knowledge of Hawaiian culture, drawing the reader far enough in at each phase to run up against further complexities. To look at its mentions of particular birds, topographical features, winds, and to feel that there are further stories behind each reference, can step up and frustrate the desire to know. *La'ieikawai* abounds in magical scenes (a girl followed by a rainbow), marvelous contests (one champion's *mo'o* biting off the ears of the other's fighting dog), and visual images (a woman balancing on the wings of a bird), but it is so textured with figurative language, puns, and references that a reader like myself feels at once enticed and productively disabled.

Particularly enabling to local students (and instructors) for conceptualizing the ongoing potential of texts like Hale'ole's to modify habits of perception and reading is Richard Hamasaki's essay, "Mountains in the Sea," (1993) which presents a *verticalist* vision of Hawaiian traditions as percolating up and through and sometimes synthesizing with the various sedimented layers of post-contact history (including the records left by explorers, missionaries, whalers, colonialists, immigrants). Such a vision never denies the potential value of what crosses the beach into Hawai'i, but recurrently insists on the precondition to any ethical and informed assessment of the epistemological stakes behind the encounter of attending to the indigenous. Those providing scholarly resources for hearing where indigenous works *come from*, and for decolonizing reading practices, insist that all epistemological contestation within representation is importantly contemporary, and that any postcolonial analysis of Hawaiian or "local" literature not grounded in the vertical will tend toward committing the violations it ethically deplores: ungrounded critiques of globalization's effect on the "local," that is, tend to serve the ends of globalization itself.

REFERENCES

Benham, Maenette and Ronald Heck, 1998. *Culture and Educational Policy in Hawai'i*, Mahwah, New Jersey: Lawrence Erlbaum.

Cheyfitz, Eric, 1995. "What Work is There for Us To Do? American Literary Studies of Americas Cultural Studies," *American Literature*, 67.4 (December).

Coleman, Stuart, 1999. "Local Literati," *Honolulu Weekly*, 3/3.

Fisher, Philip, 1992. "American Literary and Cultural Studies since the Civil War," *Redrawing the Boundaries: The Transformation of English and American Literary Studies*, eds Stephen Greenblatt and Giles Gunn, New York: The Modern Language Association of America, pp. 232–50.

Fuchs, Lawrence, 1961. *Hawai'i Pono*, New York: Harcourt, Brace & World.

Fujikane, Candace, 1994. "Between Nationalisms: Hawai'i's Local Nation and Its Troubled Racial Paradise," *Critical Mass: A Journal of Asian American Cultural Criticism*, 1:2, pp. 23–57.

Fujikane, Candace and Jonathan Okamura, eds, 2000. *Whose Vision? Asian Settler Colonialism in Hawai'i*, Special issue of *Critical Mass*, 26.2.

Hale'ole, S. N., 1864, *The Hawaiian Romance of Laieikawai*, trans. Martha Beckwith, Washington D.C.: Government Printing Office, 1919.

Hamasaki, Richard, 1993. "Mountains in the Sea: Emerging Literatures of Hawai'i," *Readings in Pacific Literature*, ed. Paul Sharrad, Wollongong, Australia: University of Wollongong.

Ho'omanawanui, Ku'ualoha, 2000. "Hero Or Outlaw: Two Views of Kaluaiko'olau," in *Navigating Islands and Continents: Conversations and Contestations in and around the Pacific*, eds Cindy Franklin, Ruth Hsu, Suzanne Kosanke, Honolulu: University of Hawai'i and the East-West Center.

James, Jamie, 1999. "This Hawai'i is Not for Tourists," *Atlantic Monthly* (March).

Jay, Gregory, 1991. "The End of American Literature: Toward a Multicultural Practice," *College English*, 53, pp. 264–81.

Johnson, Barbara, 1987. *The Feminist Difference*, Baltimore: Johns Hopkins University Press.

Kame'eleihiwa, Lilikala, 1992. *Native Lands and Foreign Desires*, Honolulu: Bishop Museum Press.

Kaplan, Amy, 1993. "'Left Alone with America': The Absense of Empire in the Study of American Culture," *Cultures of United States Imperialism*, eds Amy Kaplan and Donald Pease, Durham and London: Duke University Press.

Kawaharada, Dennis, 1999. *Storied Landscape: Hawaiian Literature and Place*, Honolulu: Noio.

Lauter, Paul *et al.*, eds, 1990. *Heath Anthology of American Literature*, Lexington MA: D.C. Heath.

Morales, Rodney, 1998. "Literature in Hawai'i: a Contentious Multiculturalism" in *Multicultural Hawai'i: The Fabric of a Multiethnic Society*, ed. Michael Haas, New York: Garland.

Morrison, Toni, 1992. *Playing in the Dark: Whiteness and the Literary Imagination*, Cambridge: Harvard University Press.

Okamura, Jonathan, 1996. "Why There are No Asian Americans in Hawai'i: The Continuing Significance of Local Identity," *Our History Our Way: An Ethnic Studies Anthology*, eds Grey Yee Mark, Davianna Pomaika'i McGregor, Linda A. Revilla, Dubuque, Iowa: Kendall/Hunt.

Rosa, John P., 2000. "Local Story: The Massie Case Narrative and the Cultural Production of Local Identity in Hawai'i" in *Whose Vision? Asian Settler Colonialism in Hawai'i*, Special issue of *Critical Mass*, 26.2, ed. Candace Fujikane and Jonathan Okamura, pp. 93–114.

Scudder, Richard J., ed., 1994. *The Apology to Native Hawaiians*, Honolulu: Ka'imi Pono Press.

Silko, Leslie Marmon, 1981. "Language and Literature from a Pueblo Indian Perspective," *English Literature: Opening Up the Canon*, eds Leslie Fiedler and Houston Baker, Baltimore: Johns Hopkins University Press.

Stratton, Jon and Ien Ang, 1994. "Multicultural Imagined Communities: Cultural Difference and National Identity in Australia and the USA," *Critical Multiculturalism*, ed. Tom O'Regan, *Continuum: The Australian Journal of Media Culture*, 8:2, pp. 124–58.

Sumida, Stephen, 1991. *And the View from the Shore*, Seattle: University of Washington Press.

Sumida, Stephen, 1992. "Sense of Place, History, and the Concept of the 'Local' in Hawaii's Asian/Pacific Literatures," *Reading the Literatures of Asian America*, eds Shirley Geok-lin Lim and Amy Ling, Philadelphia: Temple University Press, pp. 215–37.

Tonouchi, Lee, 2002. *Living Pidgin: Contemplations on Pidgin Culture*, Honolulu: Tinfish.

Trask, Haunani-Kay, 1993. *From a Native Daughter: Colonialism & Sovereignty in Hawai'i*, Monroe, Maine: Common Courage.

Trask, Haunani-Kay, 1999. "Decolonizing Hawaiian Literature" in *Inside/Out: Literature, Cultural Politics, and Identity in the New Pacific*, eds Vilsoni Hereniko and Rob Wilson, Lanham, Maryland: Rowman & Littlefield, pp. 167–82.

Wilson, Rob, 2000. *Reimagining the American Pacific: From South Pacific to Bamboo Ridge and Beyond*, Durham: Duke University Press.

Wong, Sau-Ling C., 1995. "Denationalization Reconsidered: Asian American Criticism at a Theoretical Crossroads," *Amerasia Journal*, 21:1 & 2.

Part 3

Post-colonialism
in the Border Regions

10

Writing Migrations: The Place(s) of U.S. Puerto Rican Literature

Frances R. Aparicio

> Writing is motion from the local toward all unseen correspondences.
> (Víctor Hernández Cruz, *Panoramas*)

To define writing as motion, as U.S. Puerto Rican poet Víctor Hernández Cruz does in his essay "Writing Migrations" (1997), is to reaffirm the epistemological processes of writing thoughts into words, giving them shape through the motions of the pen, the very physical act of writing. Yet it is also an exploration of the linguistic and cultural (dis)location from which the bilingual, bicultural poet writes. Moreover, it is a reaffirmation of the profound connection and potential disconnection between the geographical, physical (dis)location of the writer, the place(s) from which he or she writes, and the circulation of his/her words. At these three levels, then, Víctor's essay becomes the textual place from which I will explore a reconceptualization of U.S. Puerto Rican literature, whose boundaries and definition are being transformed by the transnational flows of capital and ideas and by the multiple circuits of migration of U.S. Puerto Rican writers during the 1990s.

Like other U.S. ethnic literatures, U.S. Puerto Rican literature has been traditionally defined, constituted and bounded by the literary production of Puerto Rican writers in the diaspora, a corpus that was based on a linear paradigm of migration from the island to the mainland. Given its historical role as the receptor city of thousands of Puerto Rican migrants throughout the twentieth century, the geocultural space of New York City has represented the center of that diasporic literary space, establishing itself as its hegemonic site. The national visibility of U.S. Puerto Rican literature gradually emerged as a result of the cultural nationalism of the late 1960s and 1970s. The Nuyorican literary movement, like its Chicano counterpart in the Southwest and the West, defiantly denounced the exploitative and inhuman conditions under which Puerto Ricans have lived as an invisible minority. This movement flourished within the community, yet unsurprisingly it remained outside the boundaries of both the Puerto Rican and the U.S. literary canons. Even today, its uneven integration into Anglo-American literature has not achieved the visibility and recognition comparable to that of African-American or even Chicano/a literature in the U.S. context.

Likewise, the emergence and development of Puerto Rican diasporic literary production has destabilized the strong binaries of Self/Other that have informed traditional Puerto Rican literature, a corpus that has been negotiating, since 1898, between the United States cultural, linguistic, and political discourses imposed on the island and a strongly constructed Puerto Rican national identity. This corpus inherited a discursive tradition of hispanophilia through which elite, male writers privileged the Spanish heritage over the African as a way of recuperating a social imaginary that would replace, or at least displace, the supposed forces of U.S. progress, modernization, and colonialism. Ironically, this privileging of the Spanish cultural and linguistic legacy has led to the exclusion of the English-writing authors from the mainland. Positioned in the interstices of both cultures, diasporic authors such as Tato Laviera, Sandra María Esteves, Miguel Algarín, Pedro Pietri, Judith Ortiz Cofer, Víctor Hernández Cruz, Aurora Levins Morales and others have foregrounded the contradictory and multiple subjectivities that constitute the U.S. Puerto Rican subject, thus questioning the essentializing elements of Puerto Rican national identity as it has been forged on the island. For these reasons, they find themselves excluded from the social and national imaginaries of both the U.S. and of Puerto Rico, yet at the same time they are politically "owned" by both the U.S. literary establishment and the Puerto Rican intelligentsia.

By the 1990s, however, U.S. Puerto Rican literature has gained visibility as part of the larger, multicultural texture of so-called "American" literature. The institutionalizing of cultural diversity in higher education since the 1980s, and the significant curricular and research contributions by Puerto Rican and Latino/a faculty have led to a revision of the U.S. literary canon that has embraced, albeit partly and in very selective ways, the multiple voices of the U.S. Puerto Rican diaspora. *The Heath Anthology of American Literature* (Lauter *et al.* 1991) for instance, represented a project that conscientiously included significant minority voices, thus allowing English literature students throughout the United States to read Tato Laviera's "AmeRícan" or Pedro Pietri's classical and foundational poem, "Puerto Rican Obituary" alongside Ezra Pound and

Emily Dickinson. The impact of these anthologizing efforts may not have been measured quantitatively, but their potential for transforming the literary canon cannot be understated. In this sense, Nuyorican literature from the 1960s and 1970s, a literary corpus that was produced by working-poor, second-generation, self-taught poets, was finally recognized, even if 15 years after the fact. That some of these voices are now being studied as part of the historical effervescence of the cultural nationalism of the 1960s and 1970s speaks to its undeniable impact in reconceptualizing U.S. culture as a multicultural rather than as a national, homogeneous space.

In contrast to Nuyorican literature, which has been centered, grounded, and produced in and from New York City, the corpus and, eventually, the canon of U.S. Puerto Rican literature in the 1990s is now including writers from the island. This transnational movement is multifaceted and informed by diverse circuits of migration of people, texts, and readers. First, the hegemonic transnational flow from north to south called upon by the New York literary market has meant that a writer such as Rosario Ferré, who has been traditionally deemed as a Latin American/Puerto Rican feminist writer, is now a "Latina author." That the Anglo-American canon is now embracing insular authors such as Rosario Ferré reveals not only a transnational gesture from north to south similar to that of the Latin American boom of the 1960s and 1970s, but it also poses a reframing of identity, location and ideal readers. Through linguistic shifts into English, the last two novels by Rosario Ferré have been marketed as part of the Latina/Caribbean literary corpus in the U.S. Who is, then, a U.S. Puerto Rican author? From where do U.S. Puerto Rican authors write and for whom? Second, the dramatic works of Pedro Pietri have been published in English by the University of Puerto Rico Press, the first, unprecedented publication in English by the island's renowned university press. This second instance of transnationalism reveals the gradual acceptance of English, historically deemed the language of colonialism on the island, as part of the corpus of Puerto Rican letters. It also signals a shift in defining Puerto Rican literature from a literature of identity to a literature of otherness in which a standard, national Spanish has been dialogized and transformed by popular orality, linguistic hybridity, black Spanish, urban working-class youth slang, and women's discourses (Rubén Ríos Avila 1995: 331, 334). Third, in the late 1980s U.S. Puerto Rican poet Víctor Hernández Cruz returned to live in Aguas Buenas, Puerto Rico, his hometown, after having spent his childhood and young adult life in New York and California. He is now writing on and from the island in

English and in Spanish. His return migration is one example of the circular and multiple relocations of diasporic writers, multiple migrations whose complexities were earlier explored in pioneering ways by Aurora Levins Morales and Rosario Morales in *Getting Home Alive* (1985). Overall, these three instances of literary migrations are characterized by the fact that English is now being written and published on/from the island and circulating towards and into a United States diverse readership, from mainstream Anglo-American readers to U.S. Latino/a communities throughout the mainland.

Thus, situating or defining Puerto Rican and U.S. Puerto Rican literature as a whole is rendered much more complex by this multiple, transnational circulation of writers and texts. Studies in transnationalism, however, have employed this term vaguely, conflating different and, at times, asymmetrical types of border-crossings. Rather, it is imperative to tease out the power differentials that inform these multiple circulations of writers, texts, and readers. While this transnational flow may be cause for celebration as the market expands and linguistic frontiers open up, more significantly it remits us to the power and agency of the U.S. literary market in redefining the U.S. Puerto Rican literary corpus and, eventually, the canon, as the case of Rosario Ferré evinces. The fact that Ferré is now writing in English is concomitant to the New York literary market's "discovery" or "invention" of a Spanish-reading audience within the U.S. and internationally, which has led to the systematic translation into Spanish of U.S. Latino/a literature. The Nuyorican texts of the 1970s that have been informed by a specific, marginal socioeconomic experience and by oppositional, denunciatory texts are now being dis/re/placed by the bestsellers of Rosario Ferré and Esmeralda Santiago, whose novels substitute the contestatory perspectives of the Nuyorican works with narratives of seamless assimilation, as in the case of Santiago, and of political integration through statehood, as in the case of Ferré. But then, what about Víctor Hernández Cruz? Can we still consider him a diasporic, U.S. Puerto Rican poet when he now writes from the homeland, and from the mountains of Aguas Buenas? Is Rosario Ferré a Latina writer, as she has designated herself publicly? While both writers write from the island, they are not both U.S. Puerto Rican writers, nor are they both "Latino/a," in the same ways. On the one hand, transnational flows dictated by the needs of capital, such as the labeling and marketing of Rosario Ferré as a Latina writer, will privilege the bourgeois writer. On the other, the forced migration or return migration of working-class U.S. Latino/a writers, whose linguistic and cultural hybridity is not strategic but the results of imposed, colonial dispossessions, becomes less visible/readable to the mainstream. These power differentials render problematic the conflation of subaltern U.S. Latino/a writers with Latin American and Caribbean authors from the elite.

On May 5, 1996 Rosario Ferré wrote a short article for *The San Juan Star*, Puerto Rico's only English newspaper, entitled "On bilingual trespassing." This piece constituted her personal defense and response to the ensuing criticism and accusations of cultural betrayal on the part of linguistic purists and cultural nationalists that followed the publication of *The House on the Lagoon*, her first novel originally written in English. In this piece, she contests such accusations by redefining herself as a strategic, bilingual writer. She states that: "Bilingual writers make themselves so out of necessity," referring to Samuel Beckett and Joseph Conrad as examples. She explains that writing in English has given her "an enormous advantage" since it allows her the emotional distance to write about particular issues that were "too emotionally charged" for her in Spanish. She then moves on to contextualize her first English novel as part of the boom of Latino writers who write "with a rumba zapateado or merengue rhythm to it," that is, writers such as Julia Alvarez, Sandra Cisneros, Ana Castillo, Cristina García, Esmeralda Santiago, and Oscar Hijuelos, who have contributed new, tropicalized ways of writing English and who are being marketed by the major publishing houses in New York. It is not surprising that Ferré equated herself to the above names of mainstreamed Latino/a voices, and did not include any of the Nuyorican counterparts, such as Pietri, Laviera, Hernández Cruz, Levins Morales or even Judith Ortiz Cofer. She concludes her defense of the right to write in English by locating her novel as a Latino text "because it travels both cultures. It is about Puerto Rico, but it is also about the U.S., where ethnic and cultural diversity is a reality we have to deal with on a daily basis" (Ferré 1996: 20). As a self-designated "Latina writer" who writes in English, she says she has "unwittingly become the spokeswoman for a minority which (sic) is claiming its future in the U.S. as it never had before" (20). She hopes her novel "helps this group achieve a sense of dignity and self-worth which has long been denied it" (20).

This particular effort on the part of Rosario Ferré to cross over from her location as a Puerto Rican and Latin American feminist writer to a "Latina writer" is not only controversial and debatable, but also very revealing of the effects of transnationalism on the U.S. Puerto Rican literary corpus and canon. I will not debate Ferré's stance point by point, since Margarite Fernández Olmos, in her own response to Ferré's piece, has already done so in a lucid, informed, and succint way. Olmos critiques Ferré's self-relocation as a Latina writer because this gesture capitalizes on the fact that the U.S. literary market and the average U.S. reader do not distinguish between Latin American and U.S. Latino/a writers, thus erasing "important differences in their literary traditions, social, class, and national origins" (Olmos 1996). She adds that Ferré has "the luxury to choose what may be more marketable at any given time" – the term "Latina" over the racialized "Puerto Rican" one – whereas many Puerto Ricans in the United States have not had that choice, but rather have had to negotiate the diverse, racialized identities imposed by social institutions such as schools, the media and the criminal system. Olmos rightly concludes that writing in English and bilingualism, for Ferré, "is an outcome of middle-class private schooling as is often the case on the island," in contrast to the bilingualism developed in the U.S. Puerto Rican communities, which is the direct result of the colonized and racialized conditions in which they live. Olmos lucidly concludes by separating Ferré's right as an individual writer to write in English, which the former respects, from Ferré's self-designated claim as a representative of the U.S. Puerto Rican community, a role that, according to the U.S. Puerto Rican critic, will take "more than just that [writing in English], I'm afraid. A lot more."

Rosario Ferré's linguistic shift into English marks not only a writer's strategy to deal with the "emotionally charged" aspects of her life. Because of its timing, it has also become a symbolic act by which the personal mirrors the political. In other words, her shift to English allegorically marks the eventual shift into English that statehood calls upon as a requisite for Puerto Ricans' political integration into the American union. Ferré's 1998 op-ed statement in *The New York Times* reaffirms the integrationist agenda behind her recent literary production. She exhorts U.S. readers to recognize Puerto Ricans on the island as equal Americans and explains the dilemma and paradoxes of the Puerto Rican subjectivity, one that "prize[s] their American citizenship" while at the same time "cherish[ing] our language and culture" (21). Yet, at the end, she contradictorily (but not unsurprisingly) reaffirms her vote for statehood based on her "passionate commitment to the modern world" (21). This suggests that, for her, modernity can only be located within the English-speaking and writing world, thus rendering impossible being modern in and through Spanish. This discursive construct, a clear echo of the imperial discourse of Britain and the United States in the teaching of English as a second language throughout the world, reveals the ideology behind Ferré's linguistic shift into English (Pennycook 1994). Like statehood advocates on the island, and like her father, Luis A. Ferré, past governor of the island, millionaire, and statehood advocate, Ferré can only conceive of modernization through United States laws, political structures, and institutions, that is, through an Anglo State. This discourse, then, erases the historical process of modernization of Puerto Rican society, which has been mediated and articulated in Puerto Rican Spanish since the 1950s.

Ferré's allegiance to English as the exclusive tool to achieve modernity and a "civilized" society also represents a shift from her previous reflections on the use of English by U.S. Puerto Ricans. In her essay, "On Destiny, Language, and Translation; or, Ophelia Adrift in the C. & O. Canal" in *The Youngest Doll* (1991) which she herself translated into English, the island author judged the loss of Spanish of U.S. Puerto Rican working-class families as "cultural suicide," making colonized and racialized individuals accountable for the processes of dispossession initiated by U.S. social institutions. Yet she defends what is the agenda for Puerto Rico of U.S. English, the political group that has been advocating for the linguistic prerequisites for statehood and which have lobbied to make the island an English-only territory. Ferré's elision of this fact is not unique, since the debates about statehood, language, and cultural identity on the island have been limited to the national, insular context. Ironically, the obvious future of Puerto Rican Spanish in the face of statehood is already evident in the diglossic, monolingual environments and policies that have affected the linguistic practices of U.S. Latino/as, both Puerto Rican and Mexican-American, in the domestic arena.

Ferré reinvents herself as a transnational writer in order to increase her Anglo audience. In order to achieve this readership, it seems that she has to systematically elide the colonial conditions of her Puerto Rican compatriots in the diaspora, that other subaltern, transnational reality produced by U.S. colonialism. Her two public statements reveal Ferré's desire to insert herself within a transnational market of Latino/a writing in the U.S. without speaking to the interests of this community. This particular, straddling positionality has also been evident in the increasing numbers of elite Latin Americanists, such as Ilan Stavans, who are now engaging in "Latino/a Studies" and defining Latino/a identity from the vantage point of their own literary heritage and class-based assumptions. This self-declared identity, however, always keeps these writers at bay from the working-class community and writers that constitute the larger, U.S. Latino/a sector. A degree of disavowal and negative critiques about Latino/a linguistic and cultural hybridity are evident in the works of these self-appointed guardians of Latinidad. In *The Hispanic Condition* (1995), the Mexican writer Stavans consistently conflates Chicano/a writers with Latin American authors such as Borges, García Márquez and Cortázar and privileges the latter as much more universal and sophisticated than the barrio voices of the former. Issues having to do with the interlingual texture of Latino/a writing in the U.S. are likewise evaluated as cultural deficits, rather than historically specific forms of cultural creativity, resistance, and survival, as Ferré's early statement on the "cultural suicide" of U.S. Puerto Ricans reveals. In the *New York Times*, she equally makes reference to Puerto Ricans on the mainland as individuals who see Puerto Rico "as an almost mythical place inhabited by ancestral gods, comparable to the role of Africa for African-Americans." This double generalization (about U.S. Puerto Ricans and Blacks) reveals an anachronistic and homogeneous view of these two, diverse communities. Her disturbing race- and class-based distance from diasporic realities is evident in this observation, for she does not take into account the continuous circular migration of Puerto Ricans between the island and the mainland nor factors such as media, radio, television, news programming, and constant travel, all of which have rendered this mythical illusion an anachronism at best. Any particular myths about "ancestral gods," or the more recent Taíno recovery movement, for instance (Dávila 1998), have emerged both on the island as well as on the mainland and have served, strategically, like Aztlán for the Chicanos, as foundational symbols for building community and identity in the face of cultural, political, and territorial dispossession.

In Ferré's latest novel, and unlike *The Youngest Doll*, *Eccentric Neighborhoods* (1999), a master narrative of statehood that protects and defends the class-based privilege of her family, there is little, if any, evidence of "unlearning one's own privilege," a postcolonial discourse that is essential in order to "be able to listen to that other constituency" and to "learn to speak in such a way that one will be taken seriously by that other constituency" (Giroux 1992: 27). Ferré's turn towards English and statehood, then, has to be understood in terms of the hegemony of her social class, as well as the hegemony that she represents as an island writer to Puerto Ricans in the diaspora, rather than as a defense of U.S. Puerto Rican's linguistic hybridity. *Eccentric Neighborhoods*, in this light, can be read as a defense of Ferré's own family, social class, and industrial hegemony on the island. It is a reclaiming of the past and, as much as she foregrounds the diverse routes of migration that led to the genealogy of her family on both sides, the novel continuously justifies the consolidation of their economic and political power. This is not a novel about displacement and forced hybridity, but about possessing and protecting land and place, about being in place, and about building power and privilege.

The initial and final, closing scene that frames this autobiographical narrative inscribes Ferré's subject position and, thus, her elite ideology. As she refers to the power of the river next to her family's hacienda and to the absence of a bridge, she recalls how at times she and her mother were in the car crossing the river, but the water currents were so strong that the car would stall. Her mother, then, commanded the driver

> to honk the horn. Soon four barefoot peasants dressed in faded khakis and scraggly straw hats, who had been standing on the shore with their oxen watching our predicament, waded silently into the river.
>
> With rushing water up to their waists, they approached the car, yoked animals in tow. Clarissa opened her handbag, took out a dollar, and waved it at them from inside the window. The peasants tied the beasts to the Pontiac's front bumper with a thick hemp rope, and slowly the car began to move forward. The smell of mud grew stronger, and I stared in horror as a thin line of water began to seep in through the bottom of the door. Clarissa signaled emphatically to the men to poke the oxen more sharply with their long poles. Once on shore, she slipped the dollar bill to the peasants through a crack at the top of the window and ordered Cristóbal to start the car. The Pontiac jumped forward, its shiny blue-and-white surface dripping with mud, and took off at full speed, an anxious Pegasus flying down the road toward Emajaguas. (Ferré 1998: 6)

This narrative serves as a metonym for the privilege of money. Like many other future capitalist Puerto Rican families, the roads and paths that Ferré's family took were based on the physical, artistic and intellectual labor of the working class and of the so-called "masses." The fact that the mother hands out the dollar through a crack at the top of the car window signals the closing of class boundaries necessary for the protection of their economic and social privilege. Indeed, the earlier description of the abundance and luxury inside of the car, "full of good things to eat" and of the girl narrator and her mother, Clarissa, "dressed in [their] Sunday best," contrasts with the lack and poverty in their surroundings, a social reality that they observed like distant voyeurs or tourists from the inside of the closed car windows, but in which they refused to participate or intervene.

In this same chapter, Ferré suggests that the development of public works in the 1950s on the island, during which time the bridge was built over the Emajaguas River, occurred at the same time as the migration of thousands of Puerto Ricans to New York. Yet, she omits the fact that this mass migration was planned by both the U.S. government and then Puerto Rico's governor, Luis Muñoz Marín, to allow for economic development and population control on the island. The unspoken connection is that Ferré's family in Emajaguas does benefit from the development of public works, not just from a new bridge that would allow them to cross the river but also eventually from a growing industrial economy that leads to her family's millionaire status. This is a direct result of the dislocation of the many working-class and poor Puerto Rican families onto New York, an emptying-out of the population that made possible the economic growth of a new, Puerto Rican capitalist elite. The silenced voices, then, of those dislocated families are not articulated in Ferré's narrative, where they remain silenced ("waded silently into the river"). Rather, they have been reclaimed and articulated by poets such as Tato Laviera, who in his poem "nuyorican" denounces this particular historical and political decision: "me mandaste a nacer nativo en toras tierras, por qué, porque éramos pobres, verdad?/ porque tú querías vaciarte de tu gente pobre" (1985: 53). In his essay, "Home is where the Music is" (1997), Víctor Hernández Cruz also foregrounds how industrial progress went hand in hand with the emigration of working-poor Puerto Ricans: "In El Guanabano, the commotion of cement trucks mixed with the whirlwind of families who were organizing themselves to jump off the edge of the world. It was not the upper classes that had to leave; the bourgeois never leave where they are milking" (1997: 19). As Henry Giroux has lucidly summarized in *Border Crossings* (1992), when we speak about the politics of location and agency what is at issue is "who speaks, under what conditions, for whom, and how knowledge is constructed and translated within and between different communities located within asymmetrical relations of power" (26). It is precisely the absence of dialogism and social heteroglossia in the novel that makes Ferré's *Eccentric Neighborhoods* more of a master narrative than a postcolonial, oppositional literary discourse.

The novel closes with the narrator's last dream about her late mother, Clarissa. Again, the scene of the Pontiac crossing the river recurs, but this time with a particular discursive substitution which reaffirms the novel's defense of women's voices, but only within the class parameters of the bourgeoisie:

We were crossing Río Loco and the family's temperamental Pontiac had stalled on us again. The river was rushing past, but instead of dogs, pigs, and goats being pulled along by the murky rapids I saw Abuela Valeria, Abuela Adela, Tía Lakhmé, Tía Dido, Tía Artemisa, Tía Amparo, all swimming desperately against the current. Clarissa and I sat safely inside the Pontiac, dressed in our Sunday best. She took a dollar out of her purse, rolled down the window just enough so she could wave the bill at the men on the riverbank, who soon came and pulled us out. And as we drove away I could hear through the open window the voices of those I could no longer see, but whose stories I could not have dreamed. (340)

This time, the narrator opens the car window to hear the voices of the aunts who had represented, for her, the prototypes of femininity and feminism, yet in the process the voices and presence of the disempowered communities on which their safety depended remain even more distant from the narrator's subjectivity. The author of *Eccentric Neighborhoods* has relocated herself even further away from the working-class Puerto Rican communities on the island and in the U.S. that she purports to represent in her newspaper articles.

Rather than narratives about family genealogies, European migrations into Puerto Rico, bourgeois accumulation, industrial growth and political power, Víctor Hernández Cruz's verses and poetic essays in *Panoramas* (1997) delve into the conflicts, discontinuities, clashes, and eventual negotiations that characterize a racialized, bicultural life. In contrast to Rosario Ferré, whose bilingualism is "strategic" and politically integrationist, driven by the political tenets of statehood and by the ideology of English as a hegemonic language, Víctor Hernández Cruz also writes in English and Spanish, yet, as he puts it, "Having grown up bilingually, I now have an accent in both Spanish and English" (1997: 118). In other words, as a racialized, subaltern subject in the diaspora, the poet recognizes that his difference is inscribed and marked by his very own bilingualism, whereas Ferré's bilingualism ultimately serves to foreground to the U.S. mainstream the "Americanness" of insular Puerto Ricans, that is, to erase difference.

Panoramas is rooted in the local but, as Cruz's definition of writing suggested earlier, "writing" is "motion from the local to all unseen correspondences" (117). Whereas the book is dedicated to a specific *ceiba* tree and a boulder in the environs of Caguas, Puerto Rico, the fact that the poet defines explicitly their respective, concrete locations speaks to the centrality of place, of flora and fauna, and of movement and travel in this poetic collection. The poet's return to Aguas Buenas has led to a renewed interest in the rural and in the natural world, as opposed to the highly urban metaphors and imagery that had permeated his earlier poetry. Yet, Cruz's characteristic juxtaposition and eventual synthesis of rural icons with the urban landscape, of the past and the present, of tradition and modernity (Canclini Garcia 1995), which he defines as "the center of metaphor" (Cruz 1997: 21) and is encapsulated in the recurring conflation of the mountain as skyscraper, does not disappear altogether but assumes a new axis: the natural world of the island of Puerto Rico and, specifically, of the Aguas Buenas area. Indeed, the *ceiba* tree serves, for Víctor Hernández Cruz, as a synechdoque for that invisible, Taíno presence in Puerto Rican culture and its spiritual vestiges in present times, one of the diverse cultural strands that underline Puerto Rican culture and that the poet recovers through his imagery and discourse. The *ceiba* tree constitutes poetry as motion "from the local to the unseen correspondences."

Location and place serve as poetic centers to *Panoramas* while migration, movement and travel continue to inform how dislocations and relocations affect identity, perspective, positionalities and, ultimately, poetry. "Home is Where the Music Is" explains, as a poetic genealogy, the earlier forms of poetry that the poet listened to during his childhood (1997: 11–26). The places of poetry were the corner *cafetín* and the tobacco *chinchales*, sites of leisure and work, respectively, where men used to sing "songs' lyrics" that have stayed with [him] through all metamorphoses of regions and climates (13), thus offering the poet an aesthetic and cultural continuum and historical memory that lends coherence to his multiple migrations. Indeed, a historical coherence is established as Hernández Cruz maps and traces the transnational circulation of *declamaciones* – oratorical performances – from the island to New York City, and the circular migration of boleros and plenas, back from New York to the Caribbean (25). Likewise, Cruz maps his own Latino youth in Manhattan, listening to pachangas, boogaloos and salsa during the 1960s, and reading William Carlos Williams's poetry. The tensions here between popular forms of culture, such as music, and the so-called "literate" articulations of Anglo-American poetry, serve to highlight Cruz's own lived experience of cultural hybridity and post-modernism, not only interculturally but also in terms of high and "low" cultures. Together, the poetic essays in *Panoramas* foreground the multiple circulation of ideas, cultural expressions, words, poems, that accompanied the migration of bodies, that is, individuals, families, neighbors, and communities, a transnational flow that was socioeconomically and politically marked by Operation Bootstrap.

It is in "Writing Migrations" (117–29), however, where Víctor Hernández Cruz develops an *ars poetica* of sorts and a metalinguistic reflection on linguistic and cultural dislocations, what he terms as "exile and bilingualism." His "exile and bilingualism," he argues, are two factors that have created the conditions for poetic production in him and other poets he admires. On the one hand, his "exile" is multiply-inflected, as it could refer to his earlier migration to the mainland or, equally as well, to his self-exile in the mountains of Puerto Rico, or, symbolically of course, to the linguistic and cultural exile that is characteristic of postcolonial identities. For Hernández Cruz, as for many other Latino/a and postcolonial poets who survived a colonial education in English, writing in English embodies the very alienating process and product of colonialism.

Unlike Rosario Ferré's integrationist ideology behind English, Víctor Hernández Cruz's use of English in his poetic works "write back" to the colonizer. Among postcolonial writers in Africa, Asia, and Latin America, debates over the strategic use of English for articulating oppositionality reveal various positions: some writers have decided to go back to local languages (Thiongo) and to repudiate English as a language of political struggle, while others feel that English needs to be discursively transformed from the centralizing, imperial standard use of English to a linguistic and literary practice that embraces various local forms of "english" (Pennycook 1994). Alastair Pennycook has suggested the terms of "diremption" and "redemption," analogous to abrogation and appropriation, to identify, first, the "process of challenging both central language practices and central discourses" (1994: 270) and, second, "the use of language to represent local contexts in conjunction with insurgent knowledges and cultural forms" (270). In *Panoramas* the appropriation of English is evident: by integrating local flora and fauna, words in Spanish, cultural markers, and narratives about local and transnational Puerto Rican cultural practices, the poet renders a new, tropicalized English that articulates the hybridity and multicultural texture of being Puerto Rican in the 1990s. Communicative gaps between Spanish and English, between the working-class, racialized Puerto Ricans in the diaspora and the Anglo-cultural mainstream, become, in the ears of the poet, inspiration for poetic production. In "Preparaciones para el pasado," the poet narrates two instances of linguistic clash: while a group of Puerto Ricans in New York were playing their guitars during the Christmas holidays waiting for the subway, the employee tells them they need to buy a "token": they heard "toquen" (play), and so performed a typical song unaware that they had to pay (172). This leads, of course, to the intervention of the police who made them pay and made them stop playing their music. As an elementary school student, the poet recalls he and his friends singing "josé can you see" instead of "Oh say can you see" (173–4). They end up in the principal's office because of a perceived lack of patriotism and respect to the American flag. These two short anecdotes reveal not only the colonial circumstances that frame Puerto Rican meanings and significations in the diaspora and lead to containment, but also the discriminating skills of Cruz, whose ear for linguistic clashes finds in them poetic bursts and moments of cultural resistance and differentiation.

In "Writing Migrations" Cruz also articulates a shift in his definition and evaluation of the bilingual poet. While he has explored the linguistic dislocation of Latino poets and his "exile and bilingualism," and has reaffirmed the "motion, the tremendous coming and going, this here and there" captured by "Latino poetry, art, and music" (122), he concludes with a cautionary note about the mixing of Spanish and English that echoes the linguistic purism prevalent among the island's traditional intelligentsia. Cruz distinguishes between the bilingualism "that is a writer's interest in other languages," as Rosario Ferré's case, and "the bilingualism that is imposed affecting an entire group of people, a whole culture" (128), making a clear differentiation between elite choices and colonial impositions. Yet, he moves on to articulate some of the myths about the alingual individual who is not "competent and secure in either language," deploring the "bilingualism that "contributes to the degeneration of one of the languages, creating expressive confusion in a people" (128). He cautions against writing interlingually, as in Spanglish poetry, and expresses his current preference for juxtaposing English and Spanish rather than interweaving them. This position against interlingual writings, ironically, converges with the linguistic purism still prevalent on the island (Pérez 1998).

Yet Víctor Hernández Cruz celebrates himself now as a writer "in the Caribbean, where things are already mixed, literature is walking, poetry dancing" (1997: 116). Indeed, he celebrates "migrating back to where it [language] was related" (116), realizing that poetry is everywhere in this region of temporal dislocations and cultural relocations. Yet, the place of origins is also the space of empire and nation where prevailing linguistic policies and attitudes equate linguistic mixing with degeneration and erect boundaries to keep languages from supposedly "contaminating" each other. The fact that *Panoramas* concludes with a section in Spanish, and with a verse that echoes Spanish poet Antonio Machado, "era tan bonito el camino al andar" (187), suggests an emerging process of hispanification for Víctor Hernández Cruz, a result, indeed, of his relocation to Puerto Rico. In one sense he has become a completely bilingual poet, since he now writes complete poems in English and in Spanish, whereas his earlier poetic collections were English dominant interlaced throughout with Spanish. He has returned to reclaim the language that was subordinated and silenced on the mainland. In the process, however, he should remember that Spanish has historically been the language of empire in Puerto Rico and Latin America and that it can play an equally hegemonic role as English has in the diaspora.

The linguistic turns and shifts represented by Rosario Ferré and Víctor Hernández Cruz do not necessarily reveal a larger degree of tolerance for linguistic and cultural hybridity, but rather a linguistic relocation informed, in the case of the former, by the dictates of a transnational market and, for the latter, by his physical relocation in a Hispanic national space, which is the island of Puerto Rico. Because of her fixed class subjectivity and her denial of seeing gender through race, the anglicization of Ferré's work clearly constitutes a hegemonic move rather than a postcolonial narrative of liberation that speaks to multicultural feminisms (Fregoso 1999). Hernández Cruz's poetry, however, reveals that geographic locations inevitably impact a poet's "motion" from the local toward "unseen correspondences." The cultural politics of Spanish on the island, a historical form of resistance to English imperialism, explain the indelible shift in his interlingual poetics. His past diasporic *vivencias* and the cultural hybridity that he consistently embodies in his person and lucidly articulates in his texts will hopefully contain the emerging purist impulses of this relocated writer.

REFERENCES

Dávila, Arlene, 1998. "Local/Diasporic Tainos and Cultural Politics," *The Latino Review of Books*, 3. 3 (Winter), pp. 2–10.

Fernández Olmos, Margarite, 1996. "Latina, Puertorriqueña: What's in a Name?" Unpublished letter. Quoted by Permission of the Author.

Ferré, Rosario, 1991. *The Youngest Doll*, Lincoln: University of Nebraska Press.

Ferré, Rosario, 1996. "On Bilingual Trespassing," *San Juan Star*, May 5.

Ferré, Rosario, 1998. "Puerto Rico, U.S.A.," *New York Times*, March 19.

Ferré, Rosario, 1999. *Eccentric Neighborhoods*, New York: Plume Books.

Fregoso, Rosalinda, 1999. "On The Road with Angela Davis," *Cultural Studies*, 13.2 (April), pp. 211–22.

García Canclini, Néstor, 1995. *Hybrid Cultures: Strategies for Entering and Leaving Modernity*, trans. Christopher L. Chiappari and Silvia L. Lopez, Minneapolis: University of Minnesota Press.

Giroux, Henry, 1992. *Border Crossings: Cultural Workers and the Politics of Education*, New York & London: Routledge.

Hernández Cruz, Víctor, 1997. *Panoramas*, Minneapolis: Coffee House Press.

Lauter, Paul *et al.*, eds, 1990. *Heath Anthology of American Literature*, Lexington, MA: D. C. Heath.

Laviera, Tato, 1985. *AmeRícan*, Houston: Arte Público.

Levins Morales, Aurora and Rosario Morales, 1985. *Getting Home Alive*, Ithaca: Firebrand Books.

Pennycook, Alastair, 1994. *The Cultural Politics of English as an International Language*, London & New York: Longman.

Pérez, Luz Nereida, 1998. "Bilingüismo: Una pregunta y una contestación," *Claridad* (8–14 May and 15–21 May).

Pietri, Pedro, 1992. *Illusions of a Revolving Door: Plays, Teatro*, Rio Piedras, Puerto Rico: Editorial de la Universidad de Puerto Rico.

Ríos Avila, Rubén, 1995. "El arte de dar lengua en Puerto Rico," *Polifonía salvaje: Ensayos de cultura y política en la postmodernidad*, eds Irma Rivera Nieves and Carlos Gil, San Juan, Puerto Rico: Editorial Postdata.

Santiago, Esmeralda, 1993. *When I Was Puerto Rican*, New York: Vintage Books.

Stavans, Ilan, 1995. *The Hispanic Condition: Reflections on Culture and Identity in America*, New York: HarperCollins.

11
Diasporic Disconnections: Insurrection and Forgetfulness in Contemporary Haitian and Latin-Caribbean Women's Literature

Myriam J. A. Chancy

In the summer of 1998 I visited an island not my own, an island cradled by the waters of the Pacific Ocean. Its rocky shores were alien to me, as were the trees emerging from its soil, the sand cool beneath my feet on its sandy beaches. I walked the single road ribboning around its contours, bottled water in hand, a shirt tied around my head to keep the sun at bay. I walked. I walked and pebbles lodged themselves beneath the soles of my feet in my open sandals. Bicycles sped past. There were no cars. Others walked before and behind and beside. We walked the road together as if reenacting a vigil, a ritual or, perhaps I would like to think that the walk was less mundane than that of a tourist. I would like to believe that none of us was like Jamaica Kincaid's insufferable, neo-colonial tourist in *A Small Place* of whom Kincaid writes:

> rain is the thing that you, just now, do not want, for you are thinking of the hard and cold and dark and long days you spend working in North America (or, worse, Europe), earning some money so that you could stay in this place (Antigua) where the sun always shines and where the climate is deliciously hot and dry for the four to ten days you are going to be staying there. (1988: 4)

I am neither American nor European and the road I walked then was not in the Caribbean but off the coast of California. I walked the route that would take me round a small, small place where the ferry drops you off in front of a sign with arrows, one pointing to a beach littered with picnickers and children, the other pointing in the opposite direction towards the Chinese Detention Center. It was a pilgrimage of sorts, this walking far from home, when any island will do because

167

every small, islanded place has something more than its size in common; each holds firmly inked into its soil the blood, sweat and tears of those who were "islanded" there without reprieve, without choice. This is Angel Island and I am an islander. Wherever I walked, there were butterflies rising to meet my very breath. Every time I looked to the ocean and back towards the straw-like growth sprouting from the broken rock at the side of the road, the butterflies, yellow, orange, shades of gold, rose to meet the movement of each of us along that road. Chaos theory holds that the beating of a wing of a butterfly in one place in the world can affect the climate in a distant land. Thus, everything we do, every movement matters. This must mean, of course, that everyone who has moved in the past has left their indelible mark upon this world, the terrain they have walked, the tears they have cried, and the blood spilt in creviced soil. It occurs to me that every place that has known cataclysmic occurrences by human hands and loss of life is inhabited by butterflies; I do not know if this is true in all small places but I know it is true of islands, and islanded places. It occurs to me that every butterfly I see on Angel Island is a marker, a reminder, of the lives that have been sacrificed there.

Inscribed on one of the walls of the now deserted Detention Center, I read the following:

I left my native village to earn a living.
I endured wind and frost to seek fame.
I passed this land to go to Cuba.
Who was to know they would dispatch me to a prison on a mountain?

And I think: who was to know that entering these walls I would find myself returned to the islands of the Atlantic, my own heritage, reflected in these words, carved so long ago in these planks still standing here for those who seek to remember and name all the places they have ever been, all the places yet to know.

An island, then, is not simply a body of land cut off by a field of water; it is a repository of memory, a site to be mined for remembrance. Islands are gate-keepers. They are also hamlets of resistance from the Chinese who persisted and carved poetry into their detention walls, to the maroons in Jamaica who fled to the mountains and made poetry of song only to descend from their enclaves by the sound of the conch, a rallying to arms. As Trinidadian-Tobagan poet M. Nourbese Philip writes in "A Genealogy of Resistance," "To island is to resist" (Philip 1997: 27). For me, the butterfly is emblematic of such island resistance.

As in chaos theory, from which emerged the concept of the "Butterfly Effect," the butterfly becomes a cataclysmic sign which cannot be foretold but which nonetheless leaves traces of itself behind in the elements. I want to borrow this concept in this brief consideration of that which has kept Caribbean peoples, especially Haitians and Dominicans, divided amongst themselves for at least two centuries, despite their common heritages, shared land masses and histories of bloodshed. During the course of this history, what would first appear to be unimportant differences in race, class, and currency eventually grow to produce what would seem to be unpredictable results, such as the carnage of the 1937 sugar cane field massacres under Trujillo's regime. How does such an accumulation take place? What are the forces that conspired to produce such a cataclysmic event? Why is it that memory has been falsified in the case of the Haitian/Dominican conflict? Why have race and gender issues pertaining to the maintenance of such conflicts been dismissed as overly facile explanations? These are some of the questions this essay attempts to address through the analysis of works by Haitian and Latin Caribbean authors, namely those of Cristina García, Julia Alvarez, Edwidge Danticat, Loida Maritza Perez, and Ana Lydia Vega.

LOST AT SEA

In a short story entitled "Cloud Cover Caribbean," Puerto Rican writer Ana Lydia Vega describes the journey on the seas of three men in search of the promises of the American continent in a humoristic and allegorical fashion. The men, one Haitian, one Dominican, and one Cuban, form a sort of unholy trinity which, as Diana Vélez suggests, reflects the structure of inter-ethnic "jokes" in which the punch-line usually offers insight into who has power and by what means that power is enforced linguistically and imagistically. The punch-line in Lydia Vega's text, however, is no laughing matter as it demands that readers re-think and interrogate their perceptions of Caribbean identity in ways that engage historical and cultural specificity with an eye to understanding and then dismantling the racial and class-bound hierarchies that manifest themselves in disunity in and among the islands.

In the story, each of the men recognizes the similarity of their flight from their Caribbean nation states and their search for a new beginning within the U.S. They are in pursuit of an elusive American Dream in which the Caribbean does not figure. Lydia Vega describes the initial encounter between the Haitian and Dominican as follows: "Then and there was spoken the royal pain of being black, Caribbean, and poor, deaths by the score were retold: clergy, military, and civilians were roundly cursed; an international brotherhood of hunger and solidarity of dreams was established" (1995: 2). As they are joined by the Cuban, however, the union between the Haitian, Antenor, and the Dominican, Diogenes, disintegrates; the first bond is disrupted both by virtue of linguistic sameness on the part of the Dominican and the Cuban, Carmelo, and a deracialization of both their identities takes place so that Antenor becomes marked as undesirably "black." Diogenes, in particular, bringing to mind the antagonistic history between the two countries which share an island, refers to Haitian cane cutters in the Dominican Republic as "madamos" and to Antenor specifically as a "nigger" when demanding access to Antenor's provisions. When a fight ensues, Lydia Vega writes: "The Cuban smiled, following the struggle with the benign condescendence of an adult watching children quarrel" (1995: 5). Clearly, despite their precarious position in the boat carrying them to the U.S., a hierarchy which is likened within the piece to the volatility of the "Bermuda Triangle," has been reinstated in which superficial bonds are forged between the Cuban and Dominican men while the Haitian is scorned. In the end, the punch-line of the story is revealed when they are rescued by an American ship. Initially "tired but content" they are immediately categorized by the "Aryan" ship captain as "niggers," a categorization which is quickly confirmed by a Puerto Rican voice, which appears to occupy insider/outsider locations, telling them that once they face "la migra" there will be again no differences between them, each will be categorized and treated as "black, Caribbean, and poor."

What interests me in this story is Lydia Vega's ability to synthesize how hegemonic relationships in and among the islands have disrupted revolutionary coalitions between islands which share a common history – this state of affairs is most obvious, as the story also makes clear, between Haiti and the Dominican Republic sharing not only a past but an island. Yet, Lydia Vega's Puerto Rican perspective also includes the island of her birth as participating uneasily in this triangle which subsumes points of commonality which outside of the U.S. could herald defiance while within point to a long-standing and cyclical pattern of racial oppression. Significantly, at the only point in the story at which the three men are not insulting each other, they turn to denigrate the women of their particular homelands, testifying powerfully to the absence of women's voices and presence in the formation and formulation of national identities in all three nation states.

As Cuban scholar and artist Coco Fusco points out, 1492 was the year in which Spain expelled from within its borders what remained of 800 years of African/Moorish colonization, at the same time as it undertook the colonization of the Americas and its indigenous population. This ushered into existence the African Diaspora in the New World, making of Christopher Columbus, as Louise Erdrich and Michael Dorris have suggested (in their novel, *The Crown of Columbus*), the first slave trader of the so-called New World. Hence, the hierarchy based on constructions of race and a simultaneous pursuit of deracialization on the part of the formerly colonized Spaniards is put into motion: as a Haitian-born woman who descends from Africans, French, Spanish, Arawak from both Haitian and Dominican foreparents, I believe this racial hierarchy remains a reality in the Spanish-speaking Caribbean islands such as Lydia Vega illustrates.

RESURRECTING THE DEAD

It is no understatement to note that the Haitian Revolution which began in 1791 with the sounding of the conch by the Jamaican-born Haitian Boukman and ended with the declaration of Haiti's Independence on January 1st, 1804, has stood as a rallying point for peoples of African descent during various times of insurrection previous to the abolition of slavery in this hemisphere in the late 1800s. In a 1994 interview with Consuelo López Springfield, Ana Lydia Vega notes that, before the abolition of slavery in Puerto Rico in 1873, Puerto Rican slaves escaped to and found refuge in Haiti. She says: "It's fascinating ... . There are lots of testimonies about those who fled to Haiti. Do you know what really fascinates me, something that I would like to write about someday? When Haiti declared its independence – it was like the Cuba of its time – it had a plan to liberate all the slaves in the Caribbean" (1994: 824). This plan, of course, did not materialize except in the workings of the imagination. Nonetheless, Lydia Vega's observations here are fascinating for other reasons. The comparison she makes between the Haitian Revolution of the last century to the Cuban Revolution of the mid-twentieth century contains racialized implications since both revolutions promised to liberate disadvantaged classes within their respective nation states, classes largely populated by Black and mixed-race peoples. Racialized implications which should have us reflect on the extent to which racism remains a deeply rooted facet of the Caribbean experience that neither Haiti's *indigéniste* movement nor Cesaire's Pan-African *négritude* movement nor Latin America's *Afrocriollo* movement have deracinated. Nonetheless, particularly in Latin American letters, the rise of magic realism which is so in vogue cross-culturally in the Americas today owes its *raison d'être* to Black insurrection. Alejo Carpentier, the white Cuban writer who coined the term "marvelous realism" and gave birth to a movement in 1949 expressed it best in his preface to *The Kingdom of this World* when he wrote:

> After feeling the in no way false enchantment of this Haitian earth, after discovering magic presences on the red roads of the Central Plateau, after hearing the drums of Petro and Rada, I was moved to compare this marvelous reality I'd just been living with the exhaustingly vain attempts to arouse the marvelous that characterize certain European literatures of these last thirty years ... . With each step I found *the real marvelous*. But I also realized that the presence and authority of the real marvelous was not a privilege unique to Haiti but the patrimony of all the Americas, where, for example, a census of cosmogonies is still to be established. (Carpentier 1949: 28, 30)

Leaving aside for the moment Carpentier's, at times, admittedly racist contributions to the *Negrismo* movement which pre-dated the *Afrocriollo* movement of the 1920s to 1940s, his preface underscores the necessity to resurrect the dead and more specifically the heritage of Black Revolution which informed Caribbean consciousness in its distinctiveness from European modes of being, a distinctiveness both syncretic and African in its constitution. Of course, neither the Haitian Revolution nor the Cuban Revolution nor the literary movements taking place in the span of time between the two historical moments achieved their promise of unilateral, racial liberation as Cristina García reveals with respect to Cuba in her debut novel *Dreaming in Cuban* (1992).

In fact, the novel reveals that when it comes to racial identity, Cuba continues to experience, as do many of the islands, a loss of memory. The novel provides a window into the lives of three generations of Cuban women both in Cuba and the U.S.: the matriarch, Celia, her daughters, Felicia and Lourdes, and their own children, most notably Lourdes's American-born daughter, Pilar. Although we are told that Felicia and Lourdes's father, Jorge, is mixed-race, all but Felicia seem to acknowledge this lineage. Jorge's mother, Berta Arango del Pino and her daughter Ofelia "rubbed whitening cream into their dark, freckled faces ... to remove any evidence of [their] mulatto blood" (Garcia 1992: 41). The whitening creams, if they have no effect on the color of these women's skins, nonetheless leave a mark in the psyche of their family, which then proceeds to distance themselves or disremember this heritage. Celia gave voice to this dis-memory when she locked her children in her house during the feast day of Changó in fear of what she believed to be "the black people's god" (76). Her daughter Felicia, however, believes in African gods and dies in the pursuit of her initiation into a *santería* community. One wonders if her death can be partly attributed to the family's lack of faith and belief in a past they have failed to constructively engage as part of their identities. García writes critically of the Communist "re-education" programs in Cuba which served to re-write the past. Yet, she also confirms through Felicia's friend Herminia, the only self-identified Black character of the novel, that though the Revolution was successful in improving the quality of life of some of the Black and mixed-race underclasses, the contributions of the Black population to Cuba's history have been largely undermined. Speaking of the war of 1912 she says: "The war that killed my grandfather and great-uncles and thousands of other blacks is only a footnote in our history books. Why, then, should I trust anything I read?" (185). Ironically, Garcia's text asks us to trust what these characters have to tell us on the subject of recalling the past, activating Felicia's own contention that the "imagination, like memory, can transform lies to truth" (88). By decoding the lies of history along racial lines, perhaps a more accurate portrait of what is still left to achieve, an ideological and spiritual revolution, might be achieved.

This view is echoed in Ana Lydia Vega's *Présence Africaine* essay of 1976 where she concludes, with respect to the mis-positioning of Black identity in Puerto Rico, that

> le Nègre, c'est ce qu'il y a de plus refoulé et de plus valable dans la portoricanité. C'est ce qui lui donne sa positivité, sa véritable définition car il est symbole de la résistance devant l'injustice et l'oppression. Le Nègre est affirmation de soi devant les forces destructrices de la colonisation. La Négritude cesse alors d'être vécue comme une fatalité pour devenir un choix, un acte [the Negro represents what is most reviled and most valuable in Puertorican-ness. It is what gives it its positivity, its real definition for he is the symbol of resistance in the face of injustice and oppression. The Negro is an affirmation of the self in the face of the nihilistic forces of colonization. Negritude, then, ceases to be lived fatalistically to become a choice, an act]. (Vega 1976: 179)

The Negro thus assumes a dualistic position much like that of the Haitian contemporaneously: the ennobled ex-slave is lauded while the laborers who bear the mark of their ancestors in the very color of their skins are denied access to that heritage through their continued disenfranchisement.

BLACK OPPRESSION

As the product of a Haitian-Dominican family, I have long wondered at the animosity that fuels the relationship between Haitians and Dominicans. I never knew my Dominican grandfather, a man who, throughout my childhood, was referred to as an "espagnol," or Spanish, a euphemism for race and class privilege, though the man was, like most of us on both sides of the island, of mixed African and European heritage. Even though my grandfather seemed to benefit from an elevated status because he came from the other side of the island, it never occurred to me to think of him as better than the Haitian parts of my family: I assumed, in effect, that we were all part of the same land, that we all shared a long and exalted history.

What I have come to know of the Dominican Republic over time, however, has not been comforting. As I have garnered more knowledge about the history that has bound the two nations of this island together, it has become clear that ours is a history mired in bloodshed and distrust, one that will take conscious and consistent effort to overcome. The dualism noted by Vega, embodied by the person of African descent in the Caribbean, is particularly salient in the Dominican Republic where Independence Day is celebrated to mark the end of Haitian domination of the former Spanish colony in 1844. It is mystifying to note that late twentieth-century rhetoric explaining the reasons for Dominican oppression of Haitians today, most notably in the cane field massacres of the 1930s, are attributed as James Gaffney writes "to harsh policies and practices of Haitian domination during the first half of the 19th century" (1994: 11), a time referred to by one historian as the period of "Black Oppression" (Fagg 1965: 145) – an ironic moniker, to say the least, when one remembers that the Dominican Republic was still governed by the Spanish Crown and slavery had yet to be abolished. In histories of the Dominican Republic, then, Toussaint L'Ouverture is referred to as a dictator and subsequent leaders as tyrants. No mention is ever made of insurrections taking place on the eastern side of the island which were bolstered by those involved in the making of the Haitian Revolution. This is to say that at a time when the Dominican Republic was still governed by the Spanish Crown and slavery had yet to be abolished on the eastern side of the island, such a period could only have been oppressive for those who still looked to Europe both for governance and for identification. Left dormant in our history books is a record of the slave insurrections taking place in the Dominican Republic at this time, bolstered by the Haitian Revolution. What we do not readily know is the effect the Revolution had on the enslaved population of the Dominican Republic. All we do know is that today, in the DR, the term "negro" denotes African lineage without carrying negative connotations, but that the term "Haitiano" is pejorative at the same time as it coincides with the visible "negritude" of Haitians; blackness and Haitianness have thus become negatively synonymous. Trujillo's regime, and, ironically, Duvalier's regime as well (steeped as it was in "noirisme" but usurping its power in order to oppress the masses) underscored this negation, making of Haitians the true martyrs of a brutality contained by neither nation.

Such a history, for one of Haitian background, becomes necessarily a site of fear. I learned of the massacres which took place under Trujillo's "de-Haitianization" campaigns which came to a head in 1937 with the massacre of 12–20,000 cane workers along the Haitian–Dominican border. In a film entitled *Sucre Noir*, by Canadian journalist Michel Régnier, this death toll was reported to have been as large as 40,000. The massacre took place amid resounding silence and has only begun to be accurately unearthed. Trujillo's aim to "Dominicanize" the Dominican Republic (or to de-Haitianize the Dominican Republic) rendered the borderlands between the two countries a battleground in which Dominicans and Haitians who had peacefully co-existed together, in trade and in conjugal unions, intermarrying, and so on, were rendered enemies. Haitians, by virtue of their "Africanness" associated to their relationship to vodou and by virtue of their increasing poverty from the 1800s to the early 1900s were seen as undesirables and, though many historians contend that only ethnic difference separated the two populations, it is also clear that the de-Haitianization process hinged on the racialization of Haitians as a sub-species. This racialization process began before Trujillo's regime, especially under the U.S. occupation of the island. Writes Lauren Derby: "new formulation[s] of social lowness ... associated Haitians with all forms of bodily pollution, especially disease and contagion" (1994: 504). She notes further that the definition of nationhood thus progressively shifted, in small almost imperceptible shifts in cultural demarcations of desirables vs. undesirables: "The nation ... transformed here in meaning through the redefinition of its boundaries, as the civilized center narrows to include ... little more than healthy, employed Dominican men" (1994: 503–4). As Derby says, "the body politic was remapped" and women's bodies, associated with the market place and prostitution in exchanges between the two countries, became abject entities. What these shifts in perceptions of border trade, both of goods (through women) and of women's bodies could not predict was the degree to which they would reformulate the notion of the body politic as a Europeanized male state which such exchanges put into question. For, if the Haitian body was indistinct through years of intermarriage with Dominicans, then nationhood could not be redefined and accessed in a de-Africanized manner. The Dominicanization process set into motion a chain of irreversible changes, changes whose effect on the future could not have been predicted. The Americans occupied the island and, in that process, imposed certain codes of sanitation and hygiene connected to the trade which hinged upon cultural codes subordinating Black and female bodies, thereby setting into motion the *mechanism* for Trujillo's Dominicanization program which culminated in the cataclysm of the cane field massacres ... massacres which now emerge as only a garish symptom of a more widespread and systemic genocide of Haitians during Trujillo's regime.

... a swarm of butterflies beats its wings in one place and this fluttering causes a storm elsewhere ...

MARIPOSAS

History, thus, has a way of coming round again and it is under the dictatorship of Rafael Trujillo, the subject of Julia Alvarez's recent novel, *In the Time of the Butterflies* (1994) that we find a convergence of Haitian and Dominican destinies. Although, as have noted reviewers of the novel such as Elizabeth Martînez, the novel sidesteps issues of color and "the particularities of the Afro-Dominican experience" (1998: 41), it resurrects a period in time under the regime in which Dominicans were subject to a terrorism not unlike that being experienced on the other side of the border by Haitians under Duvalier. The novel recounts the lives and deaths of three of the four Mirabal sisters who actively resisted the Trujillo regime and were slain for their counter-government activities. Known as the "mariposas" or butterflies, their deaths on November 25th, 1960 have been commemorated in Latin America as the International Day Against Violence Toward Women. Alvarez depicts their almost naive courage, especially that of the most defiant of the sisters, Minerva, in poetic terms. When her sister, Marîa Teresa records the events of their incarceration at the end of the years of anti-Trujillo activities, she tells us of a defiant Minerva:

Where does that sister of mine get her crazy courage?

As she was being marched down the hall, a voice from one of the cells they passed called out, *Mariposa does not belong to herself alone. She belongs to Quisqueya!* Then everyone was beating on the bars, calling out, *!Viva la Mariposa!* Tears came to my eyes. Something big and powerful spread its wings inside me.

Courage, I told myself. And this time, I felt it. (1994: 238)

Clearly, the fact that the novel depicts women's roles in insurrection when our history books have largely left women's voices muted or silenced on the edges of such texts is important. And yet, another resounding silence in the novel is the nature of Trujillo's regime which did not only filter through class lines as the novel demonstrates but across the border.

In a poeticized language reminiscent of Julia Alvarez, Edwidge Danticat's short story, "Nineteen Thirty-Seven," memorializes this suppressed aspect of Trujillo's legacy. In this story, the narrator explains her mother's bitterness towards the Dominican Republic in reference to Massacre River, "the river separating Haiti from the Spanish-speaking country that she had never allowed me to name because I had been born on the night that El Generalissimo, Dios Trujillo, the honorable chief of state, had ordered the massacre of all Haitians living there" (Danticat 1995: 33). However, there is nothing poetic about the story this young narrator has to tell of a mother who watched her own mother being killed by Dominican soldiers as she tried to cross the river, who has been incarcerated on Haitian soil under the Duvalier regime for suspicion of witchcraft, for "having wings of flame," and whose only consolation resides in the statue of the Virgin Mary brought to her by her daughter on visitation days. When she expires, it is her daughter who consoles herself with the memory that the day of her birth

in the year nineteen hundred and thirty-seven, in the Massacre River, my mother did fly. Weighted down by my body inside hers, she leaped from Dominican soil into the water, and out again on the Haitian side of the river. She glowed red when she came out, blood clinging to her skin, which at that moment looked as though it were in flames. (48)

Crossing physical borders and metaphysical boundaries, the narrator's mother embodies both Dominican and Haitian identity and, in so doing, transcends their bipolarization. She too becomes a "mariposa."

I think it is no coincidence that both Alvarez and Danticat make use of the image of the butterfly in their writings when speaking on the issue of the liberation of Haitians and Dominicans, particularly of women. In *Breath, Eyes, Memory* (1994), Danticat tells the folkloric story of a woman who "walked around with blood constantly spurting from out of her unbroken skin" (87). This goes on for twelve long years until, after consulting with the goddess Erzulie, the woman realizes that the only way to end her suffering is to end her life as a human being. "The woman was tired of bleeding," Danticat writes, "so she went home and divided her goods among her friends and loved ones. Then she went back to Erzulie for her transformation" (87). Erzulie lets her choose the form of life she would like to take. After some thought, she chooses a form of life that symbolizes freedom: the butterfly. Similarly, in *The Farming of Bones* (1998), Danticat describes one of the Haitians fleeing Trujillo's regime, Tibo, in the following manner: "He opened his arms and spread them, like the rare large butterfly that drifted past us now and then, testing new wings against the unfriendly currents of the mountain air" (174). In this way, she demonstrates that the butterfly is not uniquely feminized but a symbol of hope for all Haitians. Yet, it is ironic that in both Alvarez and Danticat's work, the death of women provides the opportunity for transformation (the character of Tibo in *The Farming of Bones* also dies).

Nonetheless, Alvarez and Danticat offer the beginnings for a more thorough examination of the terrain of Haitian/Dominican identity which lies somewhere in the morass of conflicting ideas of "nationality" and "solidarity" – ideas which have everything to do with the construction and deconstruction of a permeable border not unlike the U.S./Mexico border discussed in the work of Gloria Anzaldúa. Of the latter, Anzaldúa writes: "In the Borderlands/ you are the battleground/ where enemies are kin to each other; you are at home, a stranger, the border disputes have been settled/ the volley of shots have shattered the truce/ you are wounded, lost in action/ dead, fighting back" (from "To Live in the Borderlands Means You," 1987: 194). Trujillo's despotism rendered the borderlands just such a battleground.

Dominican writer Loida Maritza Perez's recently published first novel, *Geographies of Home* (1999), provides some interesting insights into the effects of the processes of "bodily remapping" Derby has noted as taking place in the lives of Dominicans during the Trujillo years. Perez concentrates especially on those Dominicans who, from the lower socio-economic strata, have emigrated to the United States only to find that they become raced Others. Perez's female characters are clearly abject creations and they struggle to realize destinies uncircumscribed by racialized and gendered categories. The novel tells the story of one family's inability to make of the U.S. a home; the main character, Iliana, who is the youngest of three sisters in a family of seven siblings, has had the opportunity both to hold on to pieces of Dominican culture and to the opportunities the U.S. presents. Throughout the novel, her journey is one of sifting through the legacy of the past, the ways in which it has infected and affected her family, and to find how, if possible, to overcome that past in the present in order to move towards a more productive future. Iliana's relationship to one sister in particular, Marina, is pivotal. Though most of the family suffers from some form of dysfunction or another, Marina is the closest to insanity. Iliana returns home from college to find Marina suffering from a mental breakdown. She searches for clues that might have foretold this occurrence by turning to old family photos. Perez writes of Iliana:

> Whenever she tried to focus on Marina's face, her eyes settled on a single feature rather than on the whole. It was as if a door inside her had willfully slammed shut against a complete view for fear of recognizing something not in her sister but in her herself: some shared genetic trait able to hint at her own susceptibility to madness. She involuntarily found herself checking off their differences to persuade herself that although they had been conceived in the same womb it did not follow that she too would lose her mind. No. Her sister's madness had not been diagnosed as schizophrenic. At least not definitely. (1999: 41)

Though Marina may not be schizophrenic, she is presented throughout the novel as Iliana's foil or mirror-image. Interestingly, then, it is revealed that the root of Marina's self-loathing is situated in the very features of her face. Beatriz, the oldest of the four sisters claimed that "no one ... would ever consider [Marina] attractive. Not with her baboon nose and nigger lips. So Marina had better resign herself to becoming an old maid" (42). Remembering these childhood comparisons, Iliana inspects her own face in the photographs "[b]ecause she continued to think of herself as ugly" and "was repeatedly surprised when others described her as beautiful" (43). Marina never overcomes her racial shame, one compounded by her siblings and by the American mind-set to which the family has emigrated where Blackness is summarily denigrated. Although Iliana begins to appreciate her features, what she calls the "contradictory features on her face," she shares a struggle for self-actualization with her sister though on the level of sexuality. Marina, as her sister foretold, remains an old maid for fear of how her Black features will be received while Iliana hides the fact that she has not come to terms with her own sexuality, one which the text hints is as contradictory as her facial features. On more than one occasion Iliana is mistaken for a drag queen; at the end of the novel, it is Marina who finally realizes that Iliana may be a lesbian. The novel's shocking denouement occurs when Marina, in a fit of violence, assaults Iliana physically and rapes her as she attempts to prove that Iliana is a man disguised as a woman. Though delusional, her violence has profound effects; for one, Iliana realizes that they share the same blood, the same shame, a racial shame as well as an immigrant shame. After the assault, Iliana thinks:

> Had she possessed the courage, she would have cut herself open to witness the spilling of her own blood. She would have hurried home, thrust her slit wrists before her parents, told them: "This here is the problem, this blood in my veins which my sister has made me despise just as she has despised her own." She would have severed the cord connecting her to her sister and enabling her to understand, even in the midst of her own despair, why it was that Marina hated her so. She was the prodigal daughter who had returned, the one her parents now proudly offered up as an example. (311)

In the end, Iliana survives the racial and gendered violence the rest of her family suffers through, and impose on each other, by remembering one piece of her heritage that has not been lost or distorted. This piece is a truism spoken by her maternal grandmother, Bienvenida: "in our blood we carry the power of the sea" (134) – the power to regenerate, to persevere, to give birth and to take life away, to remember. Symbolically then, the sea and the blood that Marina despises to the point of craziness offer Iliana the hope contained in their coagulation. For, in the Caribbean context, the sea is not only a symbol of death and regeneration but, more specifically, acts as a tangible relic of the Middle Passage, its attendant horrors as well as the history of slave insurrections following which should have resulted in the decoloniza-tion of spirit and mind that, evidently, Perez's Dominican American characters have yet to transcend. Perez's novel suggest to me that Trujillo's de-Haitianization process has been as damaging to the Dominican psyche as they have been to the Haitian one. While the Dominican Republic, from a Haitian point of view, can easily be seen only as a site of further impoverishment and exploitation, work like Perez's reveals that for Dominicans, life on the other side of the border may be similarly harrowing.

As a Haitian, however, it remains difficult to reconcile the Dominican Republic's history vis-à-vis Haiti with the immigration of my own grandfather's family at the turn of the century to the Haitian side of the island in search of a better future. Neither can I reconcile it with the relative prosperity I understand exists beyond our mountains on the Spanish half of Hispaniola. The difference between our two countries, in the end, is one of relative access and racial privilege in a wider global economy. Haitians provide the labor that others of us benefit from: they supply the playing field with its various accouterments while others are permitted to play the game.

The Haitian coat of arms bears an inscription that reads: "L'Union fait la force." It can be loosely translated in English to mean there is strength in numbers or that in unity there is strength. The lack of unity between Haiti and the Dominican Republic will, in the long run, assure our downfall. It is an irony that in the U.S., Haitians and Dominicans can come together and come to know each other's histories of pain and suffering. On this side of the ocean, we can commiserate. We may read Julia Alvarez and Junot Diaz alongside Edwidge Danticat and Ana Lydia Vega. We find that we are more like than unlike, and that Hispaniola has enriched us in ways that few others can understand with its riches of natural resources, stunning arrays of fresh fruits, multicolored birds and traditions that hearken back to ancient Africa. We share a history of Revolution against enslavement and also the nightmare of two regimes that have left us divided even among members of our own individual families. And still, we are one people. If we cannot recognize this, then one wonders how the Caribbean as a whole can overcome the deeply rooted schisms fostered through colonization and whether decolonization will ever truly take place in our collective hearts and minds.

CONCLUSION

In her reading of Ana Lydia Vega's story, "Cloud Cover Caribbean," Diana Veléz ponders if the racism the Haitian, Cuban and Dominican men will face in the U.S. will "operate as a unifying factor." She suggests that it is the men's carrying forth of their "imagined communities" to the United States that will divide them further, concluding that "what brought them together, if only temporarily while they were adrift, was hunger, racism, and a desire to escape" (Veléz 1994: 832). I would like to suggest a different interpretation: that Lydia Vega, in dedicating the volume in which the story appears to the yet-to-exist Caribbean Federation, pleads that we not forge our bonds on the basis of our dispossession but on the basis of the history that has made the Caribbean the rich amalgamation that it is, an amalgamation forged through the sweat, labor and fierce revolutionary persistence of the Africans brought to the Americas in chains. What she is demanding is that we risk losing our nationalistic investments in identities derived from the amnesia of Eurocentric definitions of power in order to regain a true sense of who we are and where we have come from. In the stories that contemporary Caribbean women writers such as Edwidge Danticat, Julia Alvarez, Cristina García and Loida Maritza Perez have had to tell, it is also clear that in unearthing women's lost stories of insurrection we have the opportunity to see the past through new lenses. We have the opportunity to turn the ghosts of the past into the butterflies of our imagined futures: a future in which to recognize the "Negro," Haitian or Afro-Caribbean person as central to Caribbean identity is to be free. What we risk to gain is a rebirth of ourselves, of a transmutation of one energy to another from one site of memory to another so that our ancestors may be reclaimed, "bone by bone" (Alice Walker 1983 quoting Emily Dickinson), much like a swarm of butterflies causing hurricanes to form somewhere, not far, with every beat of wing, in remembrance.

REFERENCES

Alvarez, Julia, 1994. *In the Time of the Butterflies*, New York: Penguin.

Anzaldúa, Gloria, 1987. *Borderlands/La Frontera: The New Mestiza*, San Francisco: Aunt Lute.

Benitez-Rojo, Antonio, 1992. *The Repeating Island: The Caribbean and the Post-modern Perspective*, Durham, NC: Duke University Press.

Carpentier, Alejo, 1949. *The Kingdom of this World*, New York: Noonday Press, 1989.

Carpentier, Alejo, 1993. "Prologue to *The Kingdom of This World*", *Review: Latin American Literature and the Arts*, 47 (Fall), pp. 28–31.

Danticat, Edwidge, 1994. *Breath, Eyes, Memory*, New York: Soho.

Danticat, Edwidge, 1995. "Nineteen Thirty-Seven," in *Krik? Krak!*, New York: Vintage.

Danticat, Edwidge, 1998. *The Farming of Bones*, New York: Soho.

Derby, Lauren, 1994. "Haitians, Magic and Money: Raza and Society in the Haitian–Dominican Borderlands 1900 to 1937," *Comparative Studies in Society and History*, 36: 3.

Fagg, John Edwin, 1965. *Cuba, Haiti, & the Dominican Republic*, New Jersey: Prentice-Hall.

Gaffney, James, 1994. "Race and Politics Where America Began," *America*, (May), pp. 10–12.

Garcia, Cristina, 1992. *Dreaming in Cuban*, New York: Ballantine Books.

Hernández, Elizabeth and Consuelo López Springfield, 1994. "Women and Writing in Puerto Rico: An Interview with Ana Lydia Vega," *Callaloo*, 17.3, pp. 816–25.

Kincaid, Jamaica, 1988. *A Small Place*, New York: Plume.

Lydia Vega, Ana, 1976. "Négritude et libération nationale dans la littérature portoricaine," *Présence Africaine: Revue culturelle du Monde Noir*, pp. 99–100, pp. 167–80.

Lydia Vega, Ana, 1995. "Cloud Cover Caribbean," in *Rhythm & Revolt*, ed. Marcella Breton, New York: Penguin.

Martînez, Elizabeth, 1998. "Of Passion and Politics" (Review of *In the Time of the Butterflies*), *The Progressive*, pp. 39–42.

Perez, Loida Maritza, 1999. *Geographies of Home*, New York: Viking.

Philip, M. Nourbese, 1997. *A Genealogy of Resistance and Other Essays*, Toronto: The Mercury Press.

Vélez, Diana L., 1994. "We Are (Not) in This Together: The Caribbean Imaginary in 'Encancarublado' by Ana Lydia Vega," *Callaloo*, 17.3, pp. 826–33.

Walker, Alice, 1983. *In Search of Our Mother's Gardens*, New York: Harcourt Brace Jovanovich.

12

Reclaiming Maps and Metaphors: Canadian First Nations and Narratives of Place

Richard J. Lane

THEORETICAL CONSIDERATIONS

Postcolonial studies, and the concomitant application of various types of related literary theory, is often concerned with analyzing contemporary fictional narratives to discern the subtleties of *re*negotiated cultural positions within society; personal and historical behavioral models are also brought into play in this process from a variety of critical disciplines as ideological positions within fictional texts are revealed and critiqued. As a critical tool with a pedagogic function, postcolonial literary theory often takes dual analytical and interdictive (or ethical) positions; in other words, it analyzes and reflects upon acts within texts that it is argued *should* be prohibited in the world now or in the future. This essay will explore three main questions that relate to this chiasmus, or crossing of the analytical and the interdictive in postcolonial theory:

1. Can postcolonial theory account for the *traces of trauma* that exist structurally, not necessarily thematically, within aboriginal writing (for example with the Residential School experiences and/or the banning of the potlatch in Canada)?
2. How *useful* is postcolonial theory in contributing to real-world solutions for aboriginal peoples (for example, with the negotiation of treaties)?
3. When it comes to the actual implementation of real-world solutions for aboriginal peoples within a postcolonial context, how useful is postcolonial theory for analyzing the resulting explosion of related contemporary narratives from a wide range of media that often blur the boundaries between fact and fiction?

Beginning with the first question and the example of the potlatch: its banning and reinstatement exists for Canada's First Nations like a painful scar; the potlatch "itself" should not be spoken about in this singular way (an example of a postcolonial interdiction here), because it resists being categorized as a homogenized entity or practice; rather the potlatch is a group of overlapping practices, named in retrospect. In *The Potlatch Papers* (1997), Chris Bracken argues that the colonial discursive practices that lead to the criminalization of the potlatch in British Columbia are themselves an enfolding and intertwining of notions of identity and otherness; British Columbia or the Pacific Northwest is a westerly limit where the originary conceptual center falls apart once this enfolding or intertwining is recognized. In relation to these same colonial processes in British Columbia, Chief Joe Mathias and Gary Yabsley argue that:

> The economic consequence of the loss of lands and resources is easy to appreciate. What is less obvious is the extent to which federal law in particular reached into Indian communities in an effort to suffocate the most forceful elements of traditional Indian political and cultural identity. The Indian act was repeatedly used to destroy traditional institutions of Indian government and to abolish those cultural practices that defined Indian identity. For British Columbia First Nations, this assault focused on the potlatch. (1991: 36–7)

For the purposes of this essay, the interest is in the ways in which the criminalization of the potlatch registered *culturally* as trauma – akin to the known sexual and other abuses committed against aboriginal peoples in Residential Schools narrated in fictional texts such as Tomson Highway's *Kiss of the Fur Queen* (1998). The latter novel is a surrealist text that can nonetheless be examined thematically via ethical reading strategies, even though the novel's surrealism paradoxically disrupts thematic/ethical readings (for example, the boundaries between event perception and interpretative certainty concerning the reality of events, such as sexual abuse, are blurred). But how do we account for culturally traumatic events that may structure narrative at a more fundamental level? Such events may be present in or through narrative at the level of *traces*, or present as such in ways that cannot be thematized or turned into moral lessons – and I'm deliberately operating with a simplistic model of postcolonial theory here as it is a pedagogy that increasingly is taught at earlier and earlier educational stages. One critical approach is to turn to reader-response theory to investigate trauma in fictional texts, but the notion of a structural *presencing* of trauma may operate in a more fundamental and profound way. Thinking here about the historical sequence between banning and then reinstating the potlatch in British Columbia, roughly seventy years (1880–1951), there was a shift between the attempt to destroy totally aboriginal cultures and an attempt to "hand back" cultural property, reversing not only the law, but the history of colonialism. As Jean Baudrillard argues, "If there is something distinctive about an event – about what constitutes an event and thus has historical value – it is the fact that it is irreversible, that there is always something in it which exceeds meaning and interpretation" (1994: 13). Baudrillard, in his usual polemical way, is concerned with the attempted reversal of history on a grander scale, whereby a kind of millennial creative accounting wipes clean the errors of the past; he also argues that this reversal of history is a way of negating the reality of events. The official reinstatement of the potlatch in Canada can be read as an attempt (actual and symbolic) at wiping clean the seventy years of colonial interference with First Nations culture and society, an assertion that the efficacy of the potlatch (and all that it represents) is no longer an issue, in other words that this efficacy had apparently been negated or cancelled out. In relation to Baudrillard here, this is a reversal of history, as if to say, this *trauma* did not happen, and/or, if it did, it's all over now anyway. What happened in those seventy years is open to debate, not only because the potlatch was banned (yet still continued), but also because the notion of history "itself" was contested (that is, how and why the interpretative parameters constitutive of what we know as "history" are controlled).

In touching upon issues such as the mechanisms of historical construction or versioning, postcolonial theory necessarily broadens out into a form of cultural studies, or can be thought of as one more contemporary "branch" of cultural studies. The main example considered here is the Nisga'a Treaty. Put very simply, treaty negotiations involve in part a judicial recognition of forms of evidence that function outside of Eurocentric or Western frameworks of experience and knowledge. Counteracting such recognition in British Columbia until fairly recently has been the issue of precedent. Bell and Asch argue that:

> Continuity, fairness, certainty, and predictability are the rationale for this doctrine, which is viewed as crucial in maintaining a tradition of legal objectivity. The concept of fairness reflects a formal notion of equality that all people should stand equally before the law. (1998: 39)

To summarize briefly, critics have argued that the use of precedent was highly problematic in relation to aboriginal self-government. Also, evidence put forward in courts may fall outside of the parameters of tests that have been applied in the past (in other words, the evidence is not accepted as such). However, times change and precedent is not necessarily a constraining process. To quote Bell and Asch once more: "The common law evolves not only when precedent is followed but also when it is distinguished. It is not precedent itself that binds, but judicial interpretation of the past and its relevance to the present" (40). In the initial *Delgamuukw* v. *the Queen* case (a breakthrough case for the Nisga'a in a century of legal battle with the Crown), the Canadian judiciary relied upon precedents based upon an outmoded "analytical framework which was developed by the social sciences in the nineteenth century" (Bell and Asch 1998: 64). Bell and Asch argue that with the "legal theory of culture" we get the following results:

1. The legal theory of culture allows for the possibility that human beings may live in groups and yet not live in society.
2. The legal theory of culture allows for the possibility that societies can exist that are not "organized" or that may be "organized" only with respect to some aspects of social life.
3. The legal theory of culture allows for the possibility that organized societies exist that do not have jurisdiction over their members and their territory.
4. The legal theory of culture allows for the possibility that organized societies exist where there is no "ownership," particularly with respect to land. (65)

There was a positive outcome from the *Delgamuukw* case: the recognition by the British Columbia Court of Appeal that the Nisga'a had unextinguished rights to their territory and further, that negotiation would be the best way forward in solving the issue of aboriginal title, resulting in the ratification of the Nisga'a treaty (see Nisga'a Final Agreement, Web Resources and References, below).

So what has this got to do with postcolonial theory and my second question: "how *useful* is postcolonial theory in contributing to real-world solutions for aboriginal peoples?" One of the issues in the ongoing court cases that led to the final Nisga'a Agreement was the problem of what actually constituted "evidence" in courts; crudely speaking, there was a division among Western peoples, between those on the court benches who at times rejected aboriginal practices and oral narratives as evidence, and those experts who were either involved positively with putting forward (and helping to authorize) such evidence, or, who commented in anger and disbelief over its rejection. Of interest is this *division* and how postcolonial theory, in part, may be responsible for the development of a more open, although not necessarily more sophisticated, acceptance and respect for other cultural viewpoints (and this will eventually lead me to the media responses to the Nisga'a treaty). Thinking of the general response to postcolonial literatures among a wide range of readers, there is often an almost automatic interest, respect and acceptance of, for example, aboriginal spirituality, as with Australian aboriginal Dreamtime, by the very readers who reject, say, Christianity or Islam as being irrational, too fundamentalist or in some ways totalitarian. A respect for other cultures may go hand in hand with the ongoing dissection and critique of colonial misdemeanors performed in the name of Eurocentric spiritual values, or, such a respect may simply be an expression of the complete commodification of all cultural belief-systems. Regardless of these arguments, it seems to me imperative that we reach a deeper understanding of *what* such an acceptance of other spiritual or religious systems means within a predominantly secular society.

My third question was: "when it comes to the actual implementation of real world solutions for aboriginal peoples within a postcolonial context, how useful is postcolonial theory for analyzing the resulting explosion of related contemporary narratives from a wide range of media that often blur the boundaries between fact and fiction?" Hamar Foster looks at some of the extreme responses to the Nisga'a treaty, summarizing them with the following questions:

1. Is treaty government "race-based"?
2. Is the treaty a "giveaway" by "compliant politicians"?
3. Does the treaty amend the Constitution? (1998–9: 7–33)

Taking the first question only, a summarized sub-set of statements might go something like this: such a treaty is race-based and therefore a form of racism against white/Euro British Columbians, and anyway such a treaty treats aboriginal peoples differently and is therefore violating principles of equality. Foster replies: "Prejudice against Indians may be based upon race, but treaties are based upon property rights and sovereignty: in this case, property rights and sovereignty that have long been ignored and denied" (1998–9: 28). Further, the notion of equality in British Columbia's history "has been more of a flag of convenience than a true principle." Further still, "there is something distinctly hypocritical about stripping a people of their resources and then describing a complex and careful attempt to restore some of those resources as ... a violation of equality before the law" (29). In the same issue of *BC*

Studies John Borrows parodies key statements from David Black, a media baron, and statements made on the (Canadian) Reform Party's web site. Here are the statements, via Trickster: "Let's trash the treaty. Let's scrap any talk of special group rights in British Columbia. We can't countenance race-based entitlements that sanction apartheid in our midst" (Borrows 1998–9: 106), and: "We must be vigilant against government attempts to erode our democratic rights without input or participation. Too much has been done in secret; the government has kept the average person in the dark" (1998–9: 106–7). While freedom of expression is sacrosanct, such statements are made with no cultural, historical or ethical understanding whatsoever.

Perhaps the third question has more to do with methodological issues: whether postcolonial studies is part of a wider cultural studies approach, or whether it is something placed on literature courses, usually within English departments, examining almost exclusively literary texts. In the latter case, there may be no time or space made available institutionally to examine other types of narratives circulating within the media, the courts, and so on, in comparison with the selected novels, plays, and poems usually focused upon. Why is there a need for this comparison? Because the production of an ethical stance produced via postcolonial theory needs to be contextualized in relation to the various stakeholders within the communities directly affected by cultural and economic renegotiations, with the concomitant awareness of the fact that those stakeholders themselves adopt complex political positions and allegiances that can shift at a moment's notice. For example, the overriding cash benefits of, say, a treaty, may in fact play a large part in changing the attitudes of key players who, crudely speaking, are usually portrayed by simplistic postcolonial readings as "the bad guys"; I'm thinking here of projected net financial benefits for British Columbia *after* all 50 potential or future treaty settlements; in 1999 Grant Thornton Management Consultants argued that this net benefit for British Columbia would be between 3.8 and 4.7 billion dollars. Stakeholders don't always change their attitudes because they have to: say, via judicial process; other factors come into play.

RECLAIMING MAPS AND METAPHORS

To examine one literary example of contemporary First Nations writing in relation to some of the above observations and arguments, Haisla author Eden Robinson's *Monkey Beach* (2000) is a text situated historically, geographically and culturally via the colonial and postcolonial formation(s) of British Columbia. In many respects, *Monkey Beach* is a narrative reclamation of the name "Haisla"; the book is intensely funny in places as a complex piece of trickster writing. The humor is in part a survival mechanism for the protagonist, but in this case not just in relation to the personal and community catastrophe generated as an effect of colonialism, but in relation to the sheer magnitude of power unleashed through the overall schema of contemporary First Nations writing: that of sacred text. The opening pages of *Monkey Beach* explain the mis-naming, the doubling (and beyond) and the displacements of the Haisla town of Kitamaat where the events of the novel are situated:

> Early in the nineteenth century, Hudson's Bay traders used Tsimshian guides to show them around, which is when the names began to get confusing. "Kitamaat" is a Tsimshian word that means people of the falling snow, and that was their name for the main Haisla village. So when Hudson's Bay traders asked their guides, "Hey, what's that village called?" and the Tsimshian guides said, "Oh, that's Kitamaat." The name got stuck on the official records … even though it should be called Haisla … To add to the confusion, when Alcan Aluminium moved into the area in the 1950s, it built a "city of the future" for its workers and named it Kitimat too, but spelled it differently. (Robinson 2000: 4–5)

As with the multiple and contradictory naming of place, the central protagonist of the novel "Lisamarie Hill" is dealing with multiple trauma: in the narrative present, it is the trauma generated by the loss of her brother Jimmy, who has gone missing along with the fishing boat that he was working on, called the *Queen of the North*. There is another more subtle emotion at work: that of the "traumatic imperative" she experiences in reclaiming indigenous knowledge and the spiritual powers that have been degraded historically (there is also the anxiety that "reclaiming" may be something that she cannot achieve). The novel as a whole mixes an immense number of genres and modes of writing, switching rapidly from self-parody, to intense seriousness, also utilizing literary, historical and journalistic discourses. Postcolonial hybridity, however, is not necessarily regarded by the narrator as a positive fact; rather it is one of the factors that leads to this rapid discursive switching and instability that makes cultural reclamation difficult to achieve. At one fairly factual level, the novel re-imagines colonial encounters, as with the confusion quoted above about the naming of place; Lisamarie travels by boat to attempt to find Jimmy, and the journey also becomes a re-imagining of the early colonial explorers: "Early explorers traveling through the Douglas Channel were probably daunted by both the terrain and the new languages they encountered" (Robinson 2000: 193). This observation is juxtaposed with a reflection on Haisla language, and a lesson concerning how the name Haisla is pronounced:

> The actual word for the Haisla language is Xa'islak'ala, to talk in the manner of Xa'isla. To say Xa'isla, touch your throat. Say the German "ach" or Scottish "loch." When you say the first part, the "Xa," say it from far back in your throat. The apostrophe between the syllables signals both an emphasis and a pause. Say "uh-uh," the way you'd say it if you were telling a child not to touch a stove. Put that same pause between the first and last syllables of Xa'isla. Haisla is difficult for English speakers to learn partly because most English sounds are formed using the front of the mouth, while Haisla uses mainly the back. (Robinson 2000: 193)

Such pedagogic sections of the text are to be distinguished from those that occur at the level of story; for example, the narrator's grandmother teaching her how to gather native foodstuffs, how to prepare various indigenous dishes, and how to harness spiritual powers. With the example concerning the difficulty of actually pronouncing Haisla, the narrator appears to be directly addressing the reader, not only drawing the reader into the story world, but at a more subtle level attempting to transform the reader from a passive consumer to an active participant in the "lessons" of the text. In other words, the reader is treated in a way similar to that of the "audience" or participatory members of a ritual, where the efficacy of the ritual is one that affects all of the people involved. Lisamarie can be thought of not just as a mediator between two worlds (crudely speaking, the Western world and the indigenous spirit world), since she is also a conduit to another way of experiencing the world through the act of reading. The novel can be thought of as telling a story – Lisamarie's growing up, the typical events of a *Bildungsroman* – and as creating a number of incidents and lessons that form a critical constellation, in Walter Benjamin's sense (a critical constellation is a montage form, where disparate and disjunctive images and events are brought together to create shock effects). That is to say, the story *progresses* chronologically through flashbacks to Lisamarie's past, and through incidents in the narrative present after Jimmy has gone missing, and the story *develops* structurally via the reconfiguration of narrative (the fact that the novel reworks the Canadian Gothic) and knowledge (literally teaching the protagonist and the reader about the Haisla First Nation). Jennifer Andrews, in her essay "Native Canadian

Gothic Refigured: Reading Eden Robinson's *Monkey Beach*", explains exactly how Robinson's text works through and upon genre:

> the novel retains many of the traditional markers of a [Canadian] Gothic text, incorporating settings and beings that reflect the emotional turmoil of a Gothic protagonist through a first-person narrative voice. But Robinson transports the Gothic to a Native context and, rather than depicting Haisla characters who populate the novel as potential threats to the safety of a white, Eurocentric community, lets them form their own world, in which monsters exist but are not necessarily destructive. What Northey [in *The Haunted Wilderness: The Gothic and the Grotesque in Canadian Fiction*] describes as Canadian writers' ambivalence toward the New World and the dislocation experienced by early settlers is replaced in *Monkey Beach* with uncertainty about the world beyond the Haisla community. It is this external world that proves to be potentially destructive, at least for the protagonist, Lisamarie Hill, who falls into a pattern of drug and alcohol abuse when she runs away to the urban centre of East Vancouver. Furthermore, instead of presenting the Gothic as a means of exploring how Canadians are haunted by a wilderness that they find unfamiliar and threatening, Robinson negotiates a space in which her characters can examine the possibilities inherent in connecting to the natural world, monsters and all . ... In *Monkey Beach*, she traces her characters' strong relationships to a wilderness that they recognize as having a burgeoning, though not necessarily just human, population and to a powerful tribal history that is far more important than the structural imposition of white, Western standards of civility. (Andrews 2001: 10–11)

Another way of thinking about this process of re-coding the Canadian Gothic and transforming it into the Native Gothic is as a significant part of the reclamation of maps and metaphors that occur throughout the novel. That is to say, the re-coding of genre is not simply an arbitrary stylistic or literary choice; rather it is a way of writing back against the colonial literary canon and other modes of representation of First Nations time and space. Thus, when the narrator opens the novel with the paradoxes of naming and mapping, and the ways in which the two are closely interrelated, she is also suggesting that older names can be recovered and colonial maps re-drawn; in other words, reclamation, while necessarily taking into account recent cultural and historical developments, can utilize the processes of misnaming and appropriation in a positive sense, that of overturning. To read *Monkey Beach* solely through the reversal of the usual codes and conventions of the Canadian Gothic, an act of metaphoric overturning, which produces the Native Gothic, is however to minimize the fact that the novel also works, as suggested, as a critical constellation. One of the real-world solutions offered by the novel is its rejection of a simplistic and nostalgic return to the aboriginal past; rather, the novel asserts the importance of re-learning and re-appropriating aboriginal cultural and spiritual values in relation to, and as a part of, the present, without this relational awareness being totally subsumed by present-day values. As a critical constellation, *Monkey Beach* resists post-modern notions of subjectivity. For example, Lisamarie's spiritual experiences are presented via a multitude of discourses, at times expressing and poking fun at what she experiences and at other times representing them as deadly serious. The overall point, however, is that these experiences are not subjectively accessed: they are an encounter with forces that approach and constitute Lisamarie's identity. Just as Walter Benjamin "interpreted literature as objective, not subjective expression" (Buck-Morss 1989: 222), so Eden Robinson represents the recovery of First Nations identity and belief as an objective process.

HISTORICAL CONSTELLATIONS

Walter Benjamin once wrote that: "A chronicler who recites events without distinguishing between major and minor ones acts in accordance with the following truth: nothing that has ever happened should be regarded as lost for history" (1992: 246). *Monkey Beach* is a *Bildungsroman* and a chronicle, that is to say, it is not just an account of important events in the protagonist's development, but also the seemingly unimportant, the trivial, if not ridiculous ones, such as the encounter with a sasquatch portrayed in childish and stereotypical terms: "a glimpse of a tall man, covered in brown fur. He gave me a wide, friendly smile, but he had too many teeth and they were all pointed" (Robinson 2000: 16). Of course the so-called "unimportant" turns out to be central and of great consequence; the humorous and friendly meeting with sasquatch is indicative of the more positive relationship that Lisamarie can experience with the spirit world, and the world of "mythological" creatures such as sasquatch and trickster. "Chronicle" is a powerful word, indicating strong links with the story-telling of oral cultures, and also linking *Monkey Beach* with a notion of sacred text ("Chronicles" being the historical Biblical texts of the Old Testament). Narrative has long been considered to have a redemptive function, and can form a major part (even if unwittingly) of cultural and spiritual recovery and restitution; in *Monkey Beach*, the personal stories and educational journeys of the protagonist merge with those of the Haisla Nation. Benjamin argues that "To articulate the past historically does not mean to recognize it 'the way it really was'... It means to seize hold of a memory as it flashes up at a moment of danger" (1992: 247). Lisamarie's account of her life is one of moments of danger: she fears the loss of her own contemporary, Western identity precisely at those moments that she is profoundly connected to an aboriginal "past"; but this connection is something that creates a strong temporal link rather than a distance, and her task becomes not one of merely reconstructing some dead version of the past, but one of realizing the past through and as the present.

REFERENCES

Andrews, Jennifer, 2001. "Native Canadian Gothic Refigured: Reading Eden Robinson's *Monkey Beach*," *Essays on Canadian Writing*, 73 (Spring), pp. 1–24.

Asch, Michael, ed., 1998. *Aboriginal and Treaty Rights in Canada: Essays on Law, Equality, and Respect for Difference*, Vancouver: UBC Press.

Baudrillard, Jean, 1994. *Simulacra and Simulation*, trans. Sheila Faria Glaser, Ann Arbor: University of Michigan Press.

Bell, Catherine and Michael Asch, 1998. "Challenging Assumptions: The Impact of Precedent in Aboriginal Rights Litigation" in *Aboriginal and Treaty Rights in Canada: Essays on Law, Equality, and Respect for Difference*, ed. Michael Asch, Vancouver: UBC Press, pp. 38–74.

Benjamin, Walter, 1992. "Theses on the Philosophy of History," in *Illuminations*, trans. Harry Zohn, London: Fontana, pp. 245–55.

Borrows, John, 1998–99. "Re-Living the Present: Title, Treaties and the Trickster in British Columbia," *BC Studies*, 120 (Winter), pp. 99–108.

Bracken, Christopher, 1997. *The Potlatch Papers: A Colonial Case History*, Chicago & London: University of Chicago Press.

Buck-Morss, Susan, 1989. *The Dialectics of Seeing: Walter Benjamin and the Arcades Project*, Cambridge, MA and London: MIT Press, 1999.

Foster, Hamar, 1998–99. "Honouring the Queen: A Legal and Historical Perspective on the Nisga'a Treaty," *BC Studies*, 120 (Winter), pp. 11–36.

Highway, Tomson, 1998. *Kiss of the Fur Queen*, Canada: Random House.

Mathias, Chief Joe and Gary R. Yabsley, 1991. "Conspiracy of Legislation: The Suppression of Indian Rights in Canada," *BC Studies*, 89 (Spring), pp. 34–45.

Northey, Margot, 1976. *The Haunted Wilderness: The Gothic and Grotesque in Canadian Fiction*, Toronto: University of Toronto Press.

Robinson, Eden, 2000. *Monkey Beach*, London: Abacus.

Web resources and references
Nisga'a Final Agreement, Government of British Columbia Web Site
Date Accessed: January 21, 2003, 2.05 p.m.
<http://www.gov.bc.ca/tno/negotiation/nisgaa/docs/nisga_agreement.htm>

13
Thomas King and Contemporary Indigenous Identities

Laura Peters

The central incident of Thomas King's short story "Borders" is the moment in which a Blackfeet woman and her son attempt to cross the U.S./Canadian border to visit her daughter in Salt Lake City. When the woman responds "Blackfeet" to the gun-toting U.S. Customs and Immigration officer's question as to whether she is American or Canadian, she is refused entrance to the U.S. and is sent back to the Canadian border. When she offers the same reply to the Canadian Customs and Immigration officer's query as to her citizenship she is refused re-admittance to Canada. The woman and her son are relegated to the in-between space of the Duty Free store until sufficient media attention forces the Canadian officials to allow them to return to Canada.

"Borders" encapsulates the dilemma faced by the indigenous peoples of North America who have seen colonial borders/frontiers eclipse their longer-standing affiliations. Part of the central issue in the story is that the U.S./Canadian border has split the Blackfeet population nominally into Americans and Canadians; their ethnic affiliation as a group has been placed under erasure. This act of erasure is one that has also been enacted in the colonial settlement of Canada and further enshrined in various acts from the assimilation strategy of Duncan Scott, the first Minister of Indian Affairs (who early this century infamously declared that if his strategy was successful then "there wouldn't be an Indian left in Canada") to the Multiculturalism Act of 1988 which enshrines the English and the French populations as the "two founding nations." While there has been significant critical attention focusing on the distinctness of Canadian literature from American literature, there has been less attention paid to the racialized historical assumptions underlying the term "Canadian" and how those who are not descendants of the "two founding nations" negotiate this term. Of more particular interest is how those who identify themselves as indigenous not only negotiate their ethnic identity in relation to issues of national belonging, but also how contemporary forms of this identity are negotiated in relation to historical notions of indigeneity.

This essay then will consider the work of Thomas King, specifically the novel *Medicine River* (1991) in order to explore the tensions around indigeneity, nationalism and ethnic belonging that are played out in this work. Of central importance will be the figure of Will, the mixed-race protagonist of *Medicine River*, who struggles to reconcile the contradictory nature of his own ethnic makeup. This struggle will be placed in the context of King's larger project to articulate a contemporary indigenous identity which is not completely Westernized but simultaneously is not held to an "authenticity" which is both stereotypical and prehistorical in nature. However, the essay will open by using King and the figure of the indigene to question post-modernism's use of the term "nomad" as embodying contemporary identity. Finally, the essay will present some of the strategies used to problematize terms such as *American, Canadian, indigenous,* and *post-colonial.*

By relegating his protagonists to the Duty Free zone between Canada and the U.S., King challenges the post-modern celebration of Western identities as decentered and nomadic. King reveals the politics underlying the celebration of critics like Rosi Braidotti, Iain Chambers, and, to a certain extent, Stuart Hall, of "nomadic subjects in transit" (Braidotti 1994: 12). When Chambers argues for identity as a concept permanently in "transit ... [lacking] a final destination" and migrant identity as that of "being rootless, of living between worlds, between a lost past and non-integrated present ... perhaps the most fitting metaphor of this [post]modern condition" (Chambers 1994: 25, 27–8) as one in which it is no longer possible to "go back home"; he obliterates the misery of the colonial subjects who are relegated to such an in-between space, lacking in rights and stripped of their histories. A discourse that celebrates the frequenting of transit lounges as emblematic of the collapse of modernity, oppressive nationalisms, and binary oppositions, ultimately rests on the assumption (and the possession) of one of the privileged nations' passports. While Chambers is free *not* to celebrate his national identity, the resistance of this indigenous woman to the national identities established historically by acts of colonialism quickly identifies her not only as a non-citizen but as a true nomad: stateless and relegated to the Duty Free zone not in passing but with a threatened permanence. Although determined in her resistance, she is ultimately powerless against national borders that still operate on a clearly Manichean basis.

It is important to recognize that this Duty Free zone is not an ideologically neutral zone; rather it is the space of in-betweeness, being neither here nor there, neither American nor Canadian. It is the location of unassimilated difference. As such, it is not a free space but rather is a policed one – policed by myth and colonial stereotypes. King demonstrates how the colonial borders and power structures still work to put the indigenous Other identity, if not under erasure (as Duncan Scott so infamously vowed) then very firmly within the margins. Yet, the paradox contained within Canadian national identity is that it desires what it attempts to erase. The presence of the indigenous peoples serves as a constant reminder that Canadians are not indigenous in that they are not of the land, while the indigenous – as "Borders" so powerfully reveals – are not Canadians. Thus, one could argue that Canadian citizens are immigrants while the indigenous are not citizens. The presence of the indigenous Other poses problems for Kristeva's conceptualization of the other as uncanny and as "foreigner," often evoked in post-modern analyses, just as in the Canadian context the "foreigner" is not foreign but indigenous. However, where Kristeva might be useful is where she argues that the *unheimlich* offers a return to the sites of the repressed in order to resolve the feelings of estrangement that the Foreigner provokes (Kristeva 1991: 278–80). Within the Canadian context, Terry Goldie usefully talks of a process of "indigenization" (Goldie 1989) in which Canadians both desire and attempt to become indigenous; it is a phenomenon that Margaret Atwood also writes about in the essay entitled "Grey Owl Syndrome" (Atwood 1995). As such, the figure of the indigene assumes mythic proportions in Canadian culture – that is, the myth of the indigenous identity celebrated by Canadians is often an essentialized, ahistorical one (Francis 1992). Such a myth robs indigenous peoples of their difference and of their own proper identity. In the next section of this essay I will explore the myth of the indigene and, by reading the figure of Will in *Medicine River*, I will explore the struggle of a mixed-race indigene to negotiate his own and proper identity in the face of such a myth.

In the pieces "Fiction" and "Imagining Natives: White Perspectives on Native Peoples" both W. H. New and Eli Mandel identify a current pattern in the use of the image of the native as a signifier for not only Otherness but also as the outsider. W. H. New remarks that in a number of works "the Indian ... [is] the marginal figure, one of a dying culture, a dispossessed culture, a besieged culture" (New 1976: 248). Eli Mandel furthers this by arguing that all such work takes "a position sympathetic to the Native, critical of white culture and its history of exploitation and cruelty or indifference" (Mandel 1987: 44). Margery Fee also considers this use of the native as trope in "Romantic Nationalism and the Image of Native People in Contemporary English-Canadian Literature" in which she locates a

> [v]ariant of mainstream nationalism [which] uses the First Peoples' position as marginal, yet aboriginal, to make a similar claim-by-identification for other marginal groups. Those who do not wish to identify with "mainstream" Anglo-Canadian culture, or who are prevented from doing so, can find a prior and superior Canadian culture with which to identify ... The Indian stands for a dispossession larger than his own. (Fee 1987: 17–24)

Thus, the figure of the "Indian" provides a point of identification for other groups who, by virtue of their ethnicity, find themselves marginal in a multicultural country that privileges the "two founding nations." However, such identification often has a vested interest in holding the indigenous peoples to an authenticity that is essentialized and ahistorical in nature. How the protagonist negotiates these pressures and establishes a contemporary indigenous identity will be the main subject of this section.

Thomas King's *Medicine River* can be seen to center on these issues in its adherence to and inversion of the outsider/insider polemic. King's own status would argue for him as an "insider." In an interview with Constance Rooke, King describes himself as a native writer, often writing for a native audience in a way that would make these groups (native audiences), frequently viewed as outsiders or marginalized, as insiders. King overtly acknowledges that his writing "provides the Native community with that sense of being on the inside" (Rooke 1990: 74). "I do both Native and non-Native material. When I do my Native material, I'm writing particularly for a Native community ... as a Native writer I think you take on responsibilities and obligations" (Rooke 1990: 72). Yet, despite King's claim of writing as an insider for insiders in this case, this novel centers around a process of constructing identity and belonging through narration and memory (in all its forms/manifestations) of a figure, Will, who is an outsider to this inside community by virtue of his mixed race; it is Will's mixed race which denies him full Indian status in the DIA's eyes. Focusing on the issue of Will's mixed race, *Medicine River* explores the issue of ethnicity – its paradoxes and problems – through an exploration of the heterogeneity within. In this case "within" has a dual meaning: both within the individual and within the community. The novel also explores how the discourse of homogeneity within ethnic identity is policed socially (the "law" of the reservation which states "you guys have to live in town cause you're not Indian anymore ... your mother married a white," and internally (his mother's pride that would let her "go as far as the town and no farther" (King 1989: 9), while simultaneously placing ethnicity within the larger frame of being policed from the outside (the very presence of reservations, the housing complex renamed "Bentham's reserve" (1989: 44). All of these debates are represented in Will's ambiguous position as not Indian (I use the terminology of the novel here) within the Indian community yet considered Indian within the white Toronto community.

The novel works both to construct and subvert a notion of Indian ethnic identity. On the level of manifesting an individual and community ethnic identity, the representations of Big John and Eddie Weaselhead work to undermine notions of ossified authentic Indianness. Big John is considered by some to be non-traditional because of his three-piece suits (Bertha claims the suits "make us think of Whitney Oldcrow over at DIA" and queries why he cut his hair) (53). Interestingly, however, when Eddie Weaselhead, a "half-blood," "raised in Red Deer," a virtual outsider, tries to manifest a perceived authentic (yet stereotypical) Indianness in his dress by wearing "a ribbon shirt ... and a beaded buckle ... four or five rings and an inlaid watch-band ... a four-strand choker made out of real bone with brass ball bearings, glass beads and a big disc cut from on of those shells," the same Bertha claims that he looks like "a walking powwow poster" and wonders whether he "maybe give us a bad name" in a dress that she feels hints at effeminacy (55). All the same, behind this humorous parody of Big John and Eddie Weaselhead, King is exploring the hostile and exclusive nature of the policing of ethnicity: Big John rejects Eddie's claim to his Indian culture by claiming the authentic ground and calling Eddie a "pretend Indian" (56) while Eddie questions Big John's ethnic commitment by accusing him of being "an apple" (57). On the level of the ethnic community within a larger society, King also shows how ethnicity is policed by racial stereotypes from outside the community – Will is able to imagine the Custer monument attendant's fear when confronted by two "real" Indians: "that kid hiding in the dark, hunkered down behind the fender of the Bronco, his hands shaking around his rifle, waiting for U.S. to come screaming and whooping and crashing through the gate" (King

1989: 112). However, all these images of Indianness are ultimately
subverted by the figure of Lionel James, a tribal elder, who declares: "I
better get a credit card. You know, be a modern Indian" (171). Part of
what I am arguing is that one of the concerns of *Medicine River* is to
work with contemporary ethnic identities and cultural forms: what
King identifies as associational (King 1990: 12). In a telling moment,
Lionel James, the elder storyteller remarks that:

> Sometimes I tell stories about today, about some of the people on
> the reserve right now ... All the people back home like to hear that
> story ... But those people in Germany and Japan and France and
> Ottawa don't want to hear those stories. They want to hear stories
> about how Indians used to be. I got some real good stories, funny
> ones, about how things are now, but those people say, no, tell us
> about the olden days. (King 1989: 172–3)

Through the hostilities over authenticity and commitment, the exploration of dance as a meaningful cultural form and spectacle, the refusal
to listen to contemporary Indian stories, King is constantly querying
what is an Indian? What is an Indian past? One of the responses King
offers is an inversion of the myth of the Indian in contemporary
Canadian writing as a figure rooted in history with the land, in order
to offer Indians a present (through contemporary stories) and therefore
a future. One can argue that the past, in the form of the ossified
stereotype (not history generally), that so preoccupies other contemporary Canadian writers like Rudy Wiebe, is as locked to the characters of
Medicine River as the Custer monument. In order to tell these contemporary stories, the narrative works through the different forms of
memory represented through and in the present: a type of interfusion-
al (the oral and the written); the oral tradition (storyteller and tales –
Medicine River can be read as a series of short tales unified by the central
narrative consciousness); the written tradition (his father's letters to
his mother which form the basis of a sketchy understanding of the
father he never knew); plus visual traditions (photographs and
memory/flashbacks which are framed by the present narrative so that
the past can be seen as motivating understanding of the present and
likewise the present can be seen as allowing a re-evaluation, a re-ordering
of the past). Will's construction of his own ethnic identity involves
coming to know better his father, the outsider. It is also very important
to Will that he can re-invent his lost father through various narratives.

On another formal level the novel works to subvert a notion of ethnic
identity in the way that Will (the ethnic hybrid) is established as the

"lost" figure – yet simultaneously an Indian – who has the same relationship to Indian culture as someone who is more removed or is from the white community. The pattern of a lost character learning something about themselves and their past through interaction with an Indian is one which Fee identifies:

> Typically, a white speaker or main character is confused and impelled by a strong desire to know more about the past: personal, familial, native, or national. The confusion is resolved through a relationship with an object, image, plant, animal, or person associated with Native people. Occasionally, the relationship is with a real Native person ... The movement [is] from observer to participant, outsider to insider, immigrant to "native", historian to mythmaker. (Fee 1987: 16)

A good example of this is the way in which Will's narrative reveals that although the community dances were an important part of their mother's life, to Will and James the dances, aspects of their Indian roots, have become a commodity – a voyeuristic spectacle which they watched from the darkness (King 1989: 209). The refusal, or inability, to dance manifests alienation and a lack of engagement which corresponds to Neil Bissoondath's recent criticisms of ethnic cultural festivals in Canada, as a negative form of multiculturalism, in which

> [a] traditional dance performed on a stage is not a people's cultural life but an aspect of it removed from context, shaped and packaged to give a voyeuristic pleasure ... to expose ... not ... culture but ... theatre, not ... history but ... fantasy ... You come away having learnt ... little of their present ... [having seen only an] easily digested stereotype. (Bissoondath 1994: 83–4)

A crucial part of Will's construction of his own ethnic identity then is to be exposed to the cultural forms and community life that have formed the dances, in order to become a participant. Ultimately, by moving back to Medicine River, Will is exposed to culture not theater, and to the cultural present not an ossified past or a stereotypical rendition. Yet, I do not read Will's return to Medicine River as a return to an authentic place or an authentic culture because the novel mediates against that by constantly offering a multiplicity of identities. One of the best manifestations of this is the favourite bar: the bricolage of the American Hotel which is full of Indian artefacts and run by an Italian landlord (King 1989: 80).

This issue of the location and determination of ethnicity is found within debates which surround the discourses of authenticity, essentialism, purity, and hybridity but, considering the specificity of the Canadian context, I want to consider under the general rubric of multicultural-ism. I want to emphasize here that I use the model of critical multiculturalism that David Theo Goldberg articulates in his polemical essay "Multicultural Conditions," in order to explore the concept of heterogeneity that he posits. The critical multicultural model that Goldberg posits is both "anti-assimilationist and anti-integrationist" (Goldberg 1994: 9), it marks a transformation of the body politic as center managing the margins to the body politic as the site of contes-tation as new parts gain influence in mechanisms of power, bringing about a challenge from within of the hegemonizing values of the cultural dominant (Goldberg 1994: 9). In short, the model that Goldberg offers is incorporative rather than assimilationist or integrative. As such, this is the type of multiculturalism legislated for in the Canadian Multiculturalism Act of 1988 and is not to be confused with types of difference or corporate multiculturalisms which often are considered the only type of multiculturalism. This notion of the contestation of the body politic offers an interesting way to read *Medicine River*. King's project here, as in "Borders," is an attempt to transform the body politic and what better place to do so than at the national border? What Percy Walton refers to as a decentering of the perceived center while simul-taneously not replacing it can also be read in the terms of incorporation. Where Walton argues:

> By constructing a presence upon the absence of the native Other, the text avoids prioritising native culture over other cultures. It therefore also avoids positing a new center, a center that would neces-sitate the construction of new margins. King's text rejects the culturally exclusive endeavour that has marginalized the native as Other and privileges instead an inclusive and collective process that does not rest upon cultural superiority/inferiority. (Walton 1990: 79)

I would pick up on the key words which are *inclusive* and *collective*. In fact, what King could be read as doing – in the identification of the reader with Will and his movement between "centers" (much like that of the indigenous woman in "Borders") – could be argued as not a decentering move but a contestation of the composition of the body politic. The narrative strategy of *Medicine River* is not an exploration of the margins *per se*: even the marginalization experienced by Will is simultaneously counteracted by the fact that it is he who brings the community together for the final photograph. However, the complexity of Will's identity and his relationship to the reservation community at

Medicine River and the narrative's constant exploration of the issue of heterogeneity poses a problem for Walton's reading which does not take into account the levels of policing belonging to the ethnic community. The heterogeneity of critical multiculturalism challenges discourses of purity and the artifice of the homogeneous, couched in language of origination, and would add another layer of complexity to, or in fact post a problem for, David Latham's notion of King's writing as "communal origination" (Latham 1995).

In *Medicine River*, critical multiculturalism's identified challenge from within to the hegemonizing values of the cultural dominant can be located in the challenge to traditional white masculinities. The representations of all three main characters – Will, Harlen and Louise – can be read as challenges to these values. Rooke, in her interview with King, suggests that Harlen's role is more that of female inclusive strengths. Likewise, she suggests that Louise's independent character can be read as "females moving towards male strengths" (King 1989: 67), but again it is the representation of Will which poses the greatest challenge both to specific and stereotypical traditional white masculinities. Unlike his rodeo rider father, who dies in a car accident while driving when drunk, Will is 40, single, with no children. Ironically, it is Harlen, the one person who lives an incorporative ideal and respects difference, who puts the most pressure on Will to conform to a traditional notion of masculinity: "A man's not complete until he has a woman by his side ... Seeing a man live alone is sad, Will. You get all drawn out and grey and wrinkled" (1989: 27). Harlen does try to force Will into fatherhood: he ensures that Will buys South Wing the rattle and that Will "be the man" (224). Yet, when Louise wonders aloud about commitment, Will gets anxious and breaks out into a sweat (228) despite the fact that he starts to willingly embrace the role of father to South Wing (231) and buys her the top for Christmas that he never got from his father (261). Yet, paradoxically, at the moment of the community photograph when Will is settling into his masculine role in the family, Harlen interrupts and destroys it:

> The sun was warm. Louise snuggled down against my shoulder ... I was just getting settled, feeling warm, thinking about a nap, when I felt the sun disappear, and there was Harlen. "Will, get up. You're supposed to be working. Don't want to lose your good reputation by going to sleep where everyone can see you. Come on." (208)

More seriously, in the figure of Raymond Little Buffalo, a slick, dishonest, flashy conman, is the kind of negative masculinity which Will dislikes and resists.

> Most of the boys bragged on themselves from time to time ... we'd all laugh as though we believed every story. But with Ray it was different. Anything you had done, Ray had done it before and had done it before and had done it better ... Whenever Ray would start in on one of his stories, I'd snort and cough and wave my hand around. (77)

In turn, Ray tries to force Will outside of the community by commandeering the group and leaving Will waiting alone – a gesture to Will that if he does not conform to the masculine ideal he will be out.

Harlen is a figure that can be read as committed to the incorporative politics that Goldberg outlines: through the Friendship Center, the basketball team and social events, Harlen ensures that all are heard and communal values are upheld. Harlen claims Will as an Indian and works to incorporate Will into the community when he is refused money from the DIA because he is a non-status Indian. Likewise, Harlen not only offers Will a place within the community but it is Harlen who gives Will his father's letters to his mother and it is Harlen who introduces Will to members of the community who can tell him about his parents, particularly his father. The fact that Will meets Harlen when his mother dies, and that it is Harlen who persuades Will to return "home," encourages this friendship to be read in terms of a surrogate family. It is Harlen who organizes the basketball team, leads it when necessary, and takes the team to Ninastiko (a holy place) – all to create a sense of belonging and a sense of culture.

Ultimately, on a communal level, King explores the incorporative ideal by attempting to reconcile a hybrid community with itself (in the acceptance of Will into the community). In the end, much has been made of Joyce Blue Horn's "family" photograph and Will's role as photographer: Walton argues for the photograph as the trope of the text's all-inclusiveness which "swells beyond its frame" (Walton 1990: 83) and enables the margins to swell and obliterate the center. In an interview with Rooke, when asked whether "The fact of his [Will's] entering the photograph, ... breaks down the authority position," King replies:

> It also begins to break down the barriers that exist between Will and the community. But even more than that, I suppose, I'm questioning the position of the person who's making the choices, the decisions ... In that one scene, the group photograph takes itself ... In Will's case,

in the case of the artist, the important thing for me is that the artist is part of that community ... he is also part of it. (Walton 1990: 63)

But beyond these issues, what I find interesting is the fact that Will (indirectly) brings the community together in presenting the opportunity for the photograph. Will is the synthesizer and then it is the community which affirms Will's place by insisting on his presence in the photograph. The scene in which Will runs back and forth to construct the photograph and to be present within it can be read as his simultaneous occupying of the outsider/insider role. The photo does not take itself: this is hard work, an arduous process, and Will works up a sweat doing it. Yet, he finds an extended family (with the community and with Louise) in the face of losing his own. The narrative discursively locates the Blue Horn family photo alongside Will's first family photograph of himself, his mother and his brother: ultimately the two photos are literally tacked up in Will's kitchen. Both these photos represent not only family/extended family but also the endeavours of Will, his mother, and Harlen to create a sense of family.

Of the virtues Goldberg claims for his model of critical multiculturalism I have highlighted three: heterogeneity enables intersecting multiplicities in social and subject positions, thus giving voice to those that might be effaced or eclipsed; it offers complexity in social analysis to counteract a homogeneous reductive positivism; and it is committed to incorporative politics. However, the significant absences in the photograph (which hint at erasure or effacement), mediate against an easy incorporative ideal by offering examples of those such as David Plume who are not incorporated and Joe Bigbear who chooses not to be, but rather searches for something else.

REFERENCES

Atwood, M., 1995. *The Malevolent North in Canadian Literature*, Oxford: Oxford University Press.
Bissoondath, N., 1994. *Selling Illusions: The Cult of Multiculturalism in Canada*, Toronto: Penguin.
Braidotti, R., 1994. *Nomadic Subjects*, New York: Cambridge University Press.
Chambers, I., 1994. *Migrancy, Culture, Identity*, London and New York: Routledge.
Fee, M., 1987. "Romantic Nationalism and the Image of Native People" in *The Native in Literature*, eds T. King, C. Calver, and H. Hoy, Oakville: ECW Press.
Francis, D., 1992. *The Imaginary Indian: The Image of the Indian in Canadian Culture*, Vancouver: Arsenal Pulp Press.
Goldberg, D.T., 1994. *Multiculturalism: A Critical Reader*, Oxford: Blackwell.
Goldie, T., 1989. *Fear and Temptation: Images of Indigenous Peoples in Australian, Canadian and New Zealand Literature*, Kingston: McGill-Queen's University Press.

King, T., 1989. *Medicine River*, Toronto: Penguin, 1991.

King, T., 1990. "Godzilla vs. Post-colonial," *World Literature Written in English*, 30. 2, pp. 10–16.

King, T., 1993. "Borders," *One Good Story, That One*, Toronto: HarperCollins.

Kristeva, J., 1991. *Étrangers à nous-mêmes*, Paris: Gallimard.

Latham, D., 1995. "From Richardson to Robinson to King: Colonial Assimilation and Communal Origination", *British Journal of Canadian Studies*, 10. 2.

Mandel, E., 1987. "Imagining Natives: White Perspectives on Native Peoples," in *The Native in Literature*, eds T. King, C. Calver, and H. Hoy, Oakville: ECW Press.

New, W. H., 1976. *A Literary History of Canada*, eds Carl F. Klinck *et al.*, Toronto: Toronto University Press, vol. 3.

Rooke, C., 1990. "Interview with Tom King," *World Literature Written in English*, 30. 2, pp. 62–76.

Walton, P., 1990. "'Tell Our Own Stories': Politics and the Fiction of Thomas King," *World Literature Written in English*, 30. 2, pp. 77–84.

Part 4

American Post-colonialism at Home and Abroad

14

Vietnamese and Vietnamese American Literature in a Postcolonial Context

Renny Christopher

And now, many years after the end of the war, many Americans are still discussing, pondering over the Vietnam War, with nearly 7,000 books published on this topic. This shows that the American people are a responsible nation, seriously trying to draw lessons from past experience in order to formulate a better path for the future. The war has brought the two nations closer, and the day will come, I hope, when the American people will agree that an end to the Vietnam War was indeed a victory for both nations. (Luu Doan Huynh, "The War in Vietnamese Memory," (1993: 245, 246)

[I]n Vietnam, ... the term for "culture" itself, van hoa, may be translated literally into English as "the change which literature (and art) brings about." (Lockhart 1996: 5)

Vietnamese prose literature is a syncretic form, built out of the Vietnamese poetic tradition (itself based in Chinese traditions) and the French prose tradition. The literature produced by Vietnamese diaspora writers since 1975, and the literature being produced by writers in the Socialist Republic of Viet Nam (SRV), are fusing the already syncretic Vietnamese prose tradition with other influences, particularly U.S. literary influences, into new syncretic forms; a very exciting new literature is being produced. This literature represents both an opportunity and a challenge. Teaching contemporary Vietnamese literature in translation and Vietnamese American literature written in English offers an opportunity to present issues of cultural identity formation, history and the individual, and the global community. Teaching these works also presents a challenge in that they must be taught in a historical context and require discussions of national identity, multicultural and minority identity, and competing political ideologies (both between the two countries and within each country) that the writers have to negotiate.

Vietnamese writers in the SRV such as Bao Ninh (*The Sorrows of War*), Linh Dinh (*Night Again*), Duong Thu Huong (*Novel Without a Name*) and Le Minh Khue (*The Stars, The Earth, the River*), must deal with the very present past of the war that divided their country, as well as negotiating the contemporary political climate. Even while doing this, they are reaching beyond the borders of their country to work with American writers; the extraordinary anthology *The Other Side of Heaven: Postwar Fiction by Vietnamese and American Writers* (1995) edited by Wayne Karlin, Le Minh Khue and Truong Vu brings together works by writers from three sides of the war: Euro-Americans, Vietnamese Americans who fought for the Republic of Viet Nam, and Vietnamese who fought for the National Liberation front and Democratic Republic of Viet Nam. This anthology represents the ways in which a new dialogue among Americans, Viet Kieu (exiles), and Vietnamese is helping to shape a new literature.

Vietnamese American writers must deal with their status as minority writers in the U.S. Vietnamese American writers both fit into and diverge from established patterns of Asian American and immigrant literatures, because first-generation Vietnamese Americans are refugees rather than immigrants. The dynamics of the relationship between the Viet Kieu community and the home country are both in flux and central to literary production on both sides of the ocean. Vietnamese American writers such as Lanh Cao (*Monkey Bridge*, 1998), Duong Van Mai Elliot (*The Sacred Willow*, 1999), Andrew Lam (co-editor, *Once Upon a Dream: The Vietnamese-American Experience*), Khoi Luu (co-editor, *Watermark: Vietnamese American Poetry & Prose*), and Nguyen Qui Duc are writing their experiences into the fabric of American literature.

One particularly interesting subgenre of Viet Nam-related literature is "return" narratives, which began with Euro-American veterans who returned to Viet Nam to try to understand their experiences in the war. One of the early entries in this genre was William Broyles' *Brothers in Arms: A Journey from War to Peace* (1986), and the best is W. D. Ehrhart's *Going Back: An Ex-Marine Returns to Vietnam* (1987). Narratives in this genre started appearing in the mid-1980s, before diplomatic relations were established between the U.S. and the SRV; all of them report a friendly and welcoming reception for the returning veterans by the Vietnamese. Shortly after these narratives began to appear, works by Vietnamese Americans returning to their country of origin began to appear. These works follow in the tradition of the Euro-American return narratives and in the tradition of Vietnamese diaspora writers which attempts to construct a syncretic, transnational viewpoint through which to discuss issues of exile, home, and dislocation caused by war and cultural conflict, and the forging of new identities. One such work, *Where the Ashes Are: The Odyssey of a Vietnamese Family* (1994), by Nguyen Qui Duc, is of particular interest in this regard because it brings together Vietnamese literature, the exile literature of his father's generation, and the literature of a younger generation of Vietnamese exile writers. Another work in this genre, one not as well-suited to being taught as Duc's is Jade Ngoc Quant Huynh's *South Wind Changing* (1994), which is less complex, although written from a more assimilated perspective than Duc's. Duc accomplishes this by bringing his father's POW narrative, published in the U.S. in Vietnamese, into his book. Duc makes his book the story of his family, rather than purely his own story. *Where the Ashes Are* resembles other works of Vietnamese American literature in that it seeks to bring together a diverse community of readers; to bring Euro-American readers into a Vietnamese American cultural reality. It is thus a very productive text to teach because it can serve as an introduction to many of the issues of concern in Vietnamese American and Vietnamese literature.

In my book, *The Viet Nam War/The American War: Images and Representations in Euro-American and Vietnamese Exile Narratives* (1995), I argue that early works by Vietnamese American writers have been more properly defined as exile narratives than immigrant narratives because of their focus on the writers' pasts in Viet Nam, rather than on their experiences of assimilation in America. These works have also had a didactic quality, teaching U.S. audiences about Vietnamese culture, and have presented a clear preference on the part of the writers for their home country. *Where the Ashes Are* can be defined as both exile literature and immigrant literature in its construction. Duc focuses both on his own past in Viet Nam, and on his family's experiences there after he fled to the U.S. in 1975, but he also focuses on his own experiences in becoming an American. I have argued that Vietnamese exile representations are focused on cultural negotiations, on the process of becoming bicultural. This process isn't the same as assimilating, which is to leave behind one's culture of origin. This biculturality is one of the important ways in which Vietnamese American literature differs from much of the tradition of Asian American literature. Vietnamese exile authors, while becoming "American," have insisted on remaining Vietnamese. The struggle to remain bicultural, to bring Vietnamese culture to America, is a theme that has run through most Vietnamese American literature. Bharati Mukherjee refers to this process of becoming bicultural as "transnational cultural fusion," a phrase which suggests the process of culture transcending national boundaries. Duc's narrative differs from narratives by older writers in that it is much more of a struggle for him to maintain his Vietnamese identity, partially because he was very young when he left Viet Nam, and partially because he desires to forge ties with the SRV, a desire which his family does not share.

Bicultural identity and cultural fusion are not easy or painless to achieve. Andrew Lam writes in an article in *The Nation* of the experience of exile:

> Sometimes I go to a Vietnamese restaurant in San Francisco's Tenderloin district. I sit and stare at two wooden clocks hanging on the wall. The left one is carved in the shape of the voluptuous S: the map of Vietnam. The one on the right is hewed in the shape of a deformed tooth: the map of America. Ticktock, ticktock. They run at different times. Ticktock, ticktock. I was born a Vietnamese. Ticktock, ticktock. I am reborn an American. Ticktock, ticktock. I am of one soul. Ticktock, ticktock. Two hearts. (1990: 726)

Lam's "one soul ... two hearts" might serve as a description of what biculturality is. His choice of metaphor for the shape of the two clocks/countries, reveals that his affection still lies with Viet Nam, and that he is uneasy in America. Nguyen Qui Duc ends his narrative feeling uneasy in both cultures, feeling at home only in a place that exists solely in his memory.

One of the results of this bicultural stance and the lingering nostalgia for home is that Vietnamese American authors tend to write more about life in Viet Nam than about their experience of the assimilation process in America. They are interested in bringing their culture of origin into the American context of their exile. The question of literature in exile is one that is also at issue in the Vietnamese-language exile press. In an article in the Australian *Journal of Vietnamese Studies* Nguyen Hung Quoc seeks to politically define what exile literature is.

> Living abroad and writing do not make a writer someone in exile: the pro-communist writers who are living abroad are not writers in exile. The feeling of being astray in his own country, by itself, is not enough to make a writer an author in exile ... we can extract three conditions in the making of a literature in exile: (i) there must be authors in exile; (ii) there must be readers in exile; and (iii) they must be able to create a literary activity of their own, independent of the current literature in their country of origin. (1992: 26)

Vietnamese-language exile writers are creating such a literature as Quoc describes; there is a flourishing Vietnamese language publishing apparatus in the U.S. English-language Viet Kieu writers are, on the other hand, attempting to bridge the gap between their pasts, their current lives as exiles, and the English-language readers of their countries of refuge. They stand in perhaps an even more lonely place by so doing, but they also prefigure future generations, whose first language will be English, and who may think of themselves as exiles politically, but will be at home in the West culturally. In the meantime, the current generation of exile writers, no matter which language they choose to publish in, are focused on Viet Nam and the war.

Duc brings both forms of literature, exile and immigrant, together in *Where the Ashes Are* by bringing his father's POW narrative, published in the U.S. in Vietnamese, into his book, which Duc makes the story of his family, rather than purely his own story. In alternating chapters he traces his own experiences, those of his mother who stayed behind in Viet Nam to wait for his father's release, and the story of his father's 12-year imprisonment, for which Duc summarizes and quotes from his father's memoir, *Anh Sang va Bong Toi* (Light and Darkness) published by An Nghe Press in 1990.

Where the Ashes Are resembles other works of Vietnamese American literature in that it seeks to bring together a diverse community of readers; to bring Euro-American readers into a Vietnamese American cultural reality. The book is dedicated to "the memory of my sister Dieu-Quynh, and to you." It is Dieu-Quynh's ashes that are referred to in the title of the book; the dedication brings together Dieu-Quynh, who never saw America, but whose ashes rest here now, with her family, and with the American readers of the book. The book begins with "A Note on Vietnamese Names," in which Duc explains Vietnamese naming conventions. The book is printed with diacritics on all the Vietnamese names, and Duc writes all names Vietnamese-style, including Ha Noi and Sai Gon. This marks a new trend in U.S. publishing, which has previously seldom printed diacritics, and which has usually adopted the French colonial spelling "Vietnam."

Duc spends a substantial portion of his narrative detailing his family's life in Viet Nam, as most exile writers do. He begins his family's story with Tet Mau Thanh, the event that sets their eventual exile in motion. His father, the deputy province governor, is taken prisoner during the occupation of Hue, where the family is visiting Duc's grandparents for the holiday. Duc is at this time a boy of nine. He, his mother and two sisters would not see his father again for many years.

The family is from a very privileged class. Duc's grandfather had been a mandarin; "his own grandfather had been a regent through the reigns of three young kings. Forced to sign a peace treaty with the French in 1884, my great-great-grandfather had been cursed by history" (23). Duc's mother's family also comes from the highest class. "Her family had always been respected as one that produced scholars – never anyone with the least bit of interest in business or aptitude for it. Somehow in the dark days of socialism she found she had the acumen to make a living." (105–6).

Duc grows up in a house full of servants, who he calls "Uncle" and "Auntie," and whose children he plays with. His older brother Dinh goes to Bowling Green University in 1967, and his sister Dieu-Ha later joins Dinh in the U.S. The Nguyen family is fairly insulated from the war until Duc's father becomes deputy governor in 1967, and they move from Da Lat to Da Nang. Duc grows up with the cosmopolitanism typical of upper-class Vietnamese families. After his father is taken prisoner, he whiles away time reading his father's books. "I learned about Richard Milhous Nixon, Pablo Picasso, and Ma Tse Tung, as well as the poetry of Baudelaire and the philosophy of Voltaire and Rousseau" (32). Duc expects cosmopolitanism from his readers as well, including lines of untranslated French in the narrative (81). In this, also, he is in line with the majority of exile writers.

After two chapters told from his own point of view, he switches to his father's point of view, drawing from his father's memoir. His father's story is a very typical POW narrative, recounting first a long period of travel, when he, with other prisoners including two Americans, was walked up the Ho Chi Minh trail, then a five-year period in solitary confinement, followed by a six-year period during which other prisoners were gradually released, but he was held on and on for "reeducation." Duc devotes a large section of his book to his father's narrative, thus keeping a large part of the focus of the book on Viet Nam and the war. During the elder man's solitary confinement, he composed and memorized poetry, which he wrote down after his release, and included in his memoir. Duc reproduces poems at length; except for these poems, his father's narrative reads very much like many U.S. POW narratives in its depiction of the deprivations of prison life and the unbending, grim, and unimaginative demeanor of the guards.

Duc also devotes chapters to his mother's story. After 1975, waiting for her husband's release, her circumstances have moved in a downward direction, though she always seems to have relatives who have resources, so that after she loses her job as principal of a girls' lycee, she never really has to work, but only pretends to work selling soup on the street, so she will not be hassled by the authorities. "Public security men once came to search my mother's house for hidden gold and stayed for an hour ... but came up empty-handed. ... They had not looked inside the pot of rice sitting on the brick stove in the kitchen" (100).

After eleven years, Duc's mother and father are reunited in Viet Nam when she is informed of what prison he's in and allowed to visit. Shortly after, their mentally ill daughter, Dieu-Quynh, dies of kidney disease. The following year, Duc's father is finally released. Duc narrates these experiences as part of his own story – in Vietnamese fashion his story is his family's story – he does not separate himself from them narratively, although he was separated physically.

Duc intercuts his own experience as a refugee with the chapters detailing his father's and mother's stories. He leaves Viet Nam in 1975, at the age of 16, leaving his mother and his sister Dieu-Quynh behind. When he and other relatives get on the boat that will carry them out of Viet Nam he reflects that he was "suddenly aware that we had been on the losing side and now were ignominiously deserting our homeland and our ancestors. Images of my mother and sister swirled in my head. My chest and stomach burned with shame" (86).

When he arrives in America to live with his brother, he faces serious cultural dislocations and it is here where his book takes on the character of immigrant literature, detailing his process of assimilation. His brother looks like an American to him, and his brother's Euro-American wife, Becky, presents a difficulty for him. "I couldn't bring myself to say her first name. She was my elder, and in Vietnamese, I would have had to precede her name with the word Chi, "Older Sister" (138–9). Duc's brother Dinh has assimilated and succeeded in America. He has a red BMW, a house in the suburbs, a blonde wife and a son. Even his ideas about "the war back home were strangely enhanced but also sanitized by television" (146). Dinh even suggests at one point that Duc should join the U.S. Marines, unaware of the irony of what he suggests.

> I didn't tell him I had seen a few marines in Viet Nam. Dinh hadn't seen the young girls thrown off their bicycles when marines reached down from their passing trucks to yank their hats away. He hadn't seen the masses of olive green steel transporting marines on the streets of Hue and Da Nang, or seen what they did in countless villages, firing mortars and burning huts. (150)

Duc initially doesn't like U.S. culture; from the time he encounters it at a dance club in Guam while he's in transit; but he tries to reconcile the two cultures by finding similarities. When he goes looking for a job he reflects.

> I had long heard about the value Americans placed on independence and self-sufficiency. Now, living in their midst, I wanted desperately to prove that I could be self-sufficient. The Vietnamese too value independence; millions had died defending it. Though foreigners often marvel at the acceptance by the Vietnamese of their prescribed roles within extended families, self-reliance is also cherished. (145)

Duc is looking for a way to fit into U.S. culture by reaching for resources from his Vietnamese cultural background.

Nevertheless, he can't come to feel at home in America. The suburb his brother lives in drives him crazy. "For me the lawns began to stand for all that was sterile and uniform and conformist in America" (148). He heads for Canada, but because of his visa status, he isn't supposed to leave the U.S., so he goes, with a friend, to Washington DC instead. He ends up working at a fast-food place in Alexandria, Virginia, and despite his dislike of America, does begin to assimilate, although he tries to stay within the immigrant community where he can speak Vietnamese and eat Vietnamese food. He feels very uncomfortable in the high school he attends. "I could not get used to the American habit of complaining about one's parents. ... Even as I adopted their ways, I observed my friends through Vietnamese eyes" (158). He is pulled culturally in two directions, and that split, that competition for his soul, will remain with him permanently.

In 1979 he becomes a social worker in San Jose.

> I never questioned the fact that I was helping create instant Asian ghettoes and a massive bottom-rung work force serving the electronics industry. I didn't quite believe in the American Dream I was prescribing for the refugees, but enough of those I aided did eventually succeed. (162)

The ambiguity he feels is most clearly shown when he finally applies for U.S. citizenship. When the examiner asks him questions about the constitution, he gives answers out of panic and ignorance that the examiner takes to be jokes. When asked who takes over for the President, Duc answers "Alexander Haig," and the examiner passes him, saying "you're really funny" (163). But for Duc, his split identity isn't really funny at all.

He becomes a social worker at Galang relocation camp, which processed over 100,000 refugees in the course of four years. Duc is happy to be helping Vietnamese people, but again he feels his own dividedness. "The refugees watched me because I looked like them and spoke their language but did not live their lives. ... I was watching myself as well, a man transformed from a Vietnamese to an American, to a Vietnamese again." (197). In contact with Vietnamese outside America he has to face the degree of assimilation he has unknowingly undergone: "I believed that I retained in my most profound self a Vietnamese way of thinking, but outwardly I no longer acted Vietnamese. After a while the refugees' words added up to convince me how much I had changed" (198). He has become, to some extent, an American, taken on values that set him apart from the refugees.

When he returns to the U.S. to meet his parents, who have finally succeeded in leaving Viet Nam, he is racked with self-doubt. "I had earlier failed to set myself on the path of becoming the gentleman-scholar that was the aristocratic ideal of my family. Now I was prepared to abandon my Confucian duty to ease the later years of my elders" (209). He's filled with a sense of shame over his ambitions (he wants to go to London to accept a job offer from the BBC). When he meets his parents at the airport, it's his father's cosmopolitanism and worldliness that puts him at ease; the first thing his father asks is how Jesse Jackson's campaign is doing. In fact, his father copes with America better than Duc has – he immediately finds a job as a translator. When Duc asks him apprehensively how he'll get to work, his father matter of factly replies "I'll take the M line to the Powell Street station" (212). For a man who has spent eleven years in re-education camp, several of those in solitary confinement, navigating in San Francisco is no problem.

For Duc's father life in America is not difficult or fraught with dilemmas of identity. An old man already when he arrives, he knows very surely who he is, in a way that Duc, arriving in America at 16, did not know. Duc's father writes and publishes in Vietnamese, knowing his audience is the Vietnamese exile community, and he lives at peace in America, with no desire to return to Viet Nam, because the SRV is not the Viet Nam he would wish to live in. He is truly an exile, rather than an immigrant, and Duc, the immigrant, is stunned by his father's easy adjustment.

My parents came to appreciate American society. Whereas I stubbornly lamented the impersonal, work-dominated, materialistic way of life, the impossibility of continued close friendships, the hypocritical government, the racial discrimination. My parents were always willing to overlook America's faults. (215)

Yet it is Duc who is much more American than they, wanting to follow his individual ambition rather than carry out his duty to his family.

Duc does go to London, but only stays two years. He decides to return to San Francisco when his father cries as Duc is leaving after being home for a visit. Duc had never seen his father cry before, and Duc's *hieu*, filial piety, reasserts itself. But before he leaves London he meets his future wife, Gillian Anderson, there. All three of the Nguyen family siblings outmarry, something which seems perfectly acceptable to the parents, whose cosmopolitan attitude can encompass much cross-cultural communication while remaining rooted in an unconflicted Vietnamese identity.

There is an interesting tension in the book between what seem to be Duc's father's and mother's political attitudes, and what seem to be his own. He often reports incidents from his childhood in a way that reflects the prejudices of his upper-class, southern, anti-communist family, yet, especially toward the end of the book, it becomes clear that Duc himself is not particularly anti-communist. The tone of the chapters detailing his father's experiences as a prisoner seems to come from his father's memoir. For example, in one of the chapters detailing his father's experiences Duc writes "Progressive ideas had not improved things. The equality of men and women, for example, had somehow robbed the women my father met of their femininity and characteristically Vietnamese graciousness" (112–13). Duc doesn't comment on his father's old-fashioned attitude; he simply reports it. In this way Duc acts almost as a ventriloquist for a story that he is only marginally part of, both in its events and its ideology. In this way, in his fidelity to his parents' stories, he is attempting to fulfil his role as filial son, a role which he worries about fulfilling adequately because of the ways he has been changed by his sojourn in America.

His own attitudes emerge during the recounting of his own story. While reflecting on how bland he finds life in America, he thinks: "Oddly, I never blamed 'the Communists' for robbing me of my homeland. I had once feared them as ruthless enemies, but somehow I could never hate them" (147). When Duc's parents arrive in the U.S., he starts having political debates with them within a month, over which he feels very badly. "I came to accept that for my parents, Viet Nam had been destroyed by cruel men blinded by Communist propaganda. For me, however, Viet Nam still existed: it was the place that held my cultural roots, my childhood. It was my homeland" (214).

Because of this feeling, Duc arranges to go to Viet Nam with a TV crew to film a documentary about his return. His parents warn him not to go, that he will be arrested, but he is determined. In Viet Nam, he is greeted as a stranger. Several people make remarks about how "fat" he is, a fat, pale American in contrast to the skinny, dark Vietnamese. His physical change marks his cultural change. His Vietnamese family criticize him for not living with and supporting his parents. He is also shocked by the contrast of his own modest American means which look like extreme luxury next to the poverty of the SRV. "My white canvas sneakers looked obscenely opulent next to the seven pairs of ragged flip-flops" when he visits family members (225).

He wants to feel comfortable in Viet Nam. "My exile was ending, and I strained to spot a familiar face on the streets. I wanted to be home" (229). But the feeling does not come easily, if it comes at all. When he meets with old friends he is made "uncomfortable hearing about what [they] had been through after the fall of the South" (236) because he will be returning to the comforts of America. When a friend asks "What do you think of your old home, fat man?" he has no answer (242).

He ultimately finds that his "home" exists only in memory, and his memory is continually thwarted by current reality. In Hue he finds the city to be short of material goods, and "short of its old charm, also" (245), meaning that it is not the city he has cherished in his memory during his years of "exile." When he visits Ha Noi, a place he had never been before, he finds that "Oddly, [it] felt like home" (256). He finds in Ha Noi the charm that he did not find in Hue. This is because it fits his imaginary picture of Viet Nam better than his actual old home does. After his return he writes that he misses home, but he can't quite define where home is for him. He writes of memories, rather than realities, of Da Nang and Da Lat, and of Ha Noi, "a city that now occupies a beloved space in my memory, or rather my heart" (260). Although "Viet Nam is still the place I call home," it is not his true home that the word "home" now conjures up for him. He is living in the liminal space of the permanent cultural exile.

He admits that "my notions of my homeland are romanticized," (262) and that he has largely become an American, and his way of life would not fit in Viet Nam. He describes the liminal space he occupies as a quagmire, and he dreams, quite unrealistically, of raising his children in Viet Nam, completely failing to address the fact that his children will be only half Vietnamese, which will make them outsiders to Viet Nam even more than he, as an assimilated American, is.

One of the tasks that he performs in Viet Nam is to reclaim his sister Dieu-Quynh's ashes. He reflects that his other living relatives might leave Viet Nam and also live in exile.

We'd live there for ten, twelve, fifteen years, perhaps the rest of our lives. But some of us had to come back for the things we had left behind: our childhood home – the place, as the Vietnamese say, where our umbilical cords were cut. We would come back changed, but we would come back, for a loved one, and her ashes. (229)

He concludes that "Where the ashes are, one should make that home" (264), thus proclaiming that family, not land, is what makes for cultural identity. His sister's ashes, along with the rest of his family, are here, in the U.S., now; but try as he might, Duc finds that the ashes can't quite bring him home. His home remains elusive, his identity suspended between that of immigrant and that of exile.

In teaching Duc's book, there is an opportunity to explore issues of identity, assimilation, cultural preservation, generational conflict, the battle for memory and history. There is also a challenge to students to try to grasp not only the more familiar, but also the more "foreign" elements of the book, and thus reach a greater understanding of the post-colonial in-between, transnational, position occupied by a narrative such as this.

REFERENCES

Bao Ninh, 1995. *The Sorrows of War*, New York: Pantheon.

Broyles, William, 1986. *Brothers in Arms: A Journey from War to Peace*, New York: Avon.

Cao, Lanh, 1998. *Monkey Bridge*, New York: Penguin.

Christopher, Renny, 1995. *The Viet Nam War/The American War: Images and Representations in Euro-American and Vietnamese Exile Narratives*, Amherst: University of Massachusetts Press.

Duong Thu Huong, trans. Phan Huy Duong and Nina McPherson, 1995. *Novel Without a Name*, New York: William Morrow and Company.

Ehrhart, W. D., 1987. *Going Back: An Ex-Marine Returns to Vietnam*, Jefferson, North Carolina: McFarland.

Elliot, Duong Van Mai, 1999. *The Sacred Willow: Four Generations in the Life of a Vietnamese Family*, New York: Oxford University Press.

Huynh, Jade Ngoc Quang, 1994. *South Wind Changing*, Saint Paul, MN: Graywolf.

Huynh, Luu Doan, 1993. "The War in Vietnamese Memory" in *The Vietnam War: Vietnamese and American Perspectives*, eds Jayne S. Werner and Luu Doan Huynh, Armonk, NY: M.E. Sharpe.

Karlin, Wayne, Le Minh Khue and Truong Vu, 1995. *The Other Side of Heaven: Postwar Fiction by Vietnamese and American Writers*, Willimantic, CT: Curbstone Press.

Lam, Andrew, 1990. "My Vietnam, My America," *The Nation*, 10 December, pp. 724–6.

Le Minh Khue, 1997. *The Stars, The Earth, the River: Fiction by Le Minh Khue*, Willimantic, CT: Curbstone Press.

Linh Dinh, 1996. *Night, Again: Contemporary Fiction from Vietnam*, New York: 7 Stories Press.

Lockhart, Greg and Monique Lockhart, trans. 1996. *The Light of the Capital: Three Modern Vietnamese Classics*, New York: Oxford.

Nguyen Hung Quoc, 1992. "The Vietnamese Literature in Exile," *Journal of Vietnamese Studies*, 5, pp. 24–34.

Nguyen Qui Duc, 1994. *Where the Ashes Are: The Odyssey of a Vietnamese Family*, New York: Addison Wesley.

Tran, De, Andrew Lam and Hai Dai Nguyen, 1995. *Once Upon a Dream: The Vietnamese-American Experience*, Kansas City: Andrews and McMeel.

Tran, Barbara, Monique T. D. Truong and Luu Truong Khoi, 1998. *Watermark: Vietnamese American Poetry & Prose*, New York: The Asian American Writers' Workshop.

15
Politics, Pleasure, and Intertextuality in Contemporary Southeast Asian Women's Writing

Julie Shackford-Bradley

POLITICS, PLEASURE AND THE INTERTEXT

Addressing the divide between political and aesthetic approaches to postcolonial literature, Rajeswari Mohan argues that too much emphasis on aesthetics may result in readings in which "politically charged and historically urgent discursive and textual elements are reduced to purely formal and aesthetic properties of the text" (Mohan 1995: 275). Mohan reflects a concern about readers in U.S. college classrooms who are not well-versed in what might be called "transnational literacy," and suggests that only political readings sufficiently stress "the polyvalence of the text in relation to the different cultural and political contexts it straddles." For critics and readers of postcolonial literatures, this demands an "analytical suppleness" (1995: 277–8).

From the other side, Indira Karamcheti proposes that postcolonial writers and readers embrace, rather than reject, the deeply problematic notion of aesthetics because

> the appropriation of an *artistic* high ground means also the appropriation of a *moral* high ground, which is exactly where postcolonial literatures hope to establish themselves. Consequently the giving up of the discourse of the aesthetic has serious political, as well as literary consequences. (64)

Karamcheti looks to Barthes's "text of bliss" for a model of what she terms "minor pleasure." This is a text that causes discomfort, that "unsettles the reader's historically, cultural, psychological assumptions, the consistency of his tastes, values, memories, brings to a crises his relation with pleasure." At the same time, "the text of bliss" refuses "to allow us to safely separate art from politics, private from public experience from knowledge, our private selves from the body politic" (65).

Recognizing the legitimacy of both perspectives, I would like to suggest that a pedagogical approach to postcolonial literature that focuses on the strategic use of intertextuality encompasses both political and aesthetic readings simultaneously. My main purpose is to show that, while strategies of reading for the intertext are not new, they may be revisited in the context of teaching postcolonial literature in a way that emphasizes the text's representation of the "polyvalence" of the postcolonial experience. In the process, students can develop "transnational literacy," that is, a working knowledge of the particulars of cultural, religious and political *difference* and how these particulars function in larger discourses that overlap and interconnect. This is only possible through an interdisciplinary effort that draws upon two other seemingly oppositional fields, Postcolonial and Area Studies. From the readings I present below, it will be clear that the situated knowledge of historical events and cultural frames that Area Studies offers is critical for understanding both the politics and pleasure of this body of literature. Postcolonial Studies places this information in the larger, global context, and interrogates it in terms of the structures of power through which politics and culture evolve. In addition, Postcolonial Studies seeks to decenter inquiry regarding aesthetics as well as power in literature and the arts from its position in the West and its traditions. Only then can works of art be fully appreciated in their multiple cultural and political contexts.

In this essay, I discuss three novels that have appeared in the late 1980s and 1990s by Southeast Asian women writers: Jessica Hagedorn's *Dogeaters* (1990) and Wendy Law-Yone's *Irrawaddy Tango* (1993), both of which are diaspora texts written in English, and Ayu Utami's *Saman* (1998), from Indonesia. These texts use intricate forms of intertextuality to elaborate upon the workings of power in postcolonial political structures in the Philippines, Burma, and Indonesia. While demonstrating many similarities in form and content, the texts do not explicitly refer to one another and it is unclear if one has influenced the next. Their similarities may be traced to common experiences and analysis of legacies of the Cold War and the onset of globalization for characters living under harsh military rule and to influences in narrative style that best represent the dislocation and violence and their disorienting affects on the body politic. I will focus here on the ways in which the authors weave together compelling tales out of fragments and disparate narratives, while at the same time using intertextuality to reveal the hidden structures of postcolonial histories. I will then examine the authors' response to these histories through the inclusion of a discourse of international human rights, which is woven into their narratives for the purpose of exposing unseen injustices and their long-term effects on the individual and on the general populace. The Human Rights intertext transforms works of fiction into catalysts for action, a purpose associated more with social realist works of the past than post-modern or absurdist literature.

Both Jessica Hagedorn and Ayu Utami represent the socio-cultural, as well as economic traumas brought on by the U.S.-backed military dictatorships of Marcos and Suharto in the Philippines and Indonesia, respectively. In doing so, both employ a post-modern narrative style in the sense that the texts are not plot-driven, nor do they develop characters in descriptive prose. Hagedorn utilizes a post-modern form that has been described as cinematic shaped by "jump cuts" from one voice, place, situation to another (Lee 1999: 79). Utami's text, which declares itself a fragment of a larger work, is even choppier as it moves in time from the 1960s through the 1980s and 1990s, between the U.S. and the islands of Sumatra and Java, and among a set of cosmopolitan and other characters who have shifting interests and identities. In these texts, characters are participants in a socio-political environment that the writers explore, whether it be Manila or Indonesia, in the years leading up to the Velvet Revolution (non-violent transfer of power from Ferdinand Marcos to Cory Aquino) or Suharto's downfall. These atmospheric landscapes are drawn through fragments of action, conversations, newspaper clippings, letters, excerpts from colonial texts, and references to films, novels, popular culture, as well as a variety of marginal narrative perspectives. Hagedorn's narrative style mimes the spectacle of the Marcos dictatorship and the surrealism created in an environment in which gossip or "*tsimis*" is the vehicle through which truths are transmitted. By grand design, characters eventually link up across the cartography the author presents of Manila's neighborhoods and cliques, as well as its sites of military power and terror. Similarly, in *Saman*, the characters move about a terrain shaped by transnational capitalism in the form of oil companies and agribusiness, as well as a sense of cosmopolitanism that sends them to link up in New York City. Utami excels in this arena drawing a chain of causality between a self-absorbed woman from Jakarta whose primary concern is chasing a married man, a group of human rights activists, a Catholic Pastor helping a group of Sumatran Muslim farmers fight against a Chinese palm-oil plantation landowner and his military-police henchmen. The text has drawn attention from Europeans in particular for its explicit discussion of sexuality, unusual in modern Indonesian literature, which blends "eastern" and "Western" traditions. This is done through linguistic mixing of Indonesianized words such as *klimaks; orgasme* and *masturbasi*, and the Hindu-Buddhist context of *lingga-yoni* monuments to sexuality and regeneration one finds throughout the rice fields of Central Java. The vehicle for sexual discourse in the text is the character aptly named Shakuntala who represents "pure love" in the *Mahabharata*. Through the intertext, Utami draws parallels between tales of unrequited love, misdirected lust, and unfulfilled longing and the general atmosphere that encompassed Indonesia as it awaited the impending downfall of Suharto and his GOLKAR party, and the beginning of a new era.

Law-Yone's *Irrawaddy Tango* differs in narrative strategy, in that the text is shaped as a fantastic sojourn/quest tale, which, in some other era, would feature a brave and handsome hero. The tale's heroine, also named Irrawaddy Tango, takes a circular journey from her small town to the city, to the jungles of the nation of "Daya" which is a thinly veiled version of Burma (now Myanmar), and on to the very real spaces of exile, in Thailand and the U.S. The heroine's exploits are wide-ranging; she becomes the wife of the *junta*, and is later kidnapped by, then joins in solidarity with a group of rebel fighters much like the Karen ethnic minority, is imprisoned and tortured, escapes to a lonely and bitter exile in the U.S., only to return to murder the dictator some 25 years later. While Tango's first-person narrative unifies, the text is episodic, so that Tango is placed in a variety of socio-political landscapes, which are the subject of the text. In the process, Law-Yone introduces the series of postcolonial archetypes we meet in the other texts: the corrupted military henchman; the dictator's wife, the honest and heroic rebel fighter, the human rights advocate/victim of state-sponsored violence. In a meta-textual way, the reader is also always aware of the presence of the exiled writer who watches her nation disintegrate from a safe, but vexed distance.

The pleasure of these novels is experienced not through the discovery of distinct examples of embedded intertextuality, since the works are constructed out of myriad texts and discourses. Rather, it is experienced in the particular convergence of what Appadurai has called "ideoscapes" and "ethnoscapes," which help to characterize the disjunctive nature and effects of the movement of people and critical concepts in the postcolonial/globalized world (Appadurai 1999). The author traces a now-familiar sojourn, of the torture victim to the U.S. but, in fiction, is able to represent the dislocation and disorientation of this experience in a more textured way, in the sometimes humorous and absurd context of Southeast Asia's political urgencies of the late twentieth century. But Tango is obsessed with home, and her story must therefore be told in a circular narrative structure that emphasizes the real and conceptual labyrinths in which exiles and members of the diaspora find themselves.

On one level, the many pop culture references, (vaguely?) familiar news stories, and jokes about broken English among former members of the British Empire in Burma, the Spanglish and Taglish of Manila, and the colloquial English words and phrases that punctuate the Jakarta-style Indonesian in *Saman* do invoke a "postcolonial *jouissance*" or celebration of hybridized identities (Radhakrishnan 1993: 753) that so many readers can identify with. However, these elements also lead to the discomfort of the reader, as when Law-Yone's punning leads to the cynical invocation of the "Turd World," which is no place for "free tinkers," and in the absence of glossaries or other tools for navigating the complex linguistic and narrative terrains of *Dogeaters* and *Saman*. The texts create a sense of discomfort and dislocation which is representative of the flip-side of celebrated hybridity, that is, what Radhakrishnan refers to as the "excruciating act of self-production through multiple traces" (753). In these violent and complex landscapes, the main narrators and characters of these texts struggle to understand what their purpose is. Their uncertainty and discomfort are magnified by the ways in which they, along with the writers, view their nations through a dualistic, insider–outsider perspective, with the added consciousness of how their nations are viewed in the larger world. Each thus raises the specter of the "banana republic," ("*republik pisang*," in Utami), reminding readers that several Southeast Asian countries had assumed a position in the world previously held by nations of the Caribbean and Latin America.

With the invocation of the appellation "banana republic," the writers begin to contextualize Southeast Asian nations with Latin American histories as they likewise emulate Latin American narrative styles in which the real and fantastic converge to reveal larger truths. A deeper level of pleasure is encountered here, where the writers contemplate these connections both in their writing and in their subject matter. I shall discuss this in more detail shortly in terms of Law-Yone's use of the trope of the tango in her novel. However, while there is clearly a debt owed to writers like Gabriel Garcia Marquez, these writers are not content to merely emulate. Utami makes this clear in a very subtle way in *Saman*. As Saman, the Catholic Pastor is being "interrogated" (tortured), with far-fetched questions about "external agitators" and communist plots, he makes up the kind of story that one might encounter in a Marquez text. In this story, he describes his previous study of Liberation Theology in South America, which led him to provoke revolution in the Sumatran jungle/coffee plantations, and finally to create a "kingdom of Allah" in which his followers would also become Christians *and* communists (104). These embellishments please the interrogators, since they address all the fears of the Indonesian government, and they have great fictional possibility; but Utami makes it clear that Saman's actual tale is far more banal, situated as it is in the grim realities of Sumatra's peasantry. Yet, with this interlude, Utami explores a central aspect of political life in Indonesia, along with the Philippines, the endless speculation about conspiracies through discussion of the connections between local events, and between local, national, and global forces. This is central to *Dogeaters* as well, where it subsumes much of the dialog of the text, as a central source of pleasure for the characters where political "truths" are hard to come by.

In short, the relationships created through the concept of the "banana republic" are helpful in liberating Southeast Asian literature from certain realistic constraints, and in drawing parallels that place Southeast Asian history in context. One ingredient of the pleasure of these texts is the way in which the authors address these connections and their complexity in the texts themselves. At the same time, they suggest larger connections between the banal details of local conflicts in Sumatra and land reform movements elsewhere, and provoke the reader to begin making those connections across space and time. The authors explore both the dislocation of "hybridity" and the dark humor of it through their narrative styles that blend magical realism and social realism, quest tale and post-modernist response. The goal is not only to make the region visible and speak to truth, but also to move the audience out of their comfort zones and toward some kind of action.

HUMAN RIGHTS DISCOURSE IN SOUTHEAST ASIAN WOMEN'S FICTION

All three texts focus on disparate individuals from diverse socio-economic and ethno-religious backgrounds who meet up under drastic circumstances brought on by their interactions with these corrupt military regimes. As such, the characters articulate the ideas of opposition movements, which draw on an intertext of human-rights discourse that replaces social realist narratives of nobility or victimization of the past. The three texts present narratives of a state-sponsored torture and terror, in the genre similar to what we now think of as the Amnesty International testimonial. As Elaine Scarry has pointed out, these narratives make the reader more than a "passive recipient of information about torture," and "encourage his or her active assistance in eliminating [it]" (Scarry 1987: 9). What is of interest here is the ways in which this layer of narrative is woven into the text in such a way as to magnify the effects of the AI testimonial.

Both Hagedorn and Law-Yone focus on the female experience of torture, which is sexualized for the purposes of not only undermining the individual's ability to "express the most expansive potential of the human being, his ability to project himself out of his private ... needs into a ... sharable world" (1987: 41), but also, by associating pain with sexuality, scarring the individual and at the same time limiting her (literal or figurative) reproductive capabilities. Scarry notes that the purpose of torture is to "unmake the world" of the victim, by terrorizing him/her with implements and ideas of domesticity and safety. Thus, torture techniques are named after household items, such as the refrigerator, the telephone, lampshade, the bathtub. The "torture room" plays an important role in the process of transforming the domestic into a site of pain, while these sites of torture might be called the "guestroom" or even more cynically and insanely, the "tea party," or the "birthday party" (40; see also Bow 2001). Finally, implements of torture might also be familiar – the family-sized soft-drink bottle, the oven, the chair. As she puts it, "the domestic act of protecting becomes an act of hurting, and in hurting, the object becomes what it is not" (41). Both Law-Yone and Hagedorn stress the absurdities of the process, coming up with their own names for torture rooms like "the VIP lounge" at "Camp Meditation" (Hagedorn) and "the circus," and "dynamo" (Law-Yone) and focusing in on such domestic items as the electric fan and the radio playing a serial soap opera.

In *Irrawaddy Tango* and *Dogeaters*, scenes of state-sponsored torture stand out for their brutality, but are at the same time woven into the text to demonstrate the degree to which these highly ritualized techniques have become a routine way of silencing rebels/activists. One can see the authors working their narratives so as not to sensationalize these acts, and yet magnify the reality of the victim's experience. Hagedorn places the narrative of torture in parenthesis and bold type, mixed in with the transcription of a popular Filipino radio serial that is complete with jingles for advertisements. This font/style is used elsewhere in the text for interjections of gossip or *"tsismis"* which

Manilans rely upon as their news source, since the "real" news is so distorted. In the brief, sporadic descriptions of Daisy's experience at "Camp Meditation," we can see Marcos' henchman General Ledesma utilizing the strategies of "unmaking"; the newness, cleanliness, and hospitality of the place and the military "hosts" gradually disintegrate into abject cruelty, as Daisy is questioned about her birthday, reminded of her recently assassinated father, asked about her sexual activities, shown photographs of her lover Santos Tirador that include his "gouged out eyes" and "mashed testicles," then raped, while the General promises her more torture in his "VIP lounge" (216). The inclusion of the photographs in the process, together with General Ledesma's and *his* henchman Pepe Carreon's viewing of Daisy's rape, correlate with the discourse of voyeurism and violence that runs throughout the text.

Similarly, in *Irrawaddy Tango*, the narrative of torture unfolds gradually like experience itself, "following procedure" as Tango puts it. The procedure illustrates the dark side of the absurdity of it all, encapsulated in one of the officers' statements: "You have the right to a court-appointed attorney ... Unfortunately he is on leave" (166). Again the "unstartling" questions that will eventually lead to accusations regarding Tango's sexuality, and culminating in her rape with a gun. Emphasizing the relationship between the individual and communal experience of trauma, Law-Yone interrupts Tango's experience with a description of a family's ordeal in the set of torture contraptions ("the circus," "combo," "dynamo," and "houdini"). This interruption is critical, because it suggests that the viewing of the torture of someone else, in this case, a father forced to consider the rape of his daughter "by a dozen swollen pricks" is as brutal as one's own experience. This viewing of the daughter's pending rape is transferred from the father, to the "torture veteran" who has witnessed this and describes it to Tango, and then by Tango to the reader, leaving a gulf of doubt about what's real, imaginary, fictional. The ordeal is deeply personal, yet the modus operandi of those who use torture as terror is to "infect" as many as possible.

Utami's 1998 description of Wisanggeni's/Saman's "*interogasi*" has more of the feel of a litany of the routine. All the elements are there: the beatings, the kickings, the cigarette burns, the cutting of fingers, the use of electric rods that eventually move from the neck to the penis, giving the sense that this tale is familiar to all readers and such brutality, carried out in a local police station, is the norm. Saman's response is similar to Tango's in that in the midst of it all, he retains a bizarre humor that his attackers associate with insanity. For both, the terrible irony is that the humor is part of a mechanism of mind–body detachment through which sanity is salvaged, but that the same detachment is impossible to overcome once the ordeal is passed. Utami also locates the scenes of torture among many other examples of brutality; *Saman* is most pronounced in this as the author also mentions in passing the rape and murder of an activist's wife in the context of the well-known real-life case of Marsinah, the labor activist who was found tortured and beaten to death in 1993. Perhaps Utami focuses not on a woman's ordeal but on the torture of a Catholic Pastor to rouse new emotions among her readers. It is not the sexualization of the violence that is debilitating to Saman, who practices celibacy, but Indonesian readers of all faiths will be struck by the victim's ultimate loss, of God's presence in his heart.

POSTCOLONIAL HISTORY THROUGH THE INTERTEXT IN *IRRAWADDY TANGO*

Law-Yone deploys this kind of pleasure to great extent in *Irrawaddy Tango*, while at the same time, exploiting the series of possible connections readers might make in order to make the "remote" nation of Burma more visible in the global imaginary. The title immediately focuses the author's desire to link Burma's history with that of a country whose "Dirty War" is simply more familiar to American and international readers. As the character Tango laments (referring to the pseudonym Law-Yone has ascribed to Burma),

> The infrequent headlines describing the crackdown in Daya, the sporadic pictures and film footage of the shootings and beatings; the statistics and acronyms describing the bleak economy – Daya, that once bountiful nation, now a less developed country, an LDC with an abysmal GNP and so forth ... Why should it reflect on me that every other revolution, every other bid for freedom – Tiananmen Square, Wencelas Square – seem to draw sympathy but not the one tearing up that stagnant little backwater, the *Eldorado Banal*, known as the Republic of Daya? (Law-Yone 1993: 260)

This is especially unnerving because of the representation Burma does receive – at Disneyworld in the ride called "Irrawaddy Irma," in which it is blurred into a grotesque misrepresentation of the Asia Pacific region:

> Our "river" cut[ting] through jungle walls overgrown with apple-green creepers and vines, with ruins, part Mayan, part Cambodian, poking through, and around each bend, some mechanical jungle

beast poised to scare ... At the end of the ride, around the last bend, up popped a fat, agreeable American Indian in Hawaiian shorts and shirt, his belly exposed, swinging a bunch of shrunken heads in his hand. (218)

At first take, the generic "banana republic" representation of Daya/ Burma that Law-Yone presents instead is not a great improvement over the Disneyworld version, but through the trope of the tango, the author gradually places Burma's history into a larger context that invokes important questions about the remaking of the third world after colonialism.

Initially, the trope of the tango calls to mind generic and clichéd banana republic imagery. By mentioning in passing several similar regimes, Law-Yone alludes to a kind of generic *junta* of Burma/Argentina/Chile/Indonesia/Nigeria/Cambodia/Romania/ Ethiopia in the image of khaki-clad bureaucrats following the leadership of a self-perceived martyr. However, the fantastic narrative, in which Burma has become Daya, gives Law-Yone greater leeway in both exploring and rendering absurd the dynamics of political leadership in her home country. Daya's dictator – whose name, Supremo, was once just a brand name from Daya's first American ice-cream parlor, but which also signifies upon those labor-intensive exports, coffee and cigars – leaves a trail of dead bodies, broken spirits, and disoriented exiles. While the critique of Supremo/Ne Win is quite specific in Tango's mind, Law-Yone uses intertextuality to locate Burmese politics in a larger context of postcolonial politics of the 1960s and 1970s. She does so by opening the text with a quote from Coriolanus, which is only later revealed as such. The story of the Roman "hero" Coriolanus, famously chronicled in the Shakespearean play of that name, describes a statesman bloated with power until he is driven out by the citizens of Rome after refusing to acknowledge their humanity. The tale is drawn through *Irrawaddy Tango* via a series of intersections with the character of the Dayan dictator, Supremo. This is done in a subtle way, through the detail of Supremo's mother, like Coriolanus's, thrusting her son out toward the battlefield at a tender age, and the question of the number of scars – Coriolanus is rumored to have 27, while Supremo demands that Tango count his 32, the number of the scars of the Buddha. With great efficiency, the author draws a continuity between Rome, Elizabethan England, and contemporary Burma that resists the charac- terization of the "third world dictator" as anything less than a "universal monarch," as the novel puts it (81). Supremo becomes the heir of a European tradition *and* the lineage of Dayan/Burmese monarchs; but, whereas Coriolanus's scars are visible and real, Supremo's amount mainly to "a mole here, a wart there, the stain of a birthmark, the occasional speck," as Tango discovers when ordered to "find them all!" The whole idea of the scars is rendered absurd, along with the idea of the "universal monarch" itself, in the contexts of both international and Burmese/Dayan history. It is the perpetuation of these contrivances that is of issue here, as becomes clear if we follow the intertextual referencing a bit further, to Law-Yone's mention of the Ethiopian Emperor Haile Selassie whose annexation of Eritrea occurred in 1962, the same year as Ne Win's *coup d'état* and overthrow of U Nu.

The Rome–Europe–Ethiopia–Burma connection can be followed through to the realm of political theories regarding the emergence of what Max Weber first referred to as the "Bureaucratic Empire." As it turns out, this concept, which developed in regard to European history, finds its way into numerous studies of "Third World" nations, and becomes a means through which to glorify what looks on the surface like a successful and orderly transition from the feudal, oligarchic, patrimonial, to the "modern." Donald Levine's description of Haile Selassie's re-fashioning of Ethiopia after 1941, for example, demonstrates the pitfalls of this approach. Noting that Selassie's policies exhibit "an exact parallel to the characteristic policies of rulers in the historic bureaucratic empires," Levine presents a laudatory listing of Selassie's accomplishments. Included among the building of universities and infrastructure are the creation of a "large national army and police force," and the "mobilization of military resources" and use of the media to "promote new kinds of political consciousness" (179). Reading this list in conjunction with Law-Yone's description of Daya of the late 1960s and 1970s, it suddenly becomes clear that the contiguities she has created are neither fantastic nor fortuitous in the "real world." Law-Yone explores the ways in which Third World dictators, like other statesmen, studied history and political theory as well as each other not only in how to behave but how to articulate their actions and accomplishments. In the process, they convince themselves of their greatness. Through Supremo's dialogue, quoted by the narrator, Law-Yone suggests a tendency to fashion a hodgepodge of theories to fend off paranoia or justify atrocities:

"Look at that," he said, pointing out the window at the vast symmetrical stands [of teak and rubber trees]. "Our bountiful land, our golden country.

Natural resources," he said in English. "Natural resources ... " He said it again when we reached the bleak expanses of the oil fields. "Natural resources! ... Smell, just smell ... I swear the oil smells cleaner, now with those fucking capitalists gone." Again he used the English word – "ka-pee-tah-liss" – there being no Dayan word for that plague. (111)

Supremo's statesmanship is described in terms of his major pronounce-ments and declarations: his declaration of martial law to keep people "safe" from those "making selfish demands with no thought for the greater welfare of the state, the unity of the nation" (85); confrontations with "traitors" and "insurgents," because "there are things a parent must do for the good of the child, things that may not always be pleasant or understandable at the time," and his decree of Buddhism as the state religion, "that signaled the first wave of religious persecu-tion, when mosques were wrecked and Chinese temples burned down by mobs" (112). Which is Supremo, the dynamic modernizer, or the despot? Who decides?

The trope of the tango plays yet another critical role in the text's postcolonial critique. As Savigliano points out, "The tango was originally poor but moving upwards, urban with some traces of ruralness, white with some traces of color, colonized with some traces of a native barbarian in the process of being civilized" (Savigliano 1995: 110). Unlike the puppet-like "jerking, twitching, and kicking" of traditional Dayan/Burmese dance, the tango represents a fluidity and play with socio-economic and cultural boundaries that the main character craves as a vehicle for self-expression and finds lacking in her own culture. At the same time, the tango makes power relations and their intersection with sexuality explicit, featuring: "A fatal man and a femme fatale who, despite their proximity, kept their erotic impulses under control, measuring each other's powers" (Savigliano 1995: 110). The character Tango's fantastic path to power and fame via marriage to the *junta* general is a dramatization of this relationship, and it is through this tale that the author is able to explore the relationship between domestic and state violence, and the idea that the personal is political (see Bow 2001). Law-Yone goes on to reverse that phrase to argue that the political is personal, as she represents her character's homelessness, both figurative and literal, in exile.

The tango as intertext helps Law-Yone to create a Foucauldian analysis of the web of participatory violence and oppression. Tango, the narrator, describes her exploitation of her own sexuality to rise to power as Supremo's wife. "Not that I was in the same league as an Imelda Marcos or an Elena Ceaucescu ... " she muses, "But I was on the take long enough to see how power confers almost overnight a sense of entitle-ment" (1993: 84). Tango later considers her participation in a "circle of torment," wherein "the soldiers tormented the prisoners, who tormented the chickens, who tormented the worms, who burrowed their way into the ground where the soldiers would be buried" (126). Here, the narrator is a true heroine in the culture of the dance form after which she is named, which, as Savigliano writes, transcends the simplistic idea of "winners and losers" and focuses instead on the strategies of the weak – the active presence of women as "resourceful subjects" (69). The power struggle is both the means and the end, the experience, of the "reckless passion, the sweet collusion of the embrace, the languor, the swagger" that characterizes *junta* politics; but Tango is also changeable, and she experiences an epiphany after being kidnapped by, and then joining forces with, the Jesu (Karen) rebels in which she comes to understand the "freedom" of having a known purpose and committing oneself wholly to a cause. This sense of fulfilling her potential, an issue that pulls at Tango throughout the text, is short-lived however, as that recognition of self is annihilated through the processes of detention and torture and the violence of erasure in the U.S., as just another Third World woman from a war-torn country.

THE PROBLEM OF CLOSURE

Despite their many interconnections, the three texts offer very diverse conclusions to their narratives of dislocation and brutality, conveyed through equally divergent narrative strategies of closure. These differences reflect both on the particulars of each nation's histories and the years in which the texts were published, as well as the author's divergent perspectives on the efficacy of what some have called the "Human Rights regime." Hagedorn, publishing five years after the Philippines' "Velvet Revolution," anticipates this by imagining the creation of a new, idealized community, a kind of coalition of opposition forces which draws together people from the elite and the dispossessed, and urban and rural areas and draws them out of an abject individualism. In contrast, Wendy Law-Yone pursues the idea of the total dissolution of the self, which is only regained through an act of murderous revenge of the dictator, the "architect of all of our misery." Although her book was published five years after the 1988 massacre of student protesters in Burma, and the emergence of Aung San Suu Kyi and her non-violence movement, Law-Yone chooses an imaginary point just before these events occurred to fantasize about Supremo's death at the hands of his estranged wife. She emphasizes the aura of fantasy by preceding the slaying with an erotic narrative in which Tango, with advanced and purposeful sexual techniques, subdues Supremo so she can beat him to death. Here the author sends mixed signals; the reader is cognizant of the fact that Tango has long since dismissed the efficacy of human rights discourse and practice, which she believes has evolved into spectacle on TV talk shows where descriptions of torture become a vehicle through which Americans put words to their own imagined "pain." We have also seen how Tango has experienced erasure in the U.S. to become a generic "third world woman," who is not even recognizable to a fellow "Dayan." While personalized, in Tango's final act of revenge, Law-Yone gives expression to a collective exile fantasy of taking control over impossible events at "home," to unhinge the ennui that engulfs the exile in his/her position of awkward comfort. Ne Win died relatively quietly on December 5, 2002, at the age of 91. The military regime he instituted lives on, but internal conflict has resulted in death sentences for his son-in-law and three of his grandsons, who were convicted of treason.

Utami echoes some of Law-Yone's cynicism about the ability of human rights regimes to be transformative. The conclusion to *Saman* (1998), in which the Pastor is now living in New York and working for Human Rights Watch – Utami even includes the e-mail address "hrw.org" in her narrative – fades away into increasingly brief and fleeting narrative fragments. At first, he is enthusiastic, but gradually, he comes to see that:

> They're all concerned with issues like human rights, democracy, freedom of the press, all of the problems of the third world. But, how far the [HRW] office is from the location of the problems. What a great distance it is. It's incomprehensible, for the people in this building, people who've never experienced these problems directly, have never experienced what happens in other corners of the world whose distance from here is the difference of night and day – the brutality, and the humor of it. (1998: 167)

The "thousands of kilometers" of reports on human rights violations create a sense of unease, as Saman sees the actual participants in struggles back home transformed into statistics and brief testimonials. The irony of it all, Saman notes, is that those who collect information about atrocities and attempt to make it public are considered "subversives" and "terrorists," while the police are acting "legally," for the security of the "nation" (169). Gradually, Saman's observations of this sort dissipate into an emerging discourse of longing, which is translated into sexual desire expressed through letters to another human-rights worker, back in

Indonesia. The narrative fades away with these plaintive cries: "Saman, … I only orgasm when I think of you … Yasmin, … I don't know how to satisfy you … Saman, … I will teach you … Yasmin, Teach me, rape me" (196–7). *Saman's* ending encompasses both the tragic sense of dislocation of *Irrawaddy Tango* and *Dogeaters'* optimism regarding the possibilities of a community of activists with a common purpose. In contrast to those texts, Utami, writing from Indonesia, where sexuality is still framed through religious and moral discourse, also speaks to the student-centered opposition movement of the 1990s, in which sexual liberation is equaled with mental and physical liberation from various kinds of oppression.

The aesthetics of these texts, their discomforting pleasures, are found in their representations of violent, late twentieth-century socio-political landscapes in which unsuspecting individuals get caught and caught up. The writers discussed here demonstrate that fiction is perhaps the only space that accommodates a realistic rendering of situated, time-bound events in places that exceed the boundaries of the global imaginary. This is fiction that utilizes the freedom that post-modern anti-formalism offers, but it also rejects what Radhakrishnan has called "an epistemology of relativism," and "a decapitation of history by theory, [and] the celebration of subjectlessness" (Radhakrishnan 2000: 42–3) which is out of sync with the realities of the postcolonial (third) world. Through their experimental narrative form, the authors engage issues of literary and postcolonial criticism, reiterating the links between fiction and activism.

REFERENCES

Appadurai, Arjun, 1999. "Disjunction and Difference in the Global Cultural Economy" in *The Globalization Reader*, eds Frank Lechner and John Boli, London: Blackwell.

Bow, Leslie, 2001. *Betrayal and Other Acts of Subversion: Feminism, Sexual Politics, Asian American Women's Literature*, Princeton: Princeton University Press.

Hagedorn, Jessica, 1990. *Dogeaters*, New York: Penguin, 1991.

Karamcheti, Indira, 1995. "Minor Pleasures," *Postcolonial Discourses and Changing Cultural Contexts Theory and Criticism*, eds Gita Rajan and Radhika Mohanram, Westport, CT: Greenwood Press, pp. 59–68.

Law-Yone, Wendy, 1993. *Irrawaddy Tango*, New York: Alfred Knopf.

Lee, Rachel C., 1996–7. "The Erasure of Places and the Re-Siting of Empire in Wendy Law-Yone's *The Coffin Tree*," *Cultural Critique*, 35 (Winter), pp. 149–78.

Lee, Rachel C., 1999. *The Americas of Asian American Literature: Gendered Fictions of Nation and Transnation*, Princeton: Princeton University Press.

Levine, Donald, 1974. *Greater Ethiopia: The Evolution of a Multiethnic Society*, Chicago: University of Chicago Press.

Mohan, Rajeswari, 1995. "Dodging the Crossfire: Questions for a Postcolonial Pedagogy" in *Order and Partialities: Theory, Pedagogy, and the "Postcolonial,"* eds Kostas Myrsiades and Jerry McGuire, Albany: State University of New York Press, pp. 261–84.

Radhakrishnan, R., 1993. "Postcoloniality and the Boundaries of Identity," *Calalloo*, 16. 4, pp. 750–71.

Radhakrishnan, R., 2000. "Postmodernism and the Rest of the World" in *The Pre-Occupation of Postcolonial Studies*, eds Fawzia Afzal-Khan and Kalpana Seshadri-Crooks, Durham, NC: Duke University Press.

Savigliano, Marta, 1995. *Tango and the Political Economy of Passion*, Boulder: Westview Press.

Scarry, Elaine, 1987. *The Body in Pain: The Making and Unmaking of the World*, London: Oxford University Press.

Utami, Ayu, 1998. *Saman*, Jakarta: Kepustakaan Populer Gramedia.

16

U.S. and US: American Literatures of Immigration and Assimilation

Geraldine Stoneham

Full stops (periods) are useful things. They are the border guards of meaning; they form the first line of defense against misunderstanding or free interpretation. Although the significant possibilities thrown up by the juxtaposition of letters can be glimpsed through them, the educated reader understands their purpose in such prevention and respects it. The absence of stops allows the interpretative space to be flooded with the unintended and, perhaps, undesirable. Letters that should be clearly demarcated flow into one another and create undreamed-of possibilities of signification. This permits the reader to cash in on the unregulated moment, to subvert order, clarity and representation. It becomes necessary to evaluate interpretations, to screen out the unacceptable. Consider the example of this title, "U.S. and US." In the case of the U.S., full stops prevent any interpretation of the sign, given the context, than that of the initial letters of the United States. This term carries with it over 200 years of historical record and cultural achievement: histories of nation-building, democratic values, frontier heroism, European migration, freedom of opportunity, also histories of witch-hunts (distant and recent), oppression of the indigenous population, civil war, racism, and so on. There is, in addition, the issue of world dominance that allows us to assume the absent "A" of "of America." The latter, on the other hand, is an unsecured sign. Unguarded interpretations spring up to destabilize its representative value. What or who does US stand for? Is it inclusive or exclusive? To what collective identity can US lay claim? Does it represent the powerful or the disempowered?

On one level this is simply a neat metaphor for the dynamics of the relationship arising from what Gregory S. Jay calls the "tensions between two definitions of the American," that is the civic or political essence

238

and the racial and/or cultural (Jay 1997: 27); but on another level – the most basic and fundamental level – it inscribes and dramatizes (that is, performs) those dynamics. The space of representation and interpretation can be limited or delimited according to who represents (that is, who acts upon) the condition of nationhood. Literature and literary criticism – as functions of language – are therefore integral to the constructions of identity in both central and marginal proximity to the idea of nation. The aim of this essay, therefore, is to examine the codes of representation in American civic, racial, and cultural contexts and how these codes are explored, challenged and sometimes reaffirmed in recent fiction from "non-traditional" (to use Bharati Mukherjee's term) American writers of first- and second-generation immigrant identities. I have called the focus of my study "American Literatures" in order to stress the multiplicity of representations of the "American," and to suggest that what constitutes the "American" in the literatures emerging from the United States today is an open and negotiable construct. In its complexity of reference, alliances, juxtapositions (for which even the terms "immigration" and "assimilation" are too confining), this is a debate that goes beyond race, while still being firmly rooted within that discourse. It is a debate that goes beyond ethnicity, while acknowledging the politics of the struggle of marginalized groups to be heard. It is a debate that will attempt to open up some of the criteria of "American" literature to critical scrutiny. It will also, I think, help us avoid the critical cul-de-sac of Mukherjee's (and others') appropriation of the term "mainstream" – one of those border guards of cultural exclusion.

It would be useful to begin with an overview of the changes and challenges to the representation of the U.S. national ethos and the identity of the U.S. citizen. In Orson Welles' film, *A Touch of Evil* (1958), a pregnant woman waits at the frontier with the U.S. She knows that if she can get across just before she gives birth, her child will be born a U.S. citizen, thus automatically conferring citizenship on its parents. The border officials are suspicious. They've experienced the desperation of poverty-stricken illegals and it is their job to prevent it. The film's main themes of negotiation between good and evil, corruption and decay, law and lawlessness in the liminal space of the border town are threaded through with the single-minded determination of this woman to achieve the desired object. At the end of the film, while the officials are distracted by the mayhem caused by the primary characters, the woman slips through and a new U.S. citizen is born. We have witnessed a natural (natal) negotiation with the abstraction of law that reaffirms for the audience an undisputed assertion: in spite of the breach of a legal border, an ethical right – the right of the world's "huddled masses" – has been enacted. Leaving aside faint ironic echoes thrown up by the film's ambivalent attitude towards all of the major characters (Mexican and American), it is safe to say that what is represented by this minor subplot are simple concepts of (natural) right and (unnatural) wrong: hope triumphing over hopelessness, the future triumphing over the past. Beyond the chaos of the Mexican border town is the security of identity; beyond the border with otherness is the U.S./US.

There has been enormous demographic and cultural change in the United States since 1958, not least in the emergence of literature and criticism that scrutinizes and challenges the very assumptions of the U.S./US paradigm. At the level of a reductive identity politics, there is an upsurge in anti-immigration movements that have at their center clear criteria for American national identity. Veronica Ramos, in her analysis of the "collective narratives" of one of these groups, the American Immigration Control Foundation (AICF), summarizes the criteria as "speaking English, getting a job, staying out of poverty, obeying the law, acting patriotically, and, finally, being white and European" (Ramos 1997: 601). Each of the three narratives identified by Ramos, asserts the supremacy of the ordinary American individual as white, European, and Christian (see Jay 1997: 27). Yet it also portrays him/her as a victim, a fool and as a member of a society structurally weakened by liberal sympathizers (Ramos 1997: 597–9). Ironic contrasts notwithstanding, the construction that emerges is of a deeply paranoid and insecure people preyed upon by wily, intelligent and self-interested racial and cultural aliens, assisted from within by a range of business-men, bureaucrats, academics, lawyers and do-gooders.

These new narratives of American identity have found echo in a surprising range of U.S. contemporary fiction. The interesting parallel, for example, between the above constructions and some of Bharati Mukherjee's on the theme of immigration is dealt with below. First, however, I would like to consider the viewpoint of another of the American literatures of immigration. The condition of otherness in the social and cultural relations between white European America (the already-melted pot) and its more recent immigrant identities (the mul-ticultural kaleidoscope) is the subject of *The Tortilla Curtain* by T. Coraghessan Boyle (1995). It tells the story of a liberal writer, Delaney Mossbacher and his relationship with, first, his cultural and socio-economic peers, including his wife, Kyra, and, then, a couple of Mexican illegal immigrants, Cándido and América, who are squatting just beyond the perimeter fence of his gated housing estate. This estate is overseen by security guards whose job it is to keep out the alien and undesirable so that the inmates might feel themselves to be safe and homogeneous. Needless to say, crushed between these two forces, liberal credentials are tested to the limit and the novel ends in farce with Delaney trying to kill Cándido while América gives birth in a mudslide (the baby is drowned), thus threatening the future of all.

So what has changed since 1958 for the U.S./US? Here they are again, the same suffering and desperate Mexicans (including the unborn child) that we saw in 1958. They are living the same liminal life, pregnant with possibilities but prey to corruption and violence in a no-man's wasteland just inside the border. The Americans are seen to be just as ambivalent a bunch as they were in Los Robles – corrupt, violent, and mentally and physically fragile; but they are also fearful and paranoid, aware of and imprisoned by the grotesque inequalities of their situation, and yet prepared to kill in order to defend it. Nor is it simply assumed that América will give birth and a new U.S. citizen will assert some natural and collective claim on the Earth. For one thing, the law has changed and it is much more difficult to prove citizenship in an environment hostile to immigrants. For another, the welcome given to the new citizen is much more ambivalent in the context of widespread legal and illegal immigration in the intervening 40 years. U.S. is no longer synonymous with an identifiable US, but is a sometimes explosive mix of racial, ethnic, political and cultural interest groups negotiating their own space from a limited supply. It is interesting that one reviewer, while impressed by Boyle's portrait of desperate, exploited Mexicans, is less convinced by the Americans. He comments that "[Boyle's] Mexicans are totally convincing, even though he seems to have more fun with his American characters" (Cogan n.d.). United States literature has evidently become a site where it is easier to identify the Other than it is to recognize the Self. Yet, the names that Boyle has chosen for his Mexicans, Cándido and América, quite clearly link them to a classic of European culture that specifically attacks Enlightenment optimism, belief in knowledge and progress. Boyle's use of Voltaire's final instructions to his voyager that he should stay home and cultivate his (own) garden, is surely passing a reflective glass before the eyes of all Americans: established and aspiring alike.

While Boyle's allegory ends with an affirmation of some kind of basic and universal humanity, Bharati Mukherjee, in her novel, *Jasmine* (1989), uses the suffering of would-be Americans to a very different end. This is Mukherjee's best-known and most controversial work about an impoverished and virtually uneducated village girl from India who enters the United States as an illegal alien and who negotiates her way through terrorism, rape and murder, adultery and moral responsibility to emerge virtually unscathed as the prototype of the new New World pioneer. In an almost flawless reflection of the narratives of the AICF, Jyoti/Jasmine/Jane/Jase is assisted in her relentless drive toward the future and progress by a series of self-interested bureaucrats, businessmen, lawyers, academics and do-gooders. The people she meets in the American heartland are neurotic, fragile, vulnerable and weak. They are, in effect, a pushover for someone like Jasmine: one of the new immigrants, "greedy with wants and reckless from hope" (Mukherjee 1989: 241).

David Leiwei Li (1998) makes a neat case in support of Mukherjee's claim to be an "American" rather than a "hyphenated American" writer, by representing the American novel as romantic rather than realist in form. Li states that "*Jasmine* is an inspiring work of fancy; reservations about it are perhaps best expressed via Gandhi's famous response to 'American Democracy': 'I wish it were true'" (Li 1998: 100). It is over this very aspect of fantasy that the opinion on Mukherjee diverges. On the one hand, there is a discourse that represents Mukherjee's narrative of ruthless carpetbagging as "inspiring" (for whom? Aspiring illegal aliens? Second-generation Asian Americans? The children of the "black-scarfed Babushkas," whose narrative Mukherjee supplants? African Americans? Americans of 1958/1999?), but a fantasy articulating a language of "consent" that ignores a far-from-shining American history on race (Li 1998: 99). On the other, there is a response represented by critics such as Shirley Geok-lin Lim (1997), who question Mukherjee's advocacy of historical and cultural erasure and elitist appropriation of the immigrant experience. These are not questions of literary merit (which is considerable) or critical perspective. They are questions of inclusion and exclusion; questions of who controls the constitution of US in the U.S. Mukherjee's novel is not about immigration at all; it is about the wholesale appropriation of the idea of the American. However, as Boyle reminds us, the idea of the American arose in Europe and is not so different from the value-system that the British took to India in the sixteenth century. The difference in Mukherjee's American romance is that the new colonizer is everything she should be except white, European and Christian. As if she were articulating the worst fears of the AICF, Mukherjee effectively suggests that those Americans have forfeited their right to the American dream through their own folly, market forces and sheer exhaustion of breeding potential. If Jasmine is the new American, they are the new Abject. As hundreds of thousands of immigrants to the United States over the past 50 years have discovered, appropriation of the ideals of American life does not necessarily mean a change in its power structures.

The fantasy America created by Mukherjee is made possible precisely because of the illegality of the subject. Jasmine occupies the free space of unencumbered present and limitless future. In a sense, her United States is like the jigsaw puzzle that América, the Puerto Rican housekeeper in *América's Dream* by Esmeralda Santiago, finds in her young charge's room in New York: "It's a map of the United States, with Hawaii floating on the left lower corner and Alaska floating on the left upper. And nothing else. No Canada, no Mexico, no Caribbean" (Santiago 1997: 299). In other words, there are no dangerous borderlines, no awkward reflective encounters. In this image, the United States is portrayed in the image of its collective ideal: individual, self-sufficient and autonomous – and exclusive.

América's dream is for quiet, comfortable domesticity, in which families and friends, mothers and daughters, women and men live in mutually respectful harmony, which is an ideological world away from Jasmine's acquisitive, assimilationist crusade. It is also not quite what it seems. While América quite simply does not want to assimilate with American values, or to become a U.S. citizen (although as a Puerto Rican she has that option), she would like to be acknowledged as a presence, to be free from exploitation, and to be paid a more proportionate percentage of her employers' salaries for the services she renders. Instead, betrayed by her mother and daughter, brutally treated by her lover, and exploited by the rich white New Yorkers for whom she works, her life is an allegory for the relationship between the United States and its satellite territories.

Like Jasmine, América is taken to live in the very heart of affluence. Like her, too, she becomes a surrogate mother to American children, but unlike Jasmine, América finds that proximity to the white European, culturally dominant U.S. does not imply mutuality and equality. She quickly learns that, although the children learn more from her than their parents, although she lives not that differently from them in their home, her presence makes no real impact on their lives until the horrific denouement. She hopes for a meaningful relationship based on a mutual love for the children, but the reality is that their lives are contingent and tangential, each side playing out their private dramas (the Leverett's cold marriage, América's terror of discovery by Correa) under the bemused and averted gaze of the other. She becomes just another one of the Latino maids, thrown together in uneasy alliances, who frequent the parks, playgrounds and leisure facilities of New York with their charges:

> At the health club she joins other women walking briskly with their children, equally as many mothers as empleadas. She can always pick out the mothers, because they're expensively dressed. They open the door to the club with a sense of entitlement, while the empleadas seem to be apologizing for taking up room where they don't belong. The brown and black ones, anyway. The white-skinned ones behave like the mothers, with the same confidence and unapologetic decisiveness. (Santiago 1997: 228–9)

Thus Santiago grasps the issue that Mukherjee has avoided – the issue of race as the primary indicator of exclusion in U.S. cultural identity. This is reinforced in the novel in an incident in the playground where the women act instinctively after a child has fallen and hurt itself. All rush toward the child, but the white mother shrieks as she catches sight of the brown woman reaching out to her child. Although the *empleadas* make excuses for the mother, they cannot rid themselves of the knowledge that they are fundamentally excluded from free association with "Americans" based purely on their difference from the internalized norm of U.S. identity: "'She didn't mean anything,' Adela protests. 'You know how scared of strangers these gringas are.' But none of them are so willing to dismiss the woman's scornful look, the deliberate turning of her back on them" (Santiago 1997: 227).

The dilemma of inclusion/exclusion is nicely dramatized by Chicana writer, Sandra Cisneros, in her short story, "Never Marry a Mexican" which begins:

> Never marry a Mexican, my ma said once and always. She said this because of my father. She said this though she was Mexican too. But she was born here in the U.S., and he was born there, and it's *not* the same, you know. (Cisneros 1993: 68)

In a bitter diatribe, Cisneros' narrator recounts how her mother's experience had been one of class and race (she was a lower-class Mexican and a non-white American): exactly the same criteria of exclusion she herself experiences at the hands of her rich, white, married American lover. Doomed always to exist within a racial and class-cultural wasteland, unanchored by a sense of ever belonging either to her ethnic or her natal homeland, her possibilities are all destructive: "I'm vindictive and cruel, and I'm capable of anything" (1993).

Santiago's view of US suggests, then, the impossibility of identity with any simple idea of humanity and the persistence of stereotypes of difference of the most basic kind. Yet, she also describes the extraordinary multiculturalism of New York, where even the waitress in the local Chinese restaurant knows enough Spanish to take an order, suggesting that what binds the U.S./US are those socio-economic imperatives that drive immigration in the first place. When América has recovered from the brutal attack by Correa, and is dismissed from the Leverett's service, she moves to the Bronx to be near her family. She finds in the Bronx an uneasy, if vibrant, jostling of cultures that is both supportive and threatening. Her adult cousin continues to express a kind of rebellion against her parent values by choosing exclusively males from other ethnic groups (other, that is, than white European) as partners. She also notes that life on the streets in the Bronx has become vaguely menacing for the older generation of immigrants. It is, however, comforting and potentially life-affirming to be among her people, speaking her own language. América's daughter, having joined her mother in the U.S., is becoming culturally assimilated. Her assimilation, however, is not to the dominant majority, which exists elsewhere, but to the attitudes and posturing of her ethnic peers in the multicultural space of the Bronx.

It would be wrong, however, to represent race as the whole story of U.S. identity, when clearly it is not. The same values of aspiration and "individual self-possession" (if not Mukherjee's "inalienable rights" as David Li points out [1998: 102]), do unite citizens of the United States from all ethnic and cultural backgrounds. It is the role of pan-ethnic identities (such as Asian American, Hispanic American, African American) to prevent the reduction of culture and identity to race (Jay 1997: 25) and to provide groups of peoples with a visible united, and therefore powerful political presence. It would be easy, however, illegitimately to homogenize the members of such groups. As King-Kok Cheung says about Asian American literature: "Perhaps the most important reason to maintain the designation of 'Asian American' literature is not the presence of any cultural, thematic, or poetic unity but the continuing need to amplify marginalized voices" (1997: 5).

I shall conclude this essay, therefore, by considering another factor in the multiplicity of American literatures of immigration and assimilation: the perspective of the second-generation Asian American writer, Gish Jen. In spite of what has been said above about resistance to the reduction of U.S. identity to race, the quotation from the *Independent* newspaper's reviewer, emblazoned on the front cover of Jen's collection of short stories, *Who's Irish?*, reaffirms race as paramount: "Gish Jen beautifully translates what it is to see the world through Chinese eyes." This is a disappointing response in view of the fact that a significant critical issue explored both in this collection and in Jen's first novel, about the experiences of an immigrant to the United States from China, *Typical American*, is that it is precisely not a "Chinese" viewpoint. Jen's is a distinctively second-generation perspective on the condition of migration and ethnicity in the United States. Seeing parallels with another assimiliationist, Li suggests that Jen, like Mukherjee, is laying claim to a voice that is "beyond the negative embodiments of race and ethnicity" (Li 1998: 102). It may be true to say that Jen's new Americans require the same kind of "amnesiac condition" we see in Mukherjee's work, but it is also obvious that Jen is as aware of the importance of collective identity and maintaining cultural values.

In *Typical American* (1999a), the life of Ralph Chang, Jen's hapless immigrant patriarch, follows a typical assimilationist trajectory from abandonment of/by the past to an increasingly aggressive appropriation of the future. This is offset, however, by the narrator's perspective, which is distanced and at times critical of Chang's inability to keep his goals and his identity in balance. (See David Leiwei Li (1998) for a discussion of Chang's abandonment of Confucian individualism for a capitalist model of possessive individualism: 104–7.) It is precisely because Chang has isolated himself from his Chinese (American) past, and has formed a foolish alliance with the grotesquely Americanized Grover Ding that his story ends ultimately in tragedy and loss of identity.

Jen's second generation of Chinese Americans, on the other hand, suffer from their need to negotiate with both their Chinese culture and their American identity. In "Duncan in China" (1999b), Duncan's perspective on the past home of his parents, and present home of some of his relatives, is honestly presented as shock and accommodation. The sinister party *apparatchik*, Mo, however, is stereotypical of American views of the Chinese in the 1980s and anchors the story firmly in an American literary frame. Her second-generation Chinese Americans are party to everyday interethnic negotiations and multicultural accommodations that they manage with more ease and less suspicion than their immigrant parents. Just as with the first generation, however, Jen warns about the danger of losing one's cultural identity in the melting pot of American ethnicity, but she also suggests that such a downgrading of the old culture is inevitable. In an amusing note about the difficulty of maintaining meaning across cultures, when a Chinese American woman gives birth to her first child, Adam, the Chinese grandmother is reduced to choosing a homonym, Yadan, meaning "Asia Red," thus giving the child a Chinese name as meaningless as the English name is meaningful. The primary center of meaning is shifted from Chinese to English and from China to America.

One of her more despairingly apolitical characters, Pammie, in the story "House, House, Home" (1999b), articulates on more than one occasion the side-stepping adjustments in Chinese American negotiations with U.S. identity in which her claim to "American" is momentarily challenged as inauthentic. One such moment is just after Pammie's marriage to Sven Anderson, an American of European immigrant stock and a social dropout. One of their "American" friends who has prepared a celebration to follow the wedding observes about Sven's gift to his wife:

> Just the thing for a nice Japanese wife, said John.
>
> That was awkward.
>
> Chinese American, said Pammie, lifting a glass of Chianti. (Jen 1999b: 152)

Yet, the story opens with Pammie, as an infant school volunteer, finding herself guilty of attempting to force a condition of multicultural collectivity via a "children of color" lunch. At this point it is apparent to Pammie that only the black children have any inkling that they are the representatives of the eponymous group, and that her own children, along with other Chinese Americans in the class, are oblivious to their own roles in the lunch. Pammie is, at this point, so astonishingly naive and simplistic – can we really be expected to believe that such naivety is possible even in middle-class 1990s America? This suggestion of naivety is modified by Jen later when Pammie, in an argument with Sven over who was the greater outsider, the elective or the "other," acknowledges her own and her children's position in regard to their society:

> Your confidence was conferred on you by society. Your children do not look like you and will be granted no such thing. We need to think what the sources of their power will be, that they will not be constantly kicked by little people trying to make themselves feel better. (Jen 1999b: 189)

This, I think, represents the position of the immigrant – separatist or assimilationist – better than most overtly political statements. That position is always as the "other" outsider, the one who is not there by consent, but, finding themselves by choice or by birth marked by difference, must struggle to gain enough power in economic, political and social terms to fight their racial and cultural wars. It is obvious, however, that true to her individualist principles, Jen sees this as a personal struggle, not a collective movement. None of the writers I have considered in this essay call for direct political action, and all have created characters that negotiate their own way through the borders of identity. This, more than anything else, makes them writers of American literature.

REFERENCES

Boyle, T. Coraghessan, 1995. *The Tortilla Curtain*, London: Bloomsbury.
Cheung, King-Kok, 1997. "Re-viewing Asian American Literary Studies" in *An Interethnic Companion to Asian American Literature*, ed. King-Kok Cheung, Cambridge: Cambridge University Press, pp. 1–36.
Cisneros, Sandra, 1993. *Woman Hollering Creek*, London: Bloomsbury.
Cogan, Alan, n.d. Review of *The Tortilla Curtain*. <http://www.mexconnect.com>.
Jay, Gregory S. 1997, *American Literature and the Culture Wars*, Ithaca: Cornell University Press.
Jen, Gish, 1999a. *Typical American*, London: Granta.
Jen, Gish, 1999b. *Who's Irish?*, London: Granta.
Li, David Leiwei, 1998. *Imagining the Nation: Asian American Literature and Cultural Consent*, Stanford: Stanford University Press.
Lim, Shirley Geok-Lin, 1997. "Immigration and Diaspora" in *An Interethnic Companion to Asian American Literature*, ed. King-Kok Cheung, Cambridge: Cambridge University Press, pp. 289–311.
Mukherjee, Bharati,1988. "Immigrant Writing: Give Us Your Maximalists!," *New York Times Book Review*, August 28.
Mukherjee, Bharati, 1989. *Jasmine*, London: Virago.
Mukherjee, Bharati, 1999. "The Four-Hundred Year Old Woman," in *Critical Fictions: The Politics of Imaginative Writing*, ed. Philomena Mariani, Seattle: Bay Press.
Ramos, Veronica, 1997. "Images, Symbols and Words: The American Immigration Control Foundation and "True" American Character," *The Centennial Review*, 41:3.
Santiago, Esmeralda, 1997. *América's Dream*, London, Virago.

List of Contributors

CHADWICK ALLEN is Assistant Professor in the Department of English, Ohio State University, where he teaches postcolonial literatures and theory, and American Indian literature. He is the author of *Blood Narrative: Indigenous Identity in American Indian and Maori Literary and Activist Texts* (2002) and Associate Editor of the journal *Studies in American Indian Literatures*.

FRANCES R. APARICIO is Professor of Spanish and American Culture at the University of Michigan, Ann Arbor. She is author of *Listening to Salsa: Gender, Latin Popular Music, and Puerto Rican Cultures* (1998) and co-editor, with Susana Chavez Silverman, of *Tropicalizations: Transcultural Representations of Latinidad* (1997). She has written extensively on U.S. Puerto Rican and Latino/a literatures and cultures and on Latino popular music. Currently, she is working on a book about the cultural politics of bilingualism.

MYRIAM J. A. CHANCY was born in Port-au-Prince, Haiti, and has lived in Québec City, Winnipeg, Halifax, Iowa City, and Nashville. She obtained her B. A. in English/Philosophy, *cum laude*, in 1989 from the University of Manitoba, her M. A. in English in 1990 from Dalhousie University, and the Ph. D. in English in 1994 from the University of Iowa. She is the author of *Searching for Safe Spaces: Afro-Caribbean Women Writers in Exile* (1997) and *Framing Silence: Revolutionary Novels by Haitian Women* (1997). She is Associate Professor of English at Arizona State University, Tempe; she is serving a period as editor of *Meridians* and Visiting Associate Professor of Women's Studies at Smith College for 2002–04.

RENNY CHRISTOPHER is Associate Professor of English at California State University, Channel Islands. Her book, *The Viet Nam War: The American War: Images and Representations in Euro-American and Vietnamese Exile Narratives* (1995) was named an Outstanding Book on Human Rights in North America by the Gustavas Myers Center for the Study of Human Rights. Her poetry chapbook, *My Name is Medea*, won the New Spirit Press chapbook award in 1996; her poetry collection *Viet Nam and California* is from Viet Nam Generation/Burning Cities Press (1998).

CARA CILANO is Assistant Professor of English at the University of North Carolina at Wilmington, where she teaches postcolonial and global literary studies. Her recent article on Indian novelist Arundhati Roy will appear in the *Journal of Commonwealth and Postcolonial Studies*.

MARY CONDÉ teaches at Queen Mary and Westfield College, University of London. She did a doctorate on Rudyard Kipling and Joseph Conrad at St. Anne's College, Oxford. She holds Master's degrees in modern English Studies, the politics of rights, and social anthropology. She is co-editor with Thorunn Lonsdale of *Caribbean Women Writers: Fiction in English* (1999).

RICHARD J. LANE is Honorary Reader in British and Postcolonial Studies at the University of Debrecen, Hungary. His major publications include: *Jean Baudrillard* (2000), *Mrs. Dalloway: Literary Masterpieces* (2001), *Beckett and Philosophy* (ed. 2002) and *Contemporary British Fiction* (co-ed. 2003). He has published widely on postcolonial literatures and theory, and currently writes the "Canada" section for *The Year's Work in English Studies*.

PAUL LYONS is Associate Professor of English at the University of Hawai'i-Manoa. His current research centers on American Pacific Orientalism, about which he has published in *Boundary 2*; *ESQ: A Journal of the American Renaissance*; *Arizona Quarterly*, and *Inside Out: Literature, Cultural Politics, and Identity in the New Pacific*.

DEBORAH L. MADSEN holds the Chair of American Literature at the University of Geneva. Her books include *The Post-modernist Allegories of Thomas Pynchon* (1991), *Rereading Allegory: A Narrative Approach to Genre* (1994), *Post-modernism, A Bibliography, 1926–1994* (1995), *Allegory in America: From Puritanism to Post-modernism* (1996), *American Exceptionalism* (1998), *Feminist Theory and Literary Practice* (2000), *Understanding Contemporary Chicana Literature* (2000), *Maxine Hong Kingston* (2001) and *Chinese American Literature* (2002). She edited *Visions of America Since 1492* (1994) and *Beyond the Commonwealth: Expanding the Postcolonial Canon* (1999). Her current research focuses upon exceptionalism, authenticity, and the multiethnic literatures of the United States.

JOHN HUNT PEACOCK Jr. is Professor of Liberal Arts at the Maryland Institute College of Art in Baltimore and in 1994 was Senior Fulbright Lecturer in American Literature at the University of Antwerp, Belgium. He has been a Senior Fulbright Lecturer, a Mellon Fellow, a participant in two NEH Summer Seminars, and a recipient of an American Philosophical Society grant. His essays have appeared in *Ethnohistory*,

Literature/Film Quarterly, Art and Academe, Creative Screen Writing, New Art Examiner, and in several collections of essays.

LAURA PETERS is Senior Lecturer in English at the University of Surrey Roehampton. She is the author of *Orphaned Texts: Victorian Orphans, Culture and Empire* (2000) and is currently compiling an anthology on race and racial theory with David Theo Goldberg and Tommy Lott.

ALASDAIR PETTINGER is an independent scholar, based in Glasgow, Scotland. He is the editor of *Always Elsewhere: Travels of the Black Atlantic* (1998), and has published several articles on African American travellers including Frederick Douglass and Zora Neale Hurston. He is currently working on a study of the links between Scotland and the antebellum South.

JULIE SHACKFORD-BRADLEY is Lecturer at the Institute for Global Learning at California State University, Monterey Bay. She complied the bibliography *Southeast Asia: Literature by Women* (1996) and has written widely on Asian American, and specifically Indonesian, women's writing.

RAJINI SRIKANTH is co-editor of *Contours of the Heart: South Asians Map North America* (1996), *A Part, Yet Apart: South Asians in Asian America* (1998), *Bold Words: A Century of Asian American Writing* (2001), and *White Women in Racialized Spaces: Imaginative Transformation and Ethical Action in Literature* (2002). Her book, *Worlds that Matter: South Asian American Literature and the Idea of America* is forthcoming from Temple University Press. She teaches at the University of Massachusetts Boston.

GERALDINE STONEHAM is Principal Lecturer in English at London South Bank University. She works in the fields of Australian literature, postcolonial studies and women's writing. Her publications include chapters on post-modernism and postcolonialism in *Post-modern Subjects/Post-modern Texts*, edited by Jane Dowson and Steven Earnshaw and *Just Post-modernism*, edited by Steven Earnshaw. She has also published in the journal *Wasafiri*. She is currently working on a book on Bessie Head.

LEE SCHWENINGER is Professor of English at the University of North Carolina, Wilmington, where he teaches early American, ethnic American, and American Indian literatures. Author of *The Writings of Celia Parker Woolley* (1998) and *John Winthrop* (1990), he has also published recently in *Studies in American Indian Literatures* and *MELUS*.

He is currently at work on a study of American Indian literary responses to the landscape.

ANGELA NOELLE WILLIAMS is Assistant Professor in the Department of English and Comparative Literature at San Jose State University, where her work focuses on race and ethnicity in American literature and contemporary literary theory. Her most recent publications include an *Annotated Bibliography of Asian American Literature*, co-written with Shirley Geok-lin Lim, and *Crossing Oceans: Reconfiguring American Literary Studies in the Pacific Rim* (2003), co-edited with Karen Chow.

Index